Mirror, Mirror

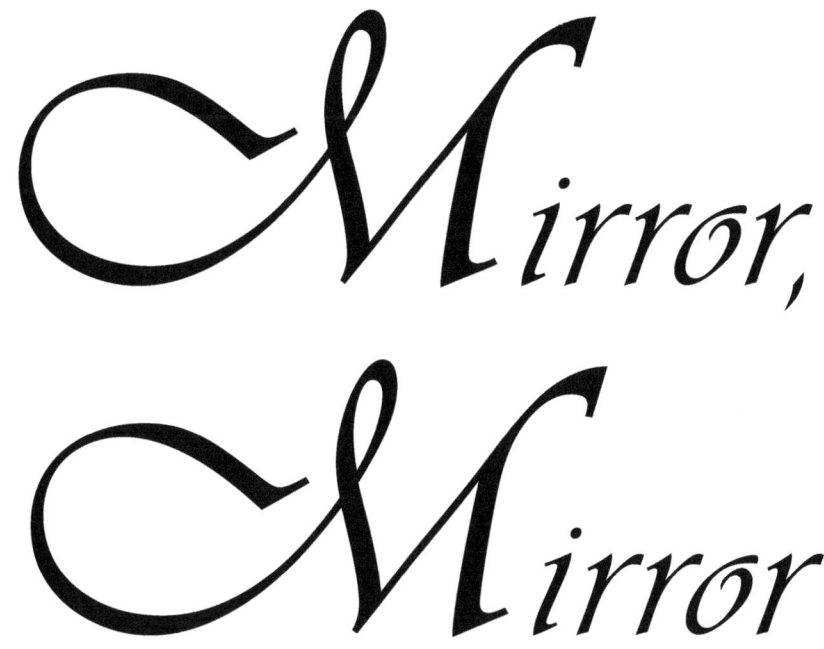

Mirror, Mirror

PAMELA FINGERHUT

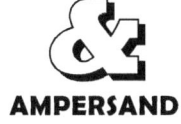

AMPERSAND

Library of Congress Cataloging-in-Publication Data is available.

ISBN 978-0-9855681-2-2

Printed in the United States of America

10 9 8 7 6 5 4 3 2 1

*I dedicate this book
to my precious grandsons,
Gabriel and Harpur,
who bring light and joy to my life.*

. . . [A}nd if a day goes by without my doing something related to photography, it's as though I've neglected something essential to my existence, as though I had forgotten to wake up. I know that the accident of my being a photographer has made my life possible.

—Richard Avedon, 1970

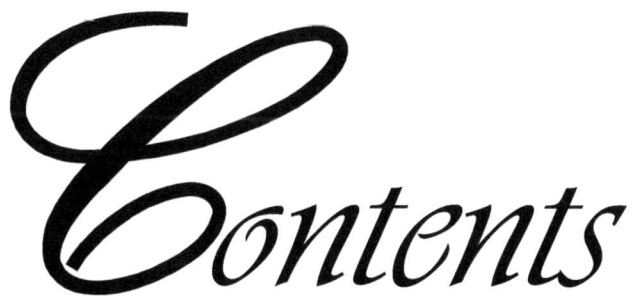

Contents

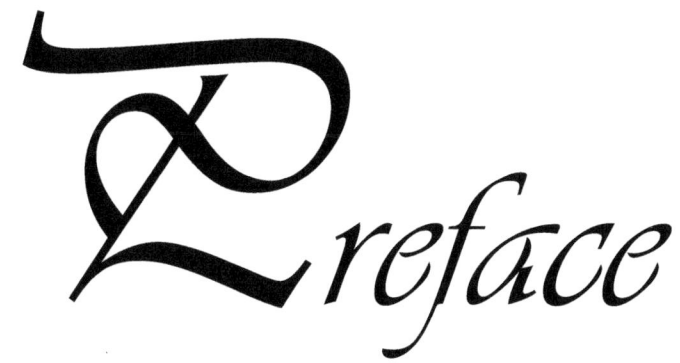

Preface

To be an artist has been my dream and passion for as long as I can remember. My parents thought I delighted in seeing colors, forms, and shadows because I spent the first month of my life without sights. I was a "premie" at 3 pounds 7 ounces and, as was the custom in those days, kept in an oxygen tank with my eyes covered until reached 5 pounds.

I remember the sheer delight in laying on the ground at the age of three and watching the clouds move across the sky. The saturated blues and the many shades of gray and white still stay in my mind.

Color mixing started around the same time. I would spin childrens books around and around to see what new colors emerged from the covers as the colors blended. While this did not improve my reading skills, it did help train my eyes to see variations in color and appreciate what it takes to mix them.

I grew up in a home surrounded by posters of Degas sketches of ballerinas and Goya's painting of Don Manuel Osorio Manrique De Zuniga, with his cat and birds in cages. The Degas sketches always pleased me with their beautiful lines and compositions but the Goya confused me because I could not figure out if the portrait was of a boy or a girl. I never asked either parent the title of that poster.

I began to learn photography in my father's darkroom, where the magic of black and white photography came alive as we dipped the exposed photo paper into the developer and an image slowly appeared. Photography was my dad's passion and he created very sensitive portraits, mostly of family members. One in particular amazed me. It was a portrait of my grandfather reading the Yiddish "Forward" newspaper. The gesture and expression of my grandpa seemed to capture his essence.

On many occasions, I sat for my father and loved seeing the results, which often showed a quieter, sweeter being than what I saw in myself.

During the second grade, my teacher spoke to my parents about my artistic talents and suggested I attend the Corcoran Museum School of Art in Washington, D.C. There I had classic training, which started with sketching Greek and Roman casts, followed by still life sketching, pastel work, life drawing, and painting the human figure. I was totally enthralled and relished each minute of study, followed by scouting different paintings and sculptures in the museum.

My friend Sharon Kahn commuted with me from Maryland to D.C. via tram and bus. We would sit and sketch the passengers quickly, then offer them our artwork for sale. At 10 cents a drawing, I made enough to feel like a professional.

Corcoran Art School was my salvation from second grade until the middle of my senior year of high school.

My college education started at the University of Maryland. I married after two years of undergraduate school and finished my undergraduate and graduate education by transferring to schools near where my husband got his Master's and his first three jobs. My BA was finished at the University of Hartford, where I graduated summa cum laude, and I completed my MBA at Long Island University, Post College. I was newly pregnant at the time and graduated three months before my first child was born.

Andrew, my son, was born in 1973. My daughter, Brooke, was born in 1976. During their formative years, I was a stay-at-home mom who adored family life, being a corporate wife, and watching the children grow into wonderful adults. On Saturdays, I would commute to New York City where I studied anatomical drawing under Gustave Rehberger and sculpture with my mentors Jonathan Shahn and Leonid Lerman.

My children have grown into bright, creative adults and are married to people I have grown to love as much as my own. Andrew now uses his creative bent to sell tattoo artists' artwork on the Internet while evolving into a hands-on dad to my two precious grandsons, Gabriel and Harpur. Brooke has blossomed into a full-time artist who creates diverse artwork, from huge semi-abstract oil paintings to book illustrations to beautiful pastry and candy creations.

Once I became an empty-nester, I could devoted myself to art full-time. First, I spent all my weekdays creating sculpture at studios in New York City, sharing studio space with twelve other sculptors and a mold maker for twelve years. Eventually, I stopped sculpting and immersed myself in photography. When digital photography was just beginning, I saw the potential to create images rather than capture them.

By concentrating on studies at the International Center of Photography, including digital photography, studio lighting, Photoshop from beginning to advanced, long-term projects, and portraiture, I became a professional photographer. I continue to add to my knowledge and stretch my imagination at master classes at Maine Media Workshop and ICP.

My CV lists the various solo and group shows I have participated in plus the various organization I am involved in, past and present.

The artists statements preceding each section of this book provide a glimpse into my brain and heart as I devote myself to my passion for art and creativity.

Recently, life has thrown me some huge curves and I hope to use these often painful happenings to grow both emotionally and artistically.

As I look into the future, I can see my photography evolving into a whole new realm. Most importantly, I want to stay open to new ideas and new technology, relying on my art education to keep my work grounded in the traditions of the past.

I sincerely hope you enjoy my this book and that my work will evoke an emotional or psychological response. My images are the window to my soul.

Thank you for spending time with my artwork.

My deepest thank-you to my cuz, Paul, who has made this book possible and enriches my life one-hundred fold.

PAMELA FINGERHUT
2014

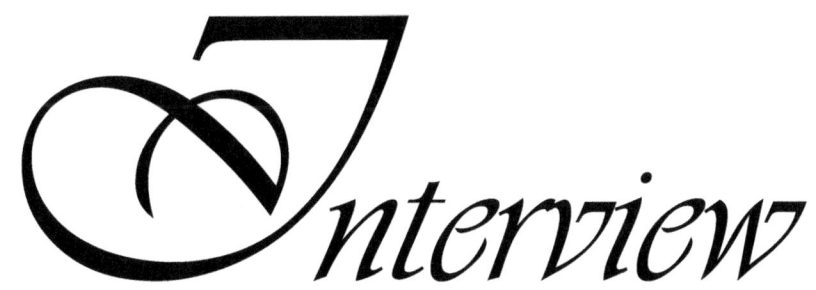

The following is the transcript of an interview with Pamela Fingerhut (PF) by Susan Barnett (SB), broadcast as an episode of the "51%" program on WAMC FM (NPR affiliate in Albany, NY) on December 18, 2008.

SB: Finally, today, it's "Art Space." This one is a tough one. When I first saw the work of artist Pamela Fingerhut, I had to look away, even though it's not gruesome or overtly offensive. Her current collection, which she calls "Female Taxonomy," digitally combines images of women and dolls to create a vision of the female form that is somehow deeply disturbing but also thought provoking.

When I saw your work and spoke briefly with you, what struck me was that it seemed important to you to rattle people's cages a little bit. Is that, in your opinion, what art is supposed to do?

PF: It can and I think it's relevant in the day and age we live in. It's not always what I start out doing when I'm creating. But more and more, lately, that seems to be the result of my work.

SB: And how is that? What's happening?

PF: I want it to become a dialog. I have a lot of concerns about women and about the difference between our subconscious and conscious thoughts. I'm concerned about what climate change is doing to women; about aging; about what young people are thinking now; what beauty, inner or outer, is; with body image; and the joys and pitfalls of being a woman. As I get older and see younger generations coming up, I want to have a dialog with the public about these and other feelings.

At the same time, I still want to deal with the formal concerns of everything in fine arts, like composition and colors; all those things are important to me as well.

SB: Does it bother you that there are people who really may be offended by your work, at least this one exhibit that I saw. It sort of hit them at a very emotional level where they seemed to say, "I can't even look at that."

PF: I know, and that surprises me. There seem to be two schools of thought on my work. Some people have said they relate to it and they think, "Oh wow, this is great," and others seem to be stricken by fear. I'm not really sure where that comes from but it doesn't bother me if that's how they're responding. At least I'm getting a visceral response from people and that's part of what I think my work is about. I'm intentionally being heavy handed because I think these are important issues. Some people find the work beautiful and funny, and others are taken aback.

SB: Well, you know Pamela, and I'm reading a lot into it, but could it also be something as simple as some people are creeped out by clowns and some people are creeped out by dolls.

PF: I think you make a very valid point. Dolls, for some people, are really frightening. And it's interesting that when I was collecting the dolls and photographing them and their owners, I heard the stories of their childhood. And these are, a lot of them, high-powered professional women. They were glad I touched their dolls. Their moms took cares of these dolls. Some had been best friends with their dolls. Some thought of them as human, others didn't. And, possibly, that transcends. I find that men are sometimes more frightened by dolls than women are.

I think, also, that all these movies with "Chucky" and so forth have done a disservice to dolls, and influenced our feelings; made them the things of horror movies rather than a part of growing up, things that young males and females want to play with.

SB: So, what are you working on next?

PF: I have a few series coming up. One is called Bible Babes. It's going to deal with women of the Bible in a contemporary setting.

SB: Oh, no! (Laughter)

PF: Yes, I know. It could be very interesting. I'm working with some rabbis and I'm working with some ministers, and I'm learning so much, and I'm setting things up in unusual places such as food stores, sidewalks, and scenes in the city, as well as the traditional kind of days-of-old thing. It's been a kick. I'm having a great time with it. And I'm also doing a Lullaby series—much tamer. I am going to be a grandma and I'm doing a series for my future grandson dealing with a lot of macro work, with tiny little objects seen through bubbles.

SB: Oh, that sounds like fun!

PF: That's a fun, upbeat one. Of course, my work tends to start upbeat then, sometimes, it takes a turn to the dark side. I and a lot of my artist friends say that we have an "Aha" moment. And, lately, I seem to have an "Oh my gosh" moment instead, or a "Yikes" kind of thing going on.

SB: (Laughs) It make you wonder what's going on in your head.

PF: Yeah, sometimes; and that's okay. I'm willing to go with it.

SB: (Background music) You can see Fingerhut's work and judge for yourself at her website, pamelafingerhut.com.

That's it for this edition of "51%." Thanks for listening. If you had any comments about today's program or ideas for future shows, please e-mail me at sbartnett@wamc.org.

For "51%," I'm Susan Barnett.

Female Taxonomy

The *Female Taxonomy* project challenges society's perceptions of women. Portraits of women representing diverse demographics are combined with images of dolls, resulting in a series of photomontages that offer yet a third persona, provoking dialogue about stereotypes.

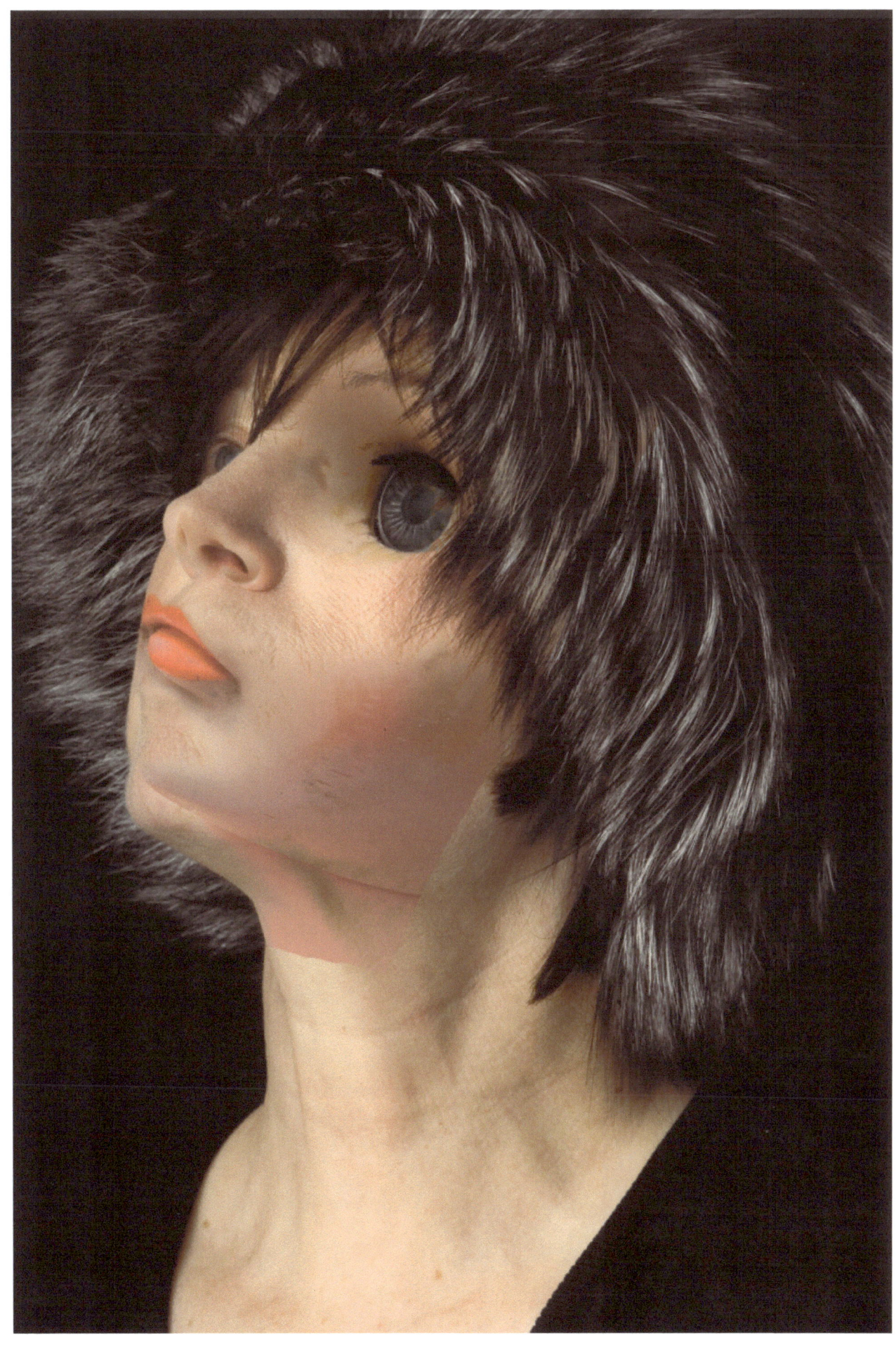

Female Taxonomy #1 (size 30 inches × 40 inches)

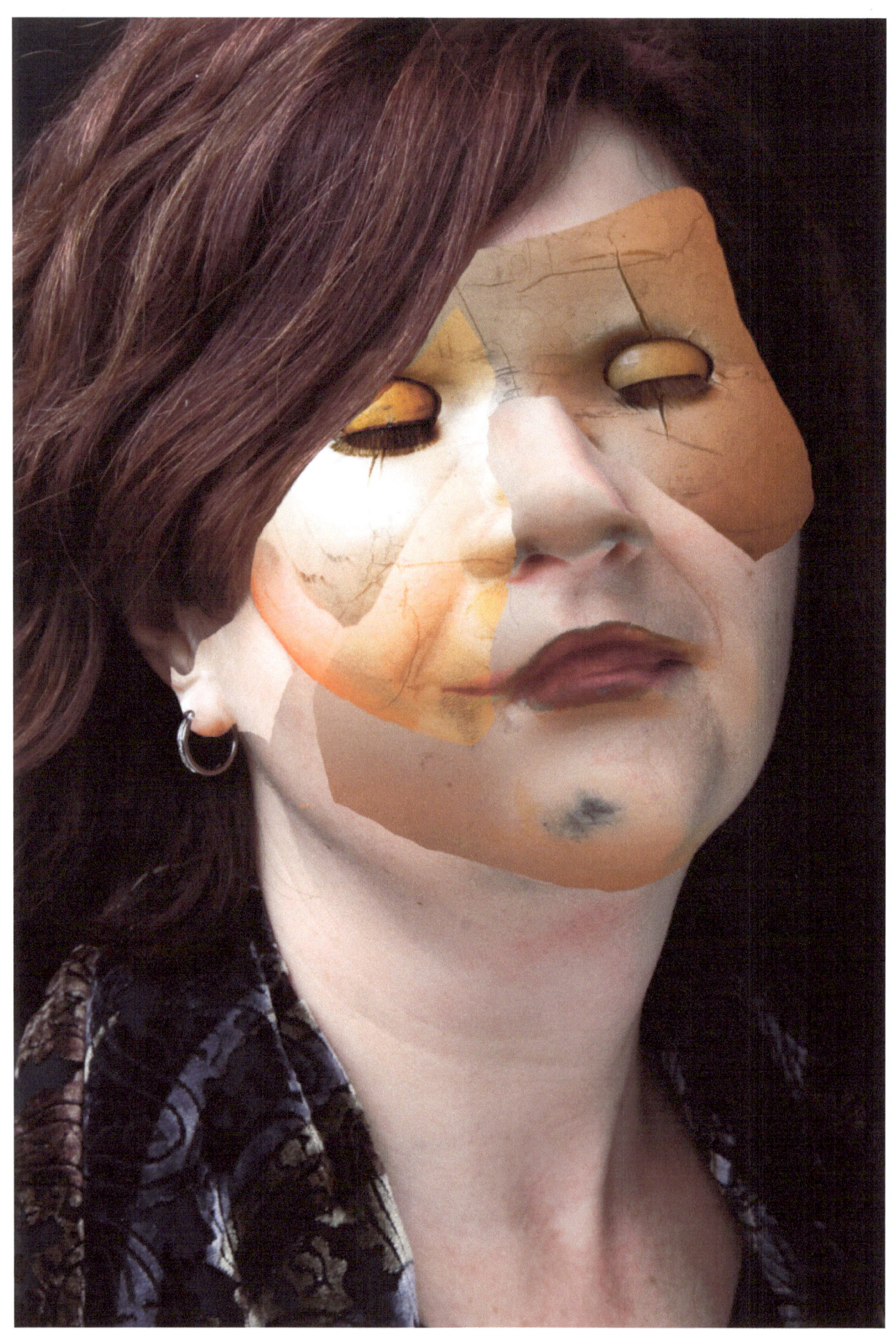

4   ℒ   Female Taxonomy #2 (size 30 inches × 40 inches)

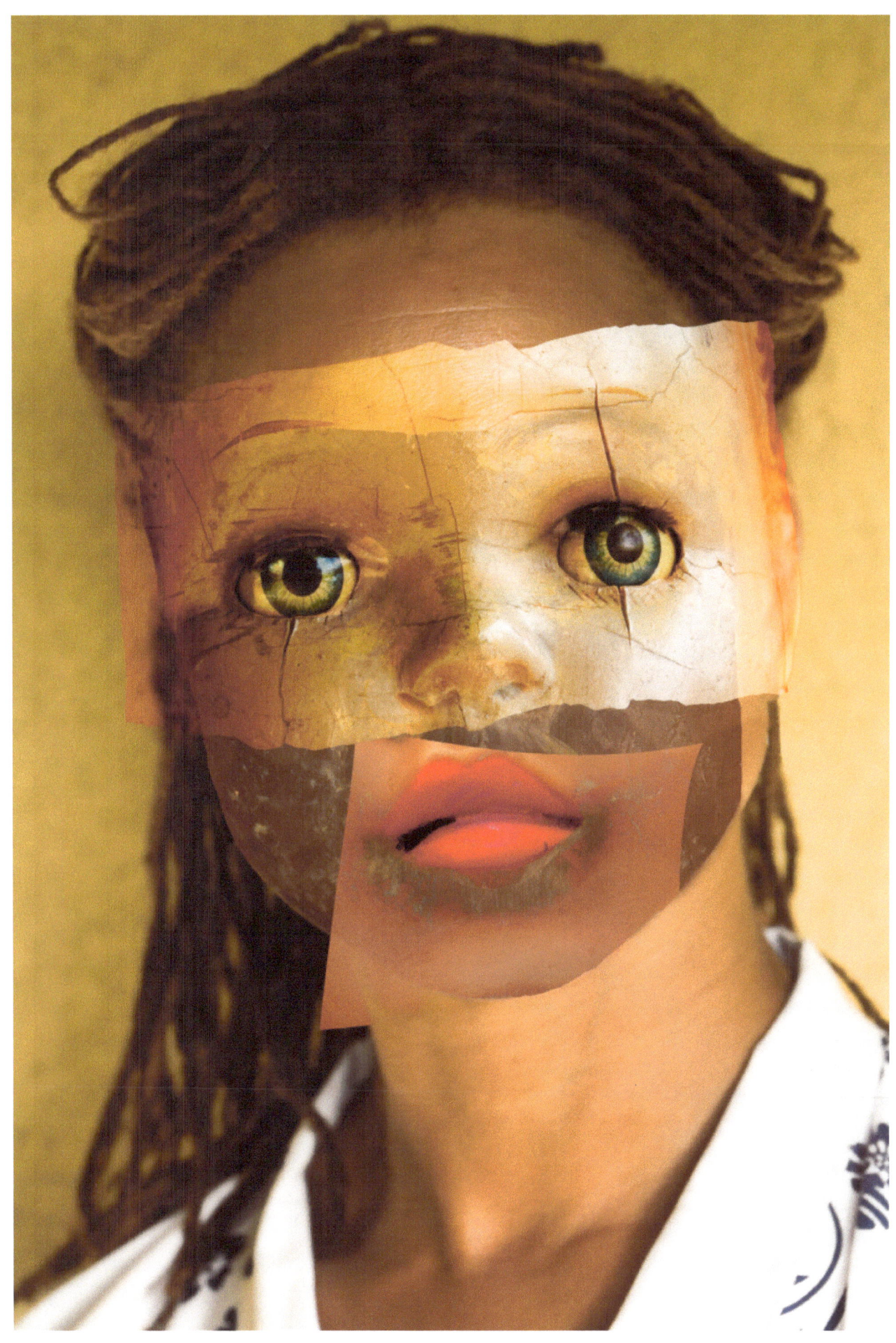

Female Taxonomy #3 (size 30 inches × 40 inches)

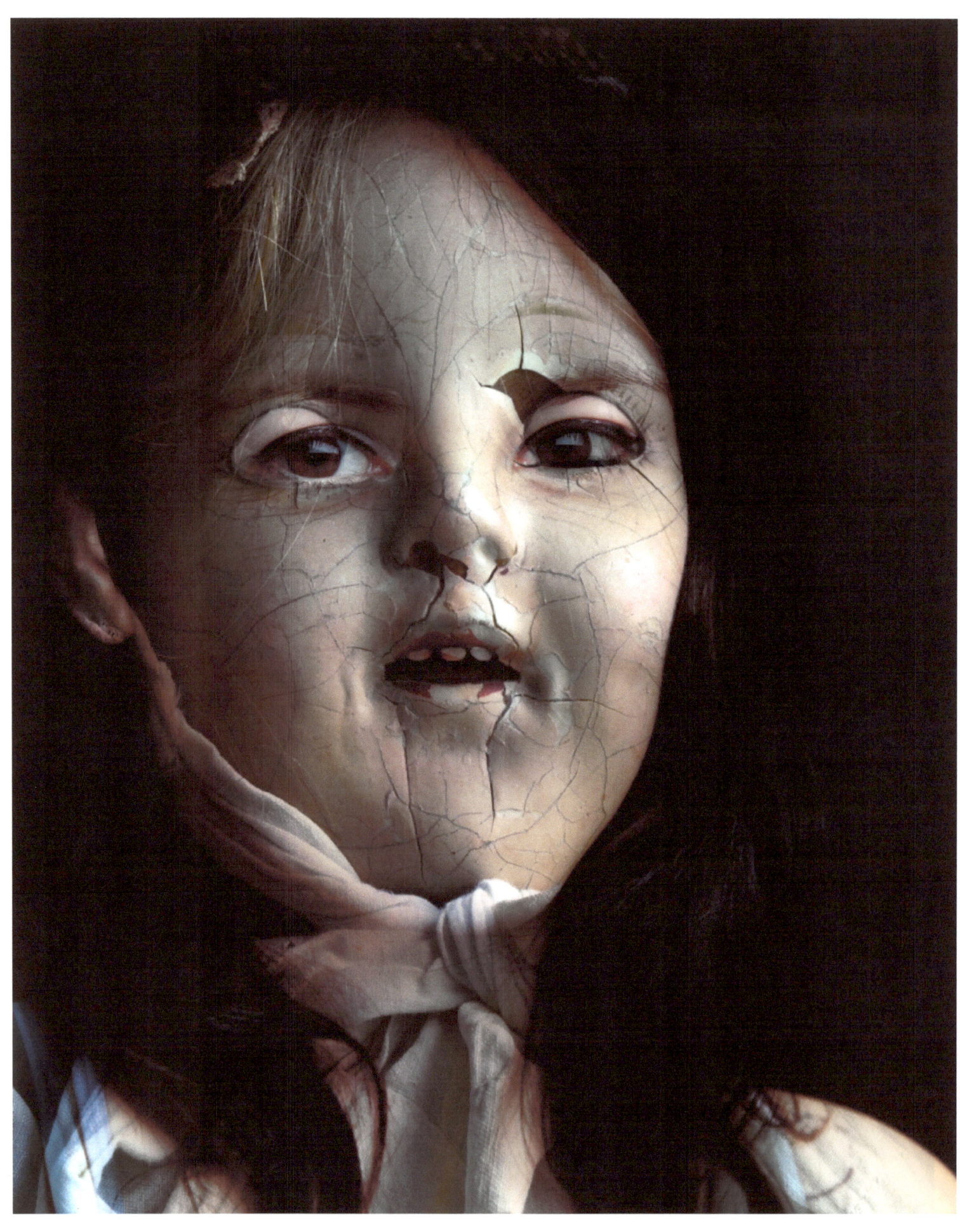

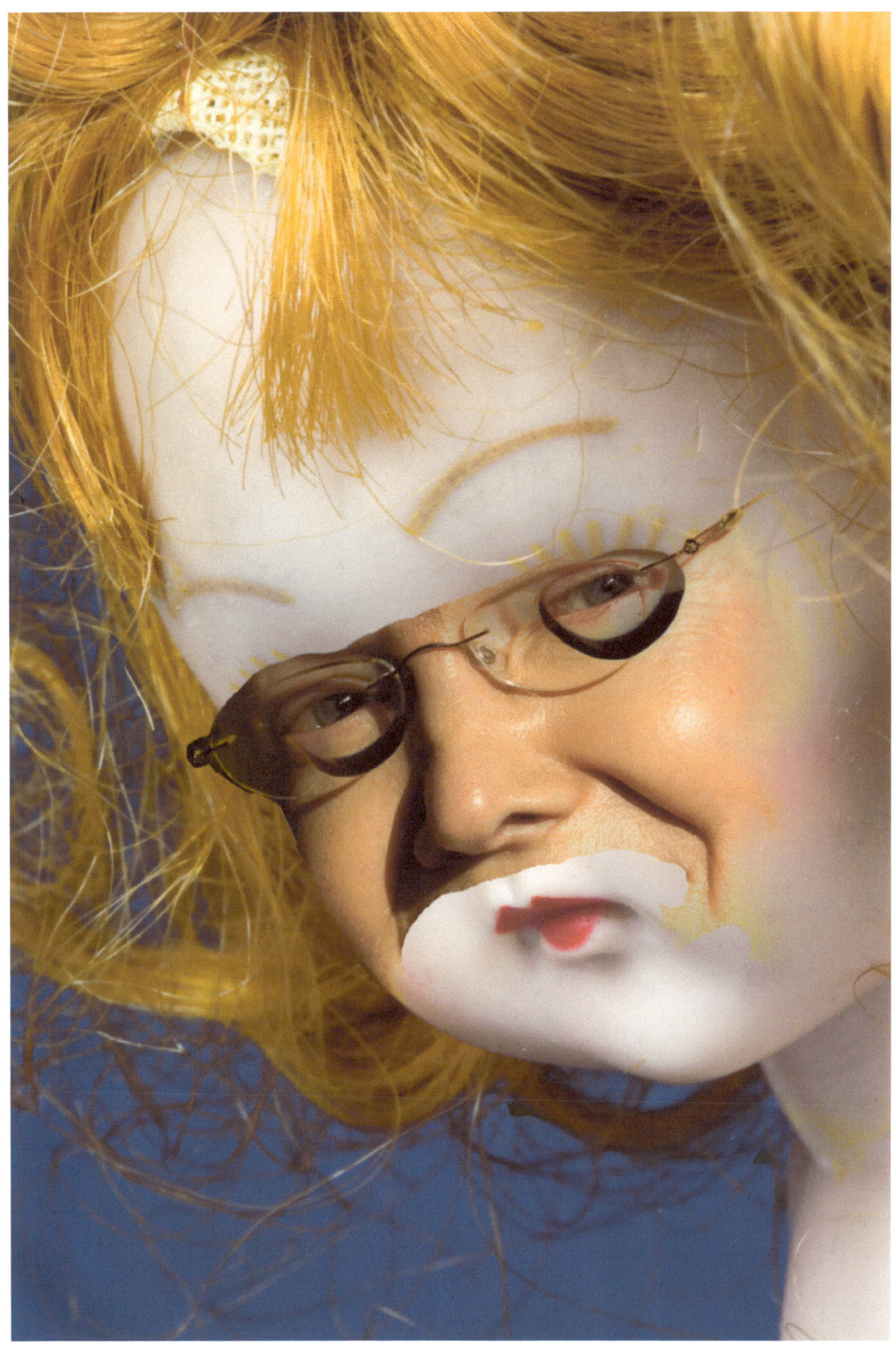

Female Taxonomy #7 (size 30 inches × 40 inches) ❧ **7**

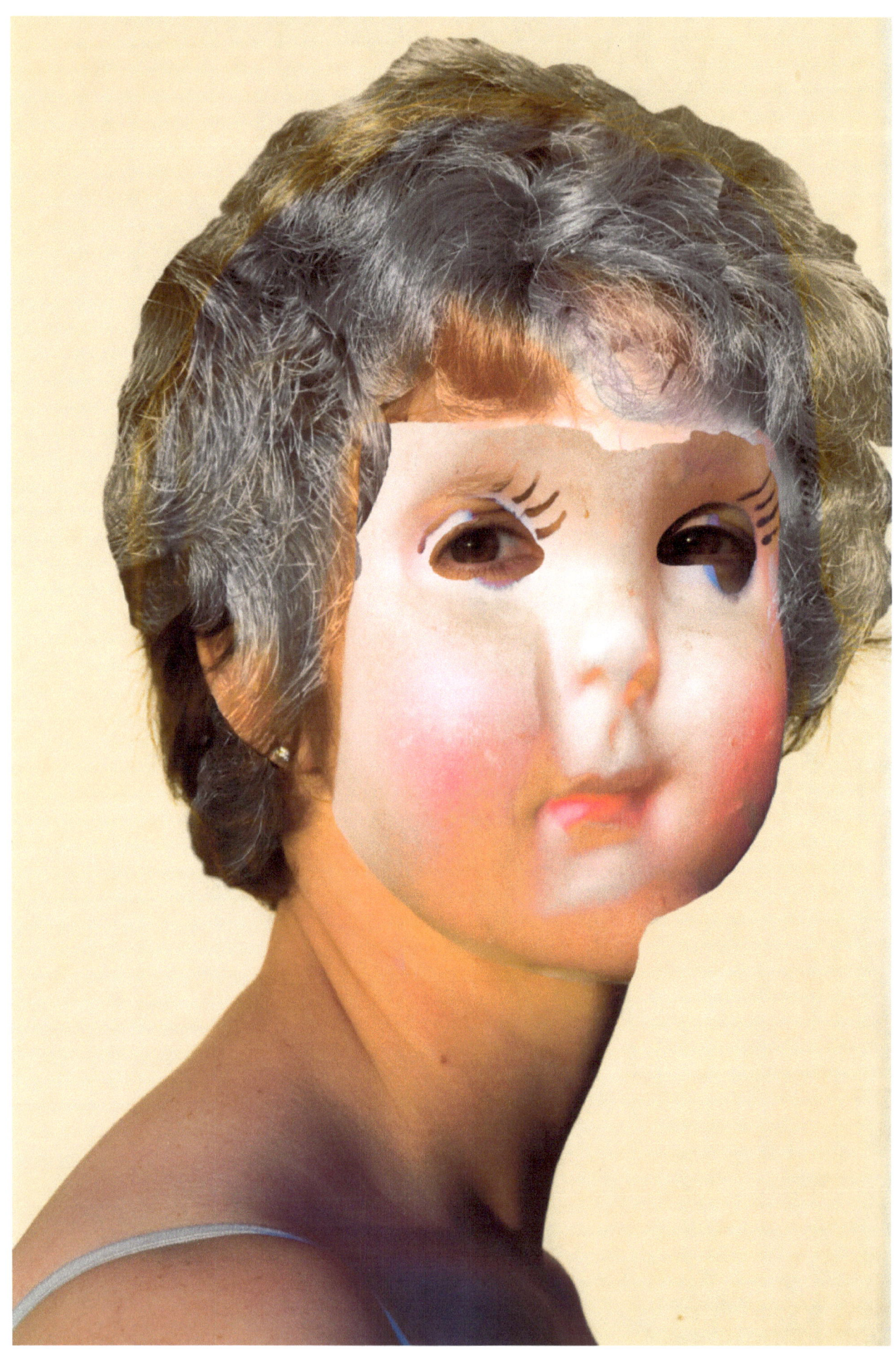

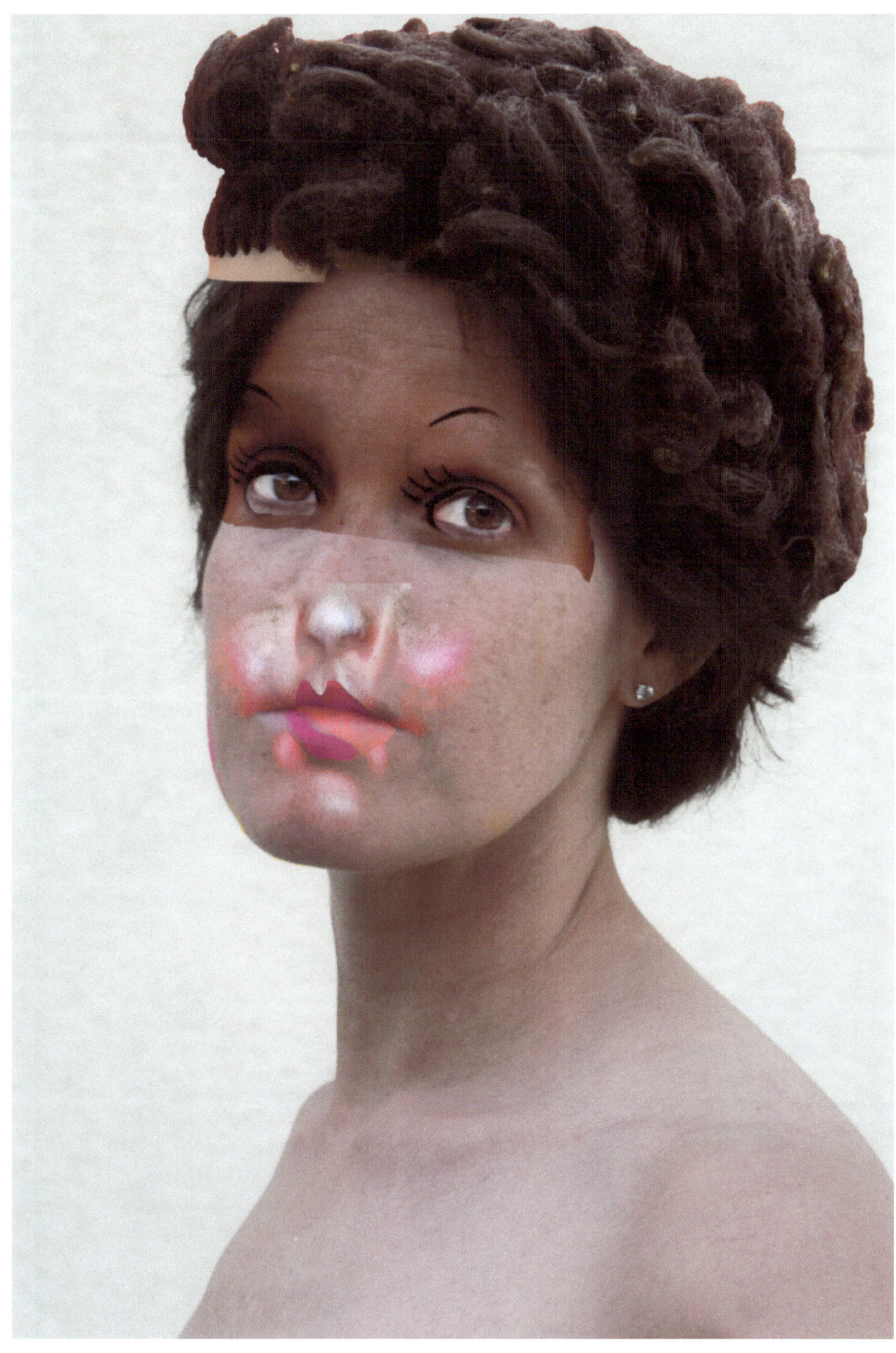

Female Taxonomy #4 (size 30 inches × 40 inches) ❧ **9**

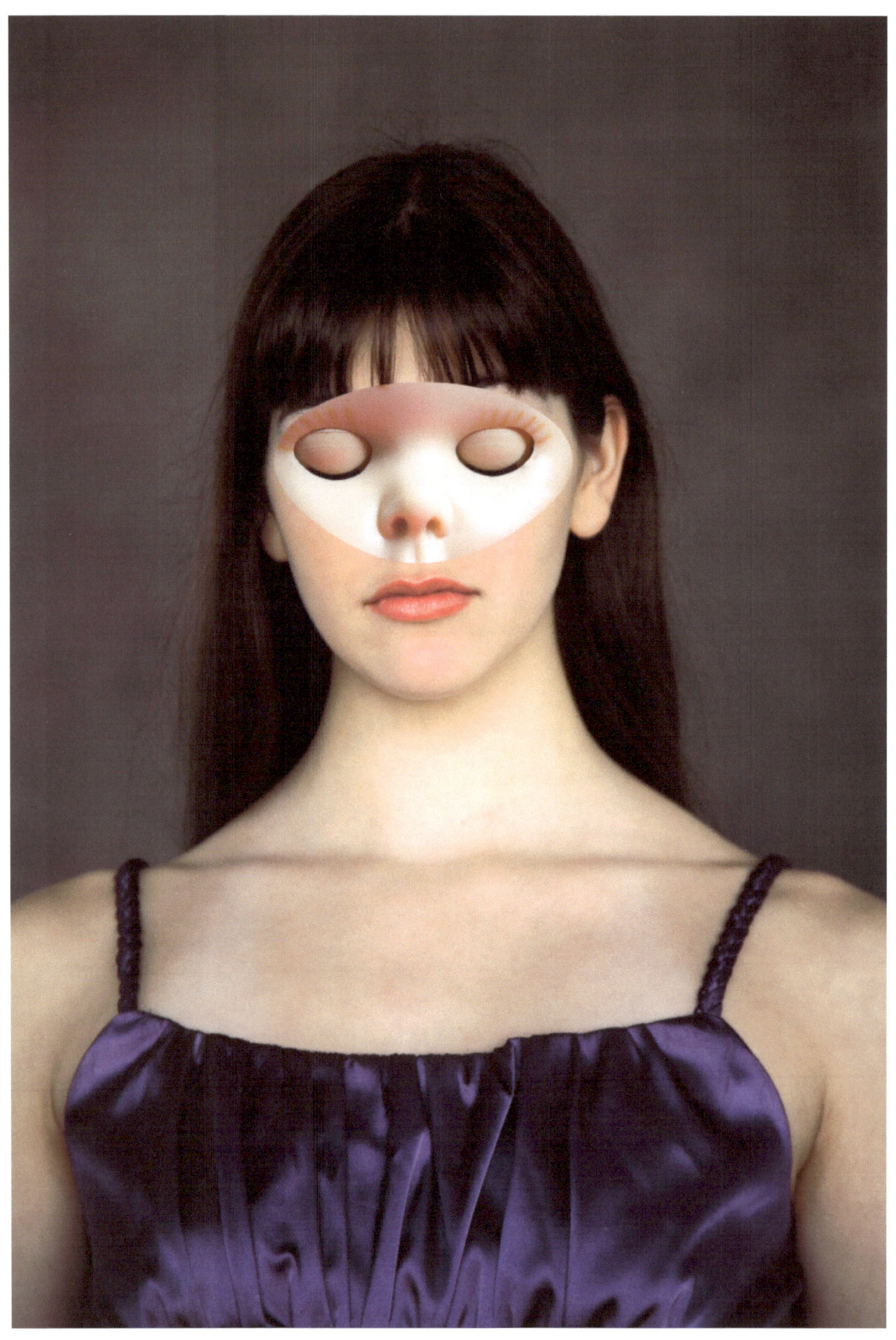

➷ Female Taxonomy #5 (size 30 inches × 40 inches)

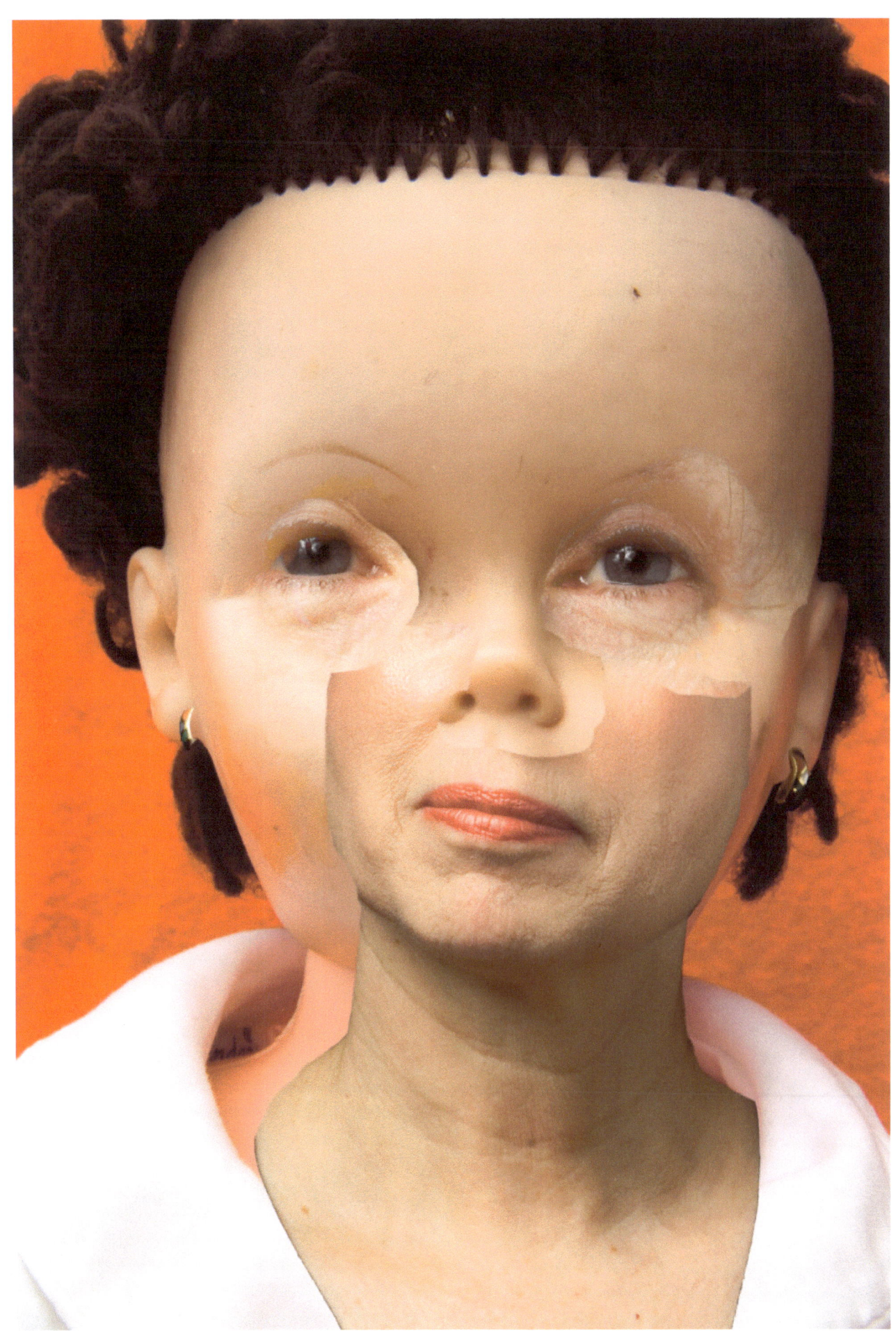

Female Taxonomy #9 (size 30 inches × 40 inches)

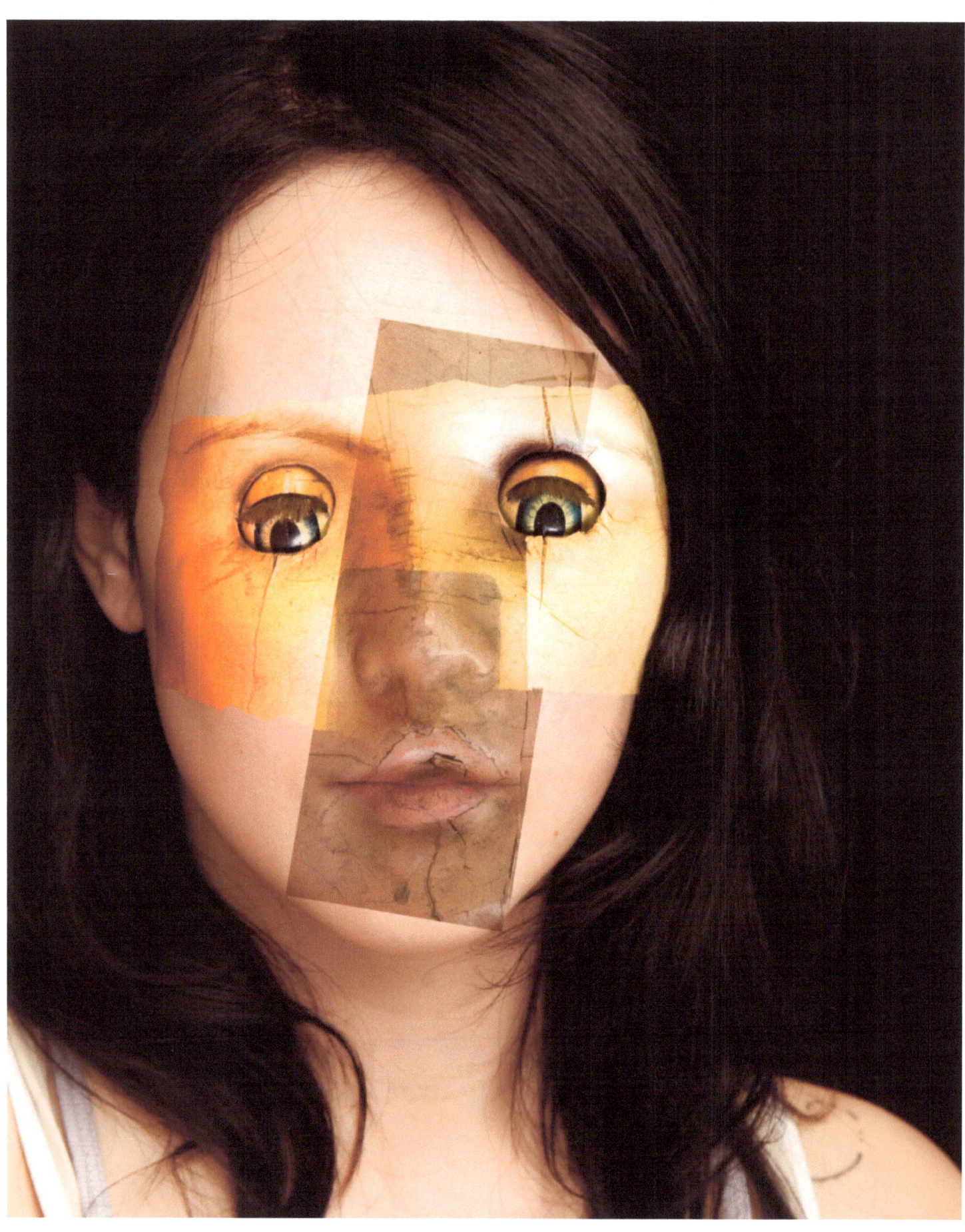

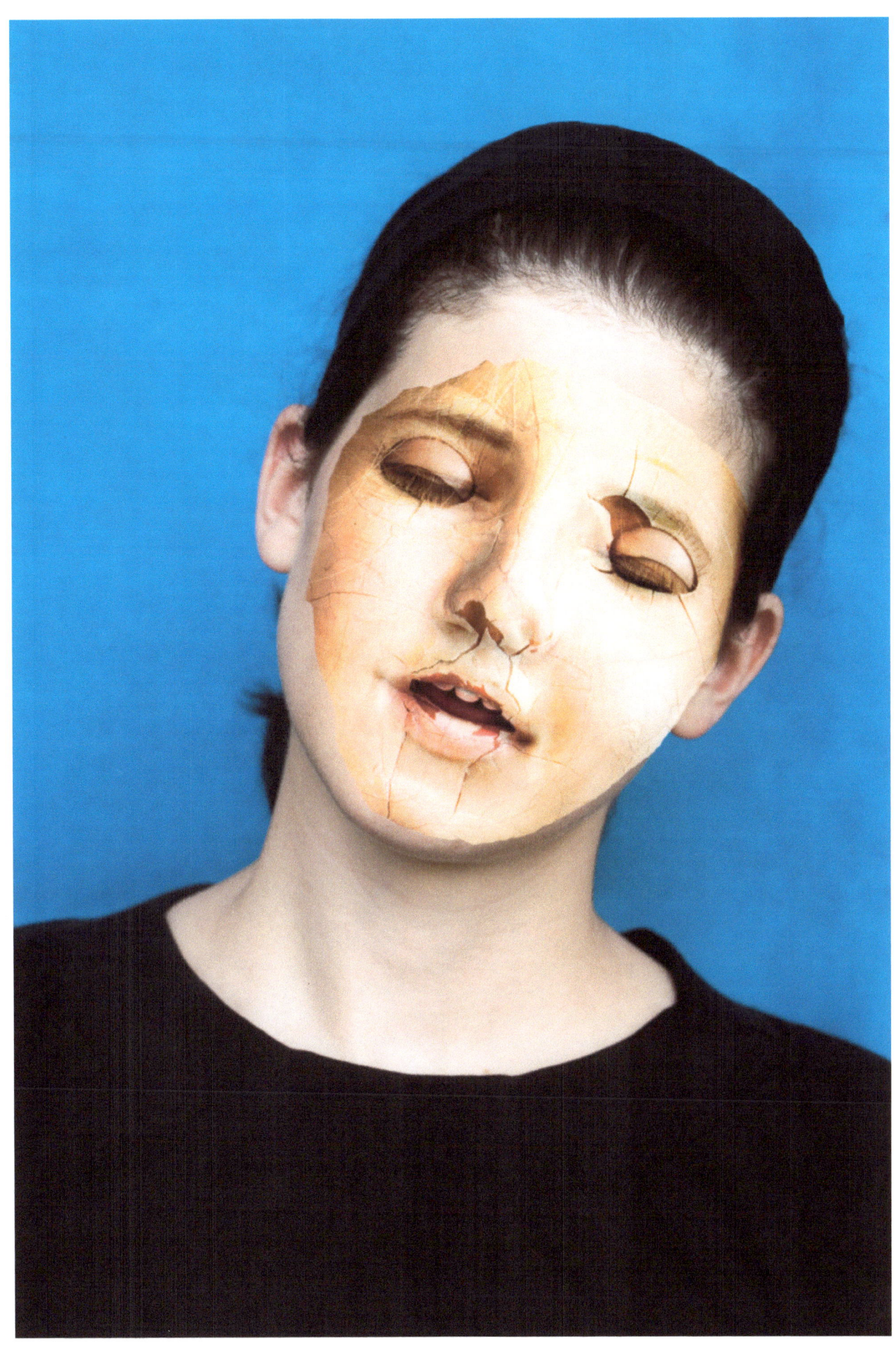

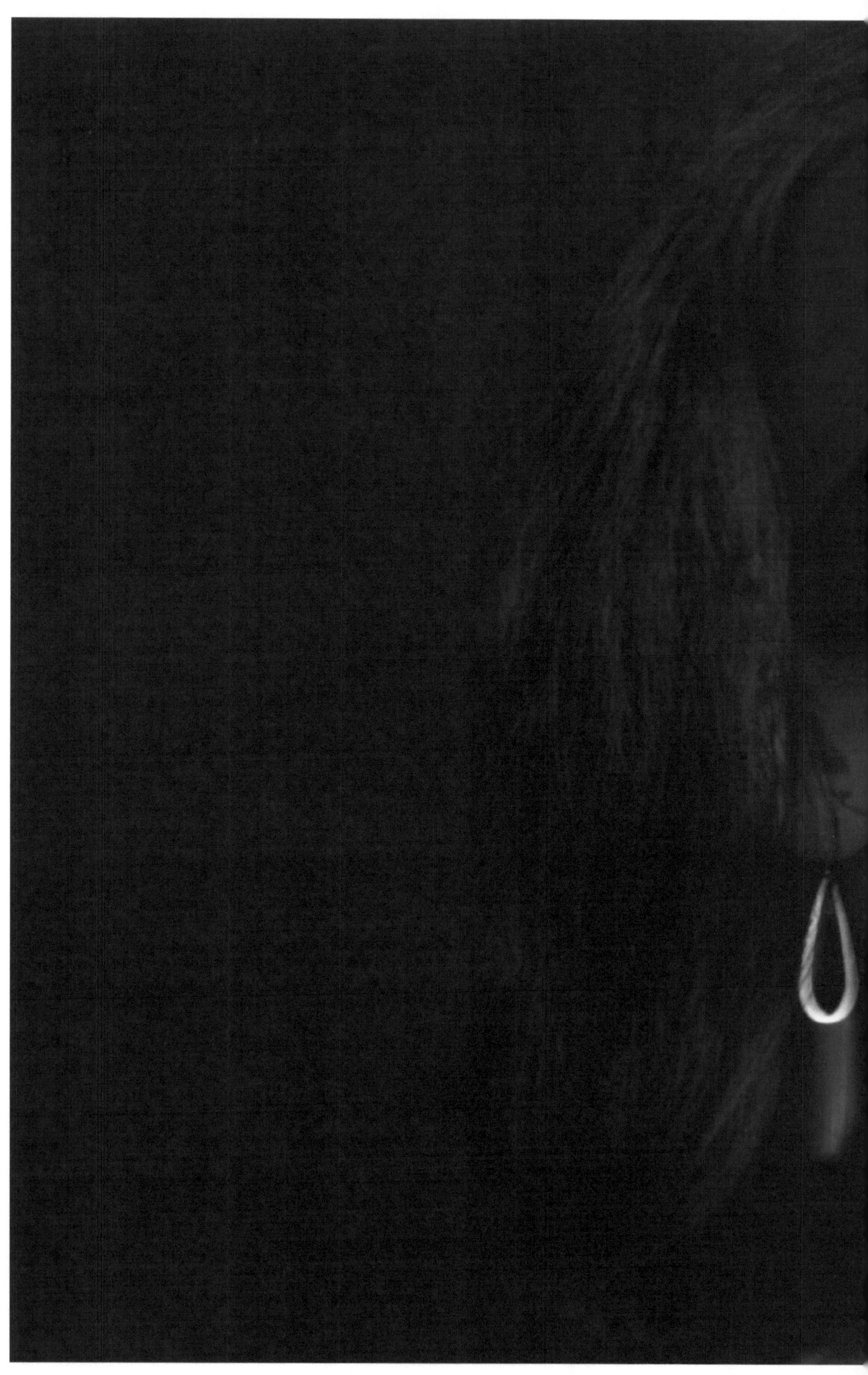

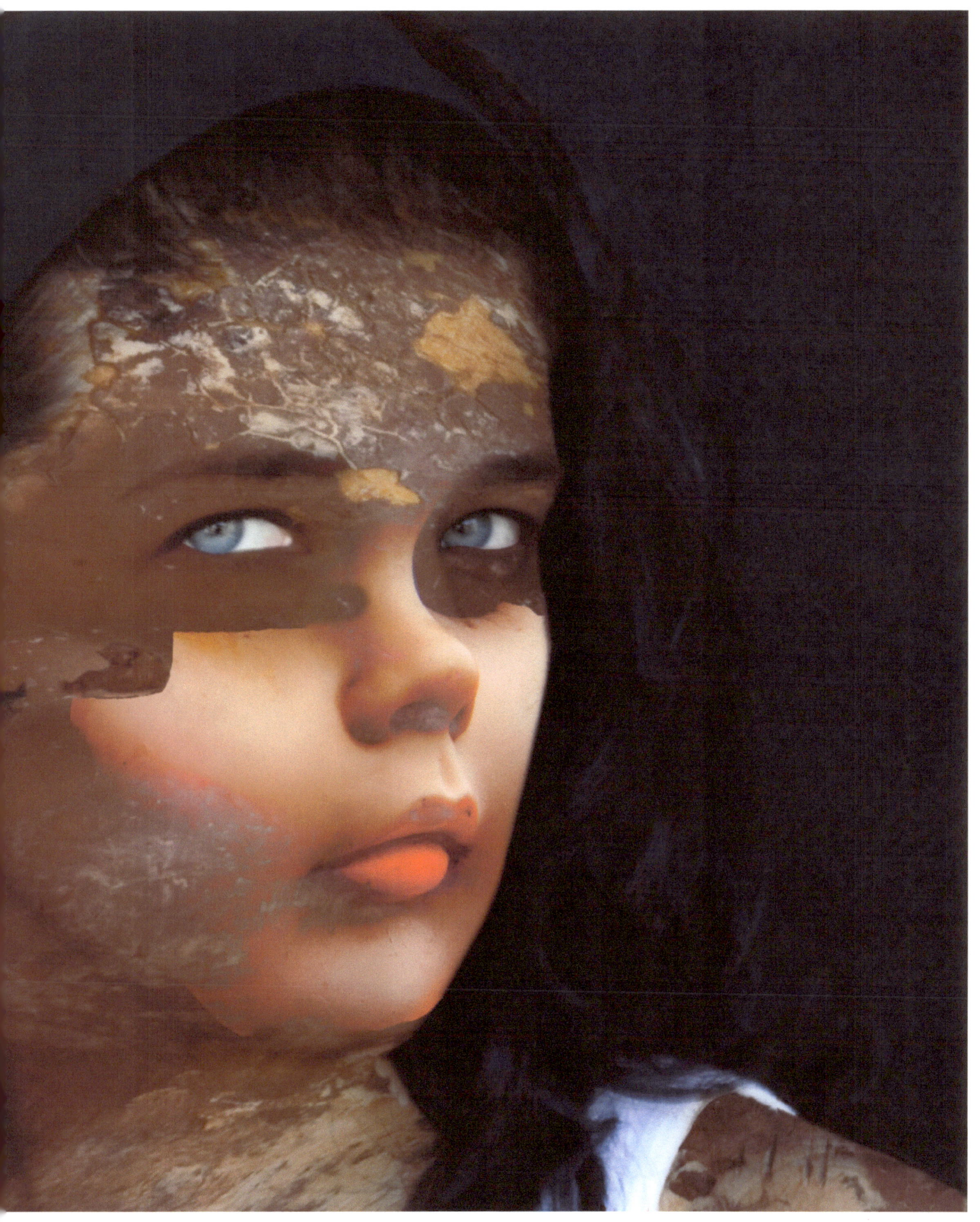

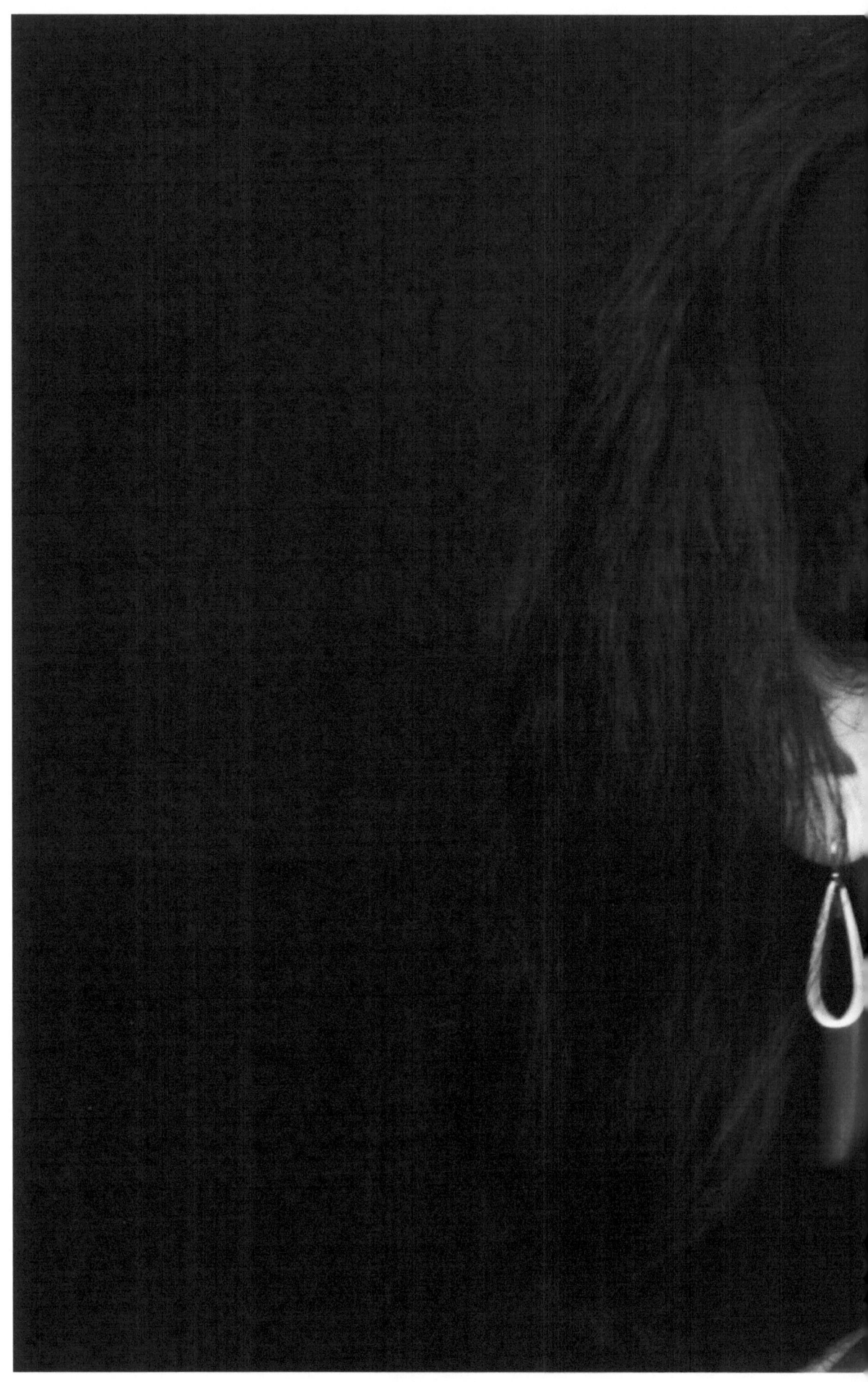

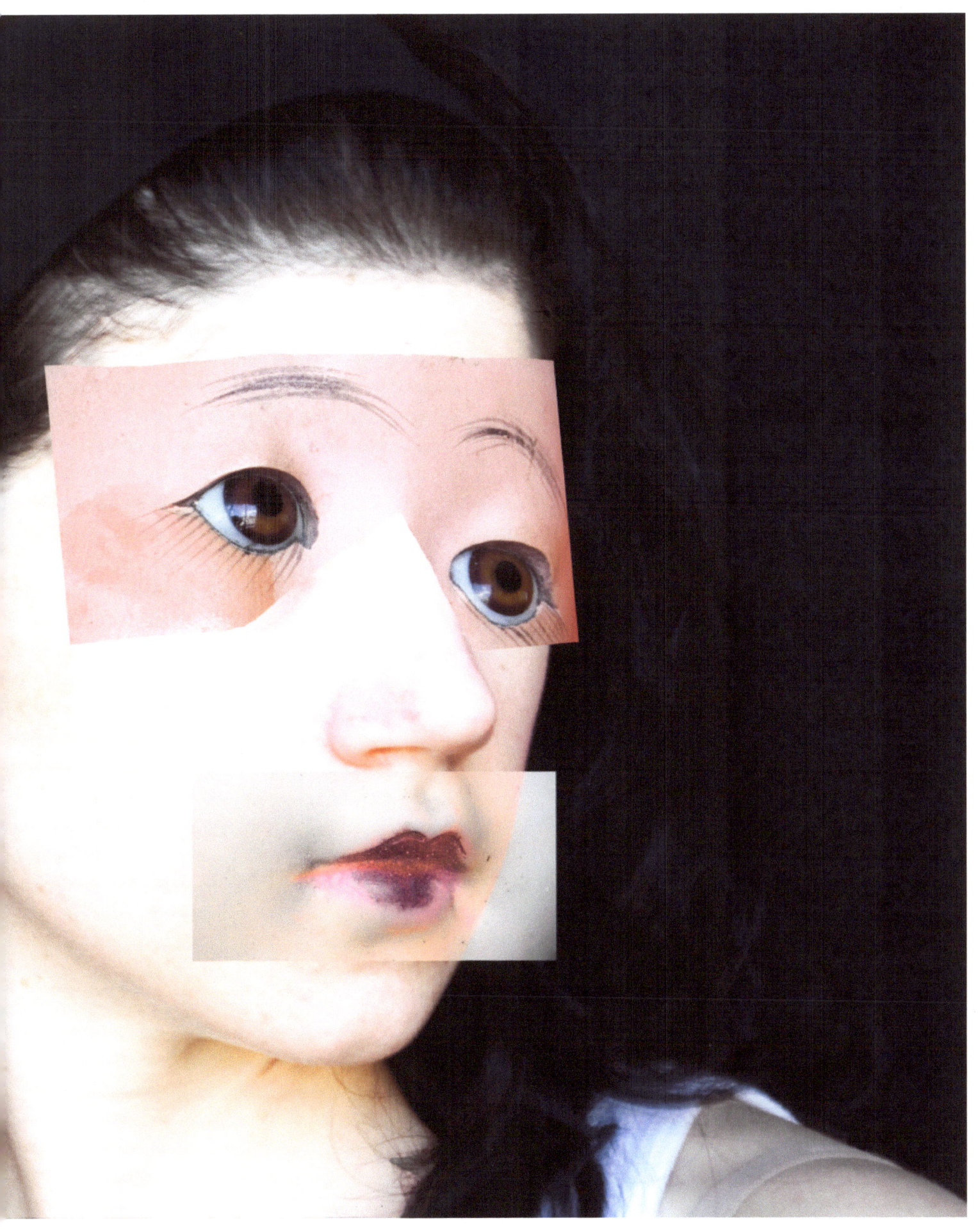

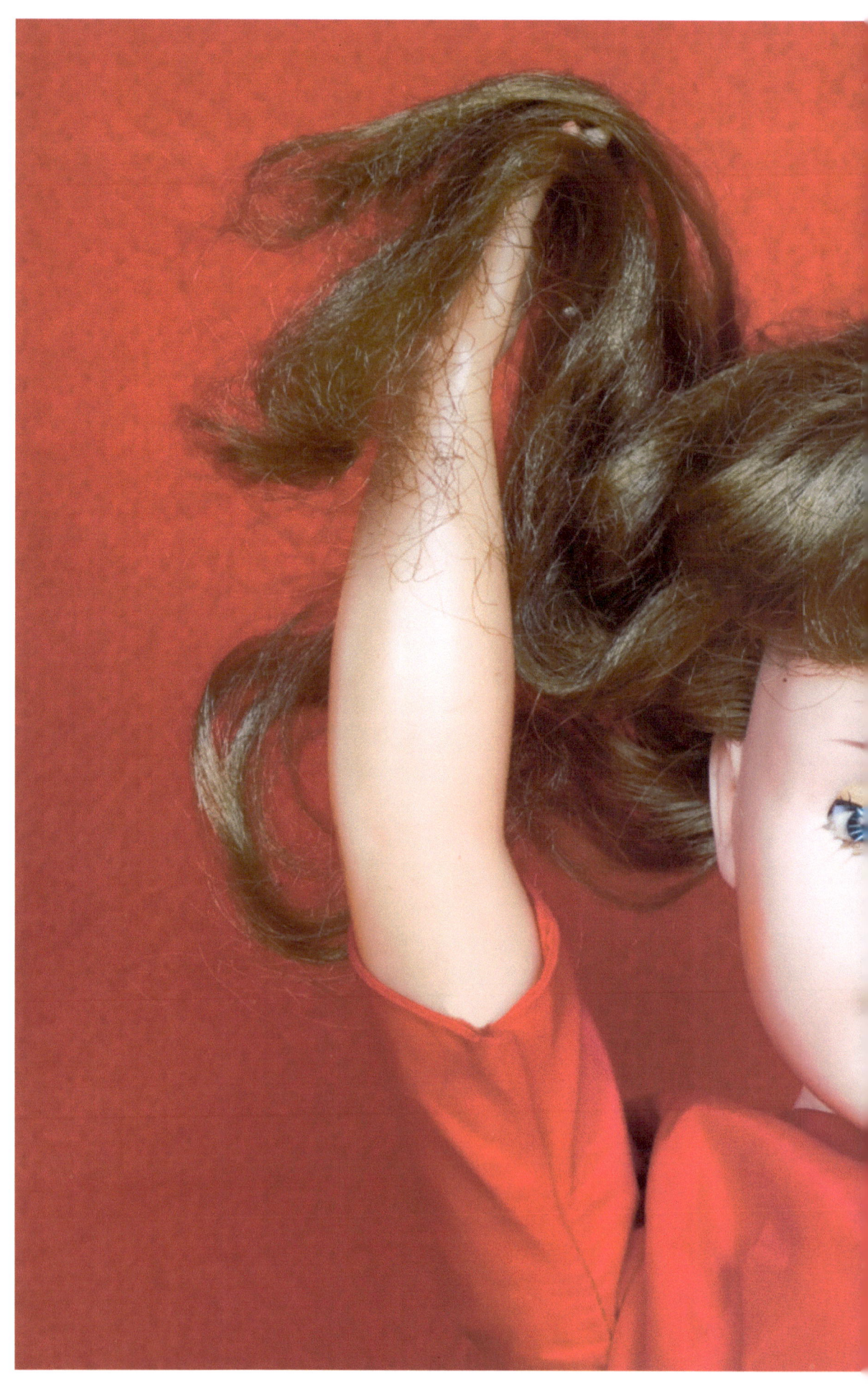

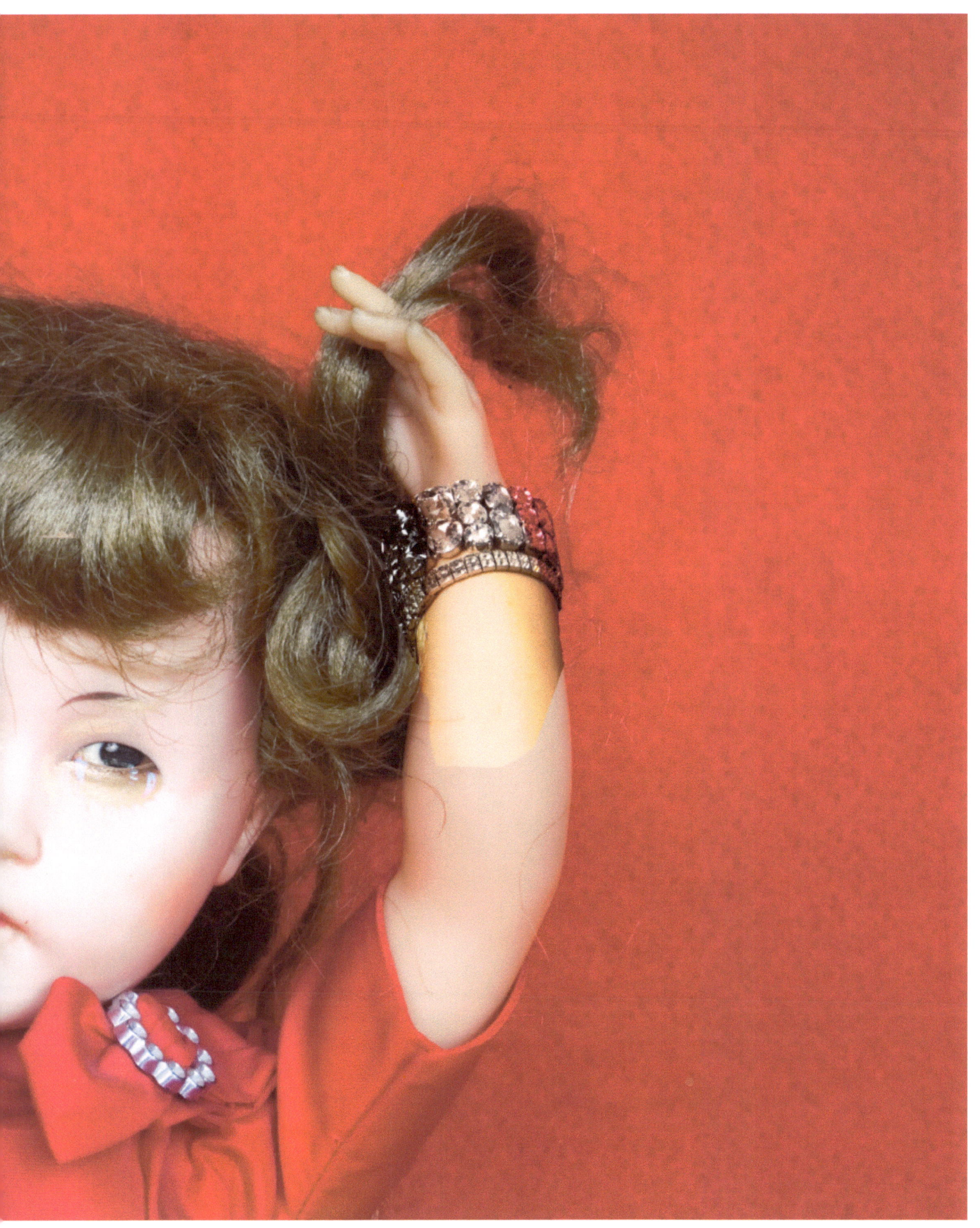

Female Taxonomy #15 (size 40 inches × 30 inches) ✍ **19**

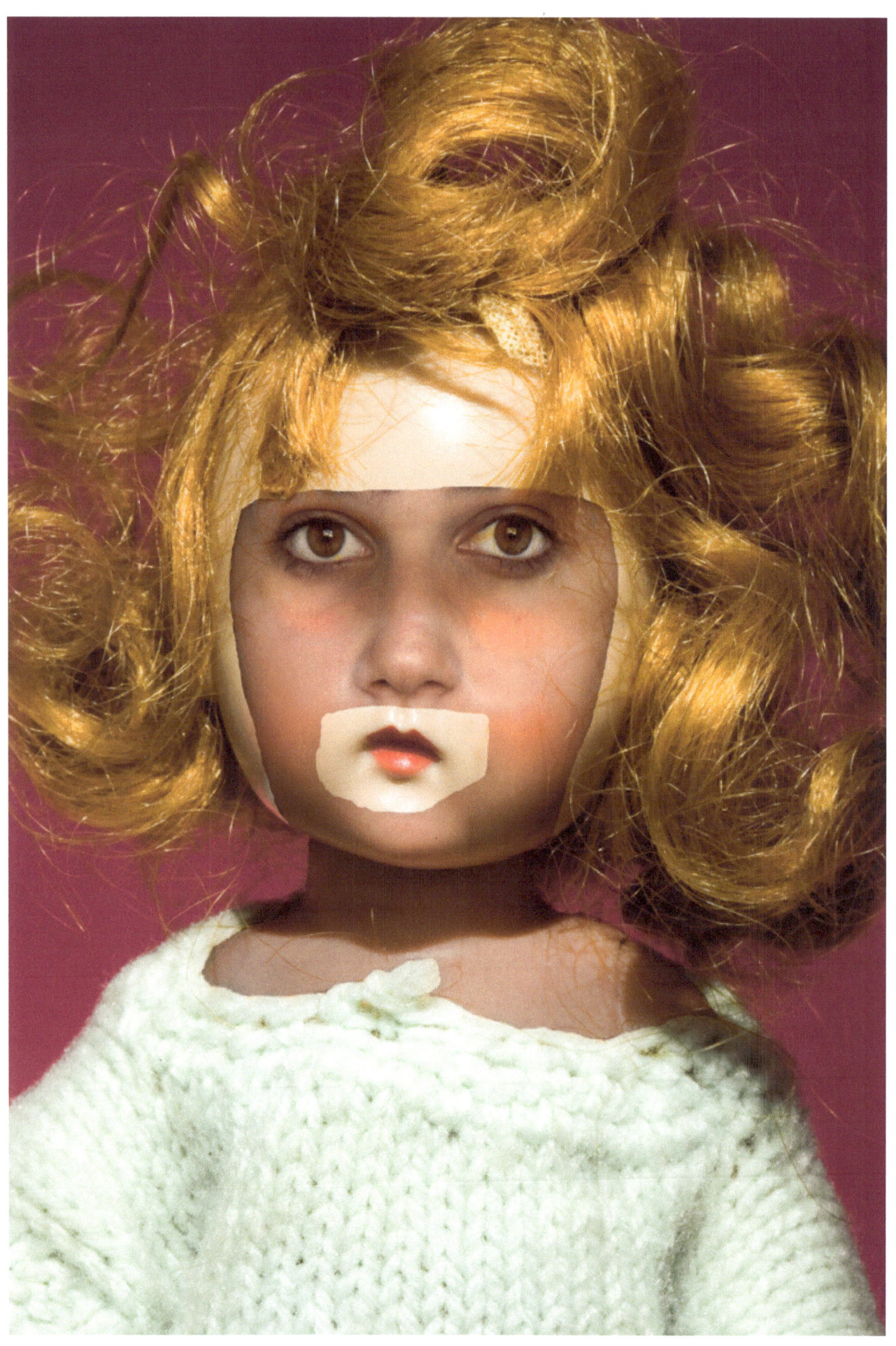

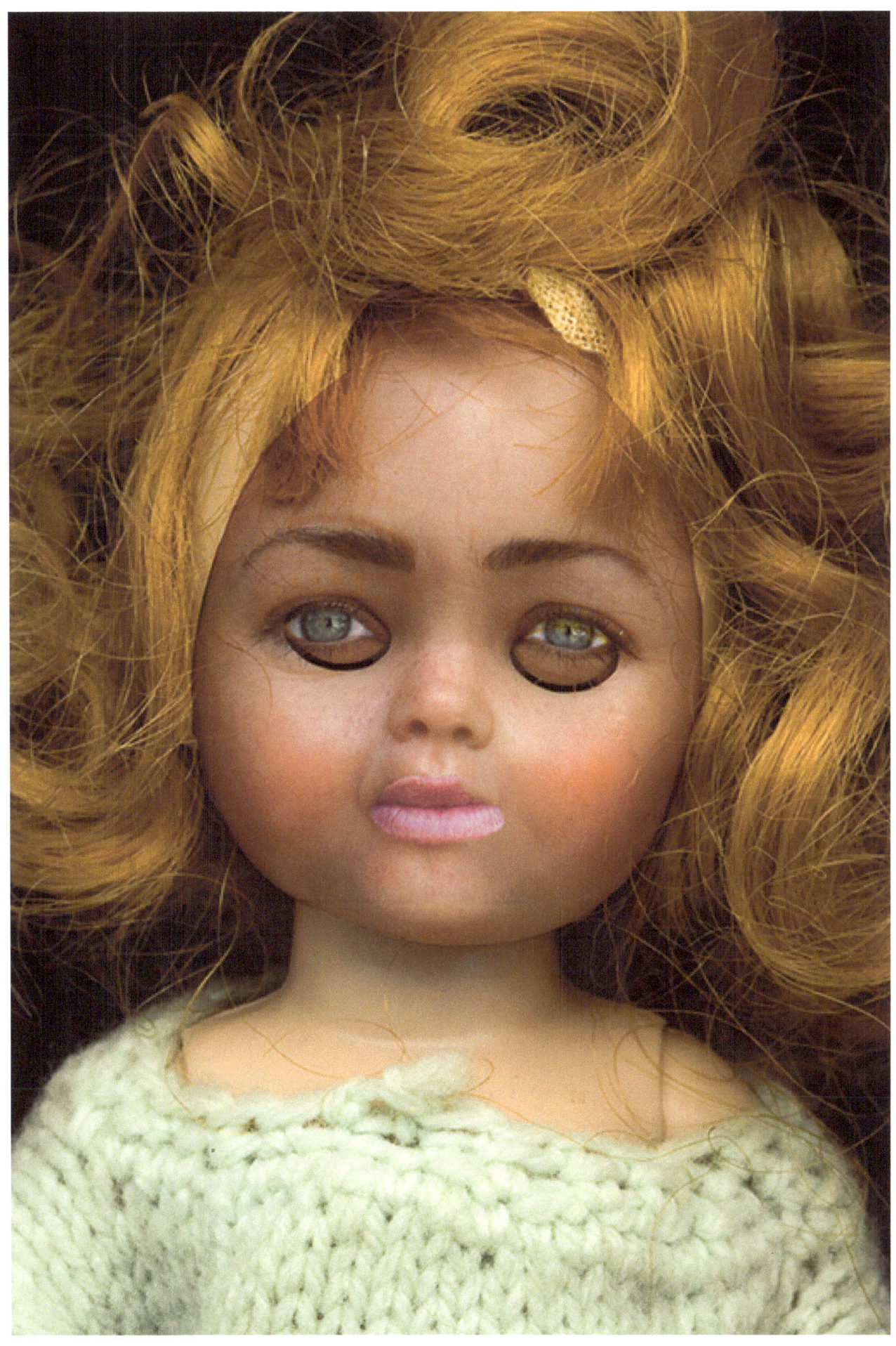

Female Taxonomy #8 (size 30 inches × 40 inches) ✎ **21**

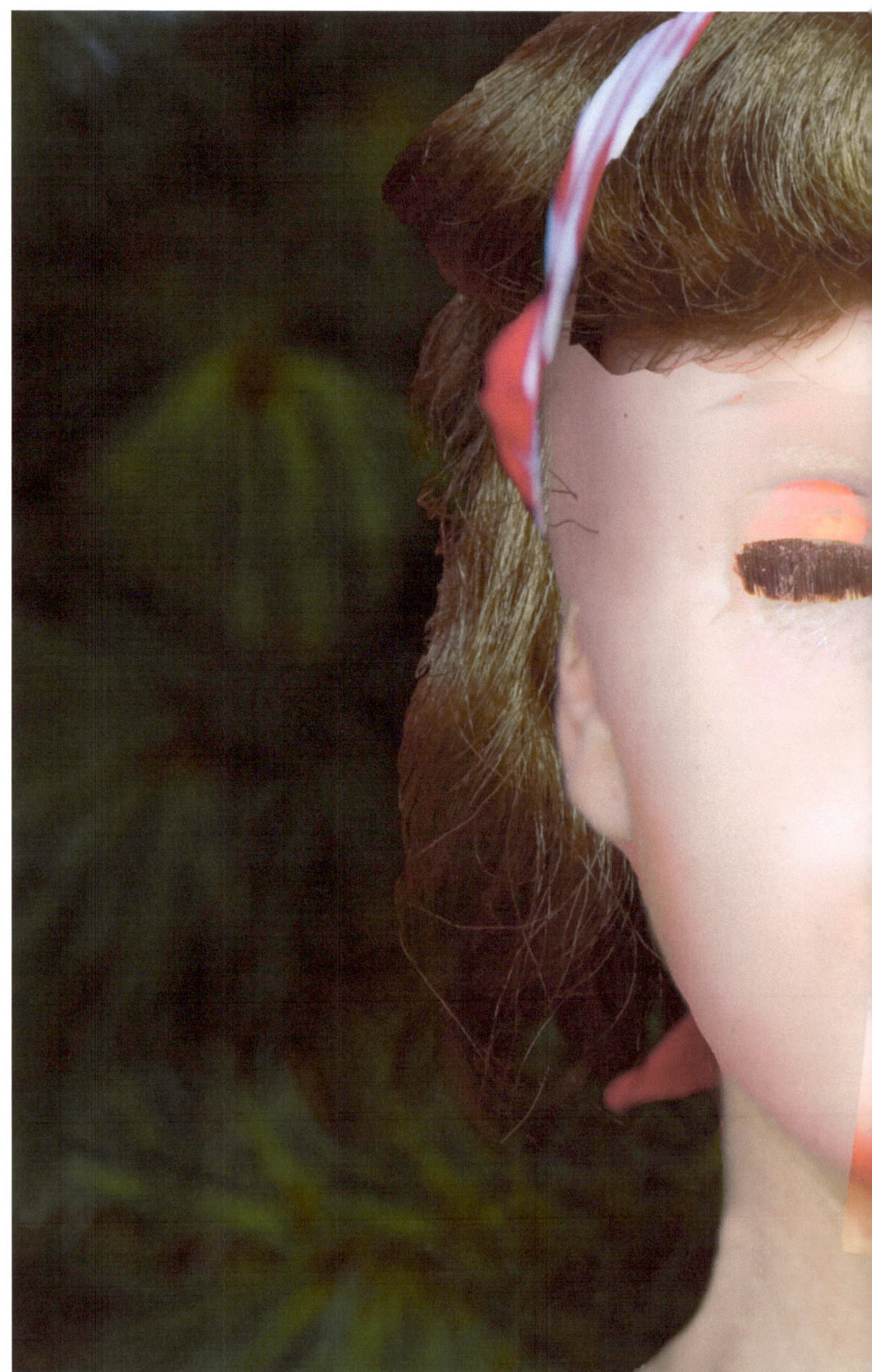

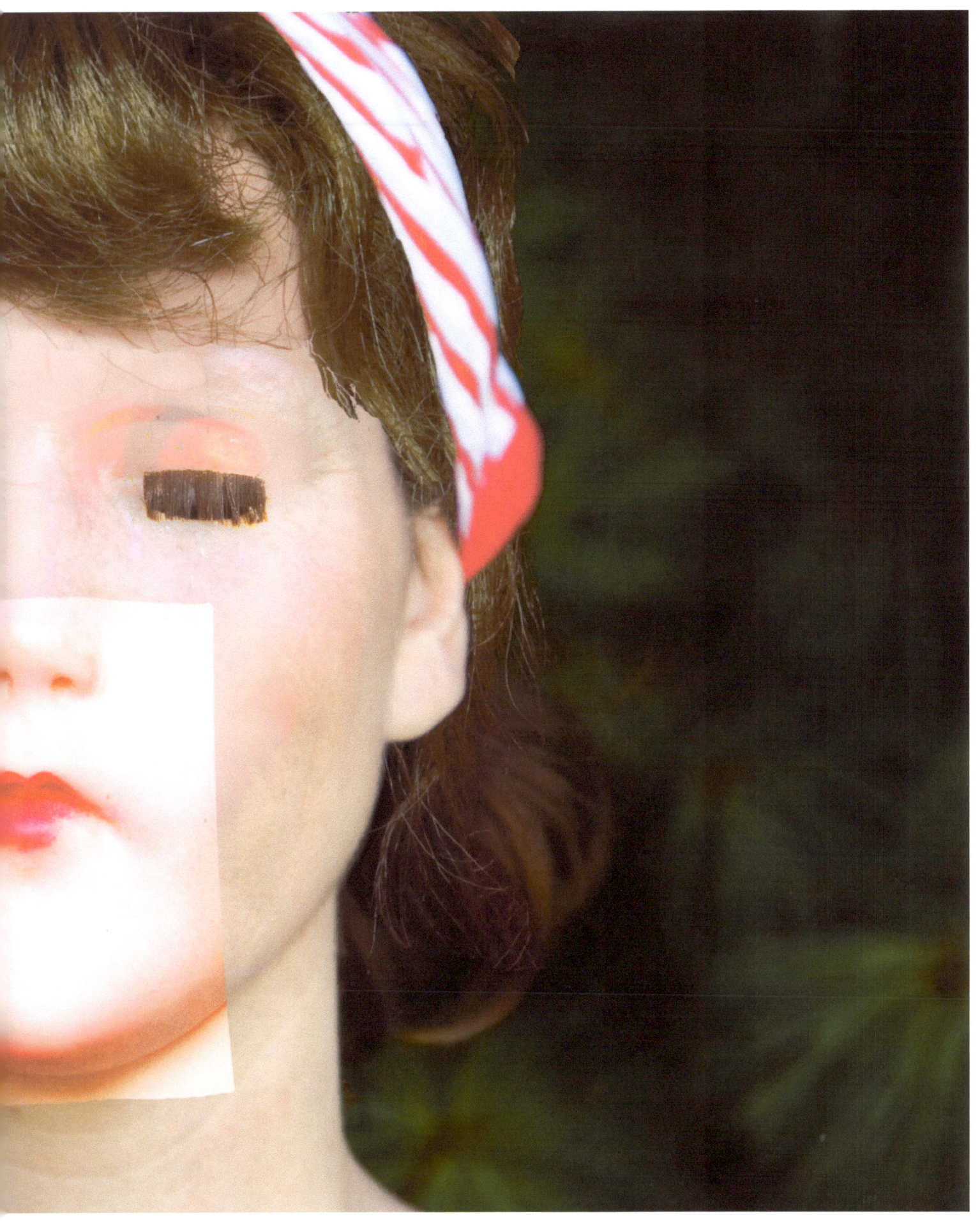

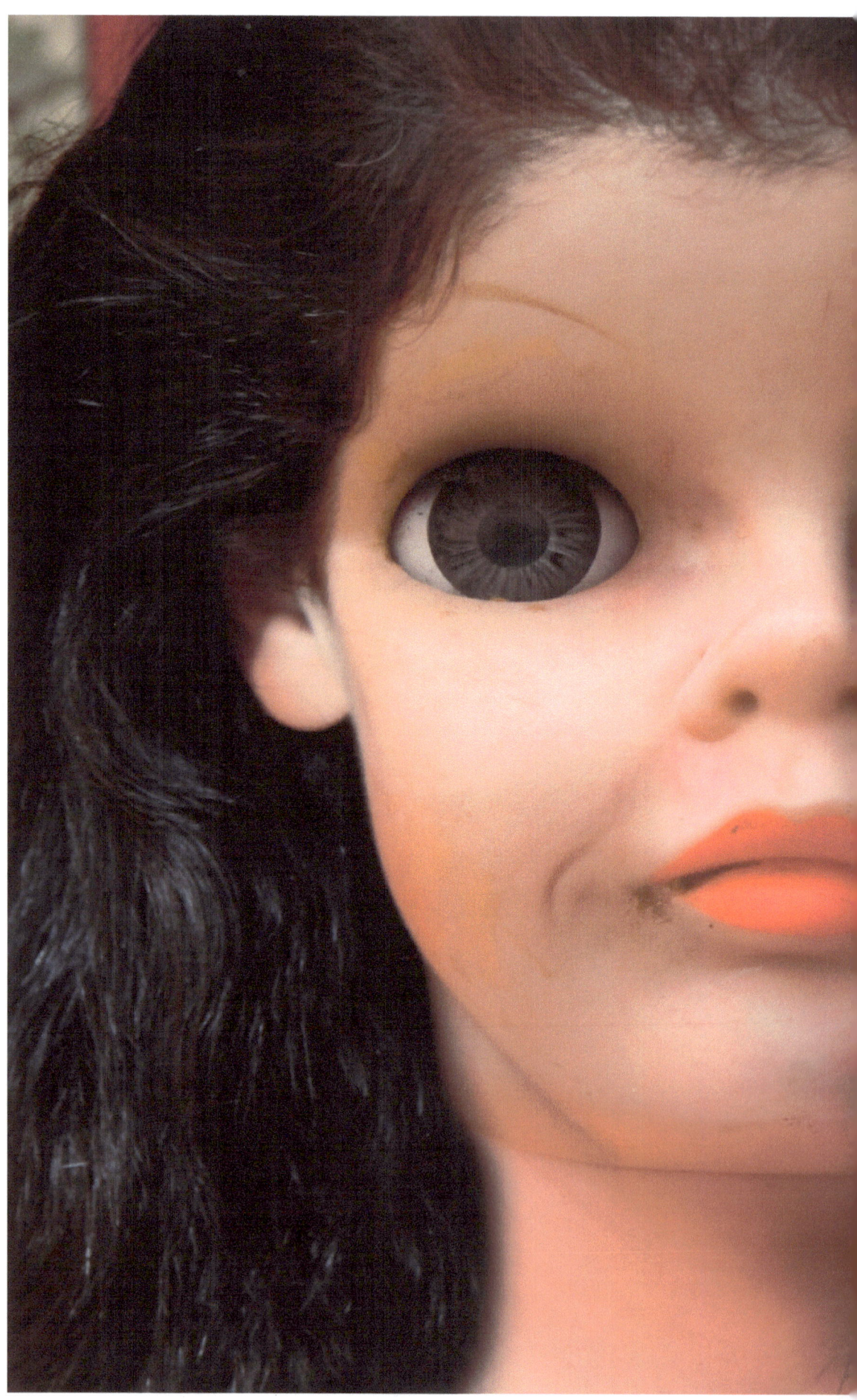

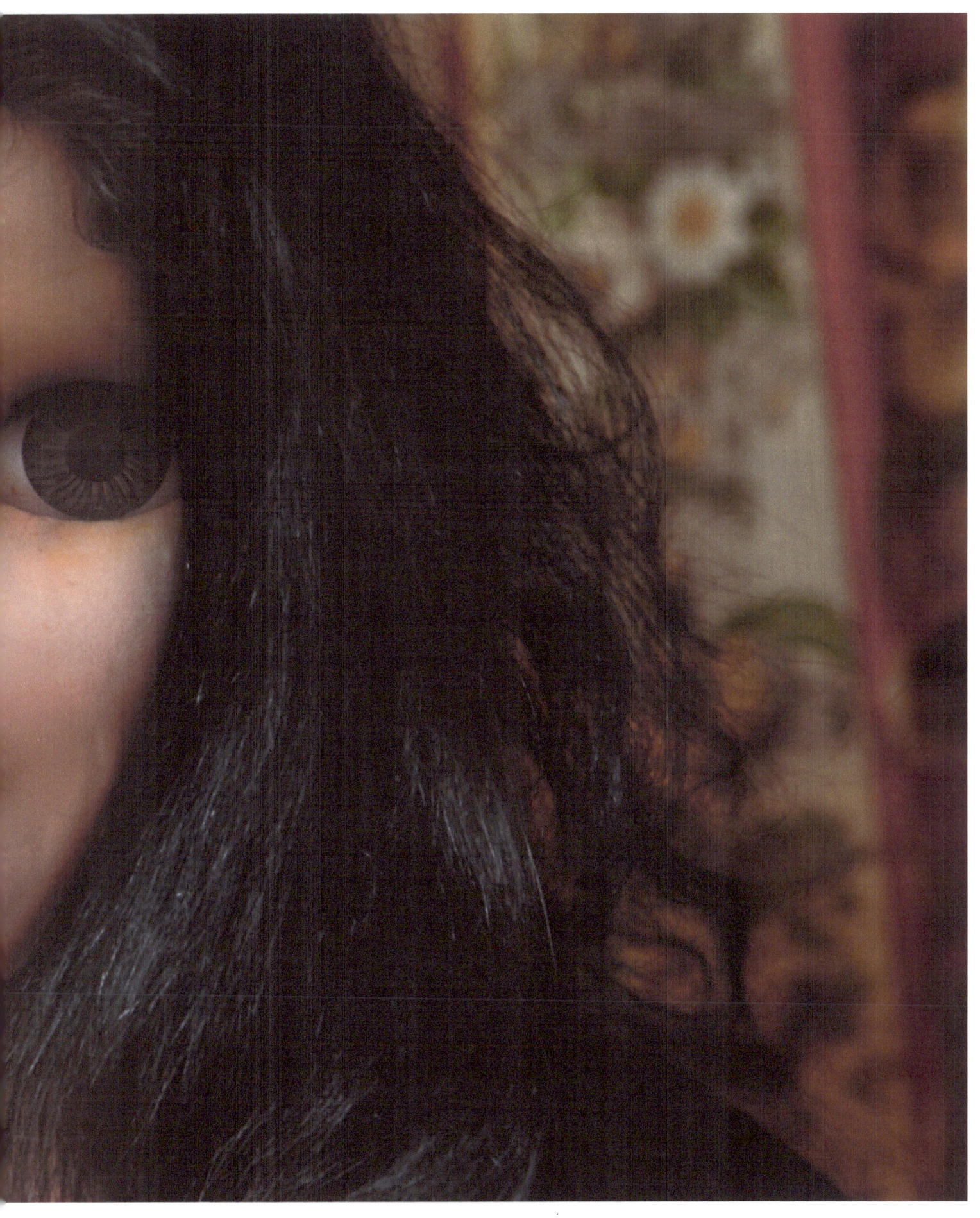

Female Taxonomy #17 (size 40 inches × 30 inches) ✖ **25**

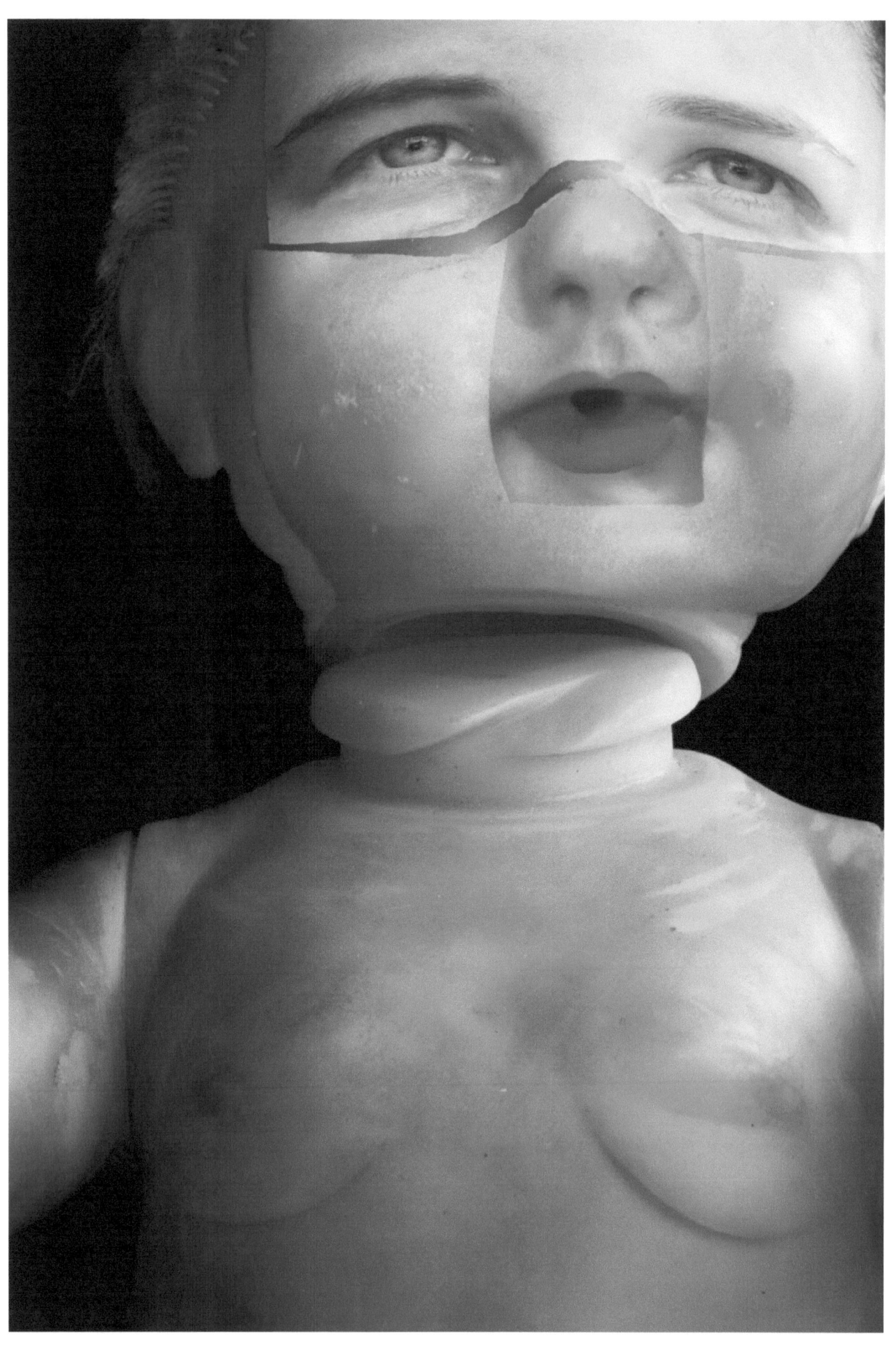

Her

Case

The *Her Case* project is the artist's reaction to the post-9/11 practice of open searches of private property in public settings. The camera-eyed voyeur creates still lifes of women's handbags, exposing their contents and investigating capsule identities and secrets.

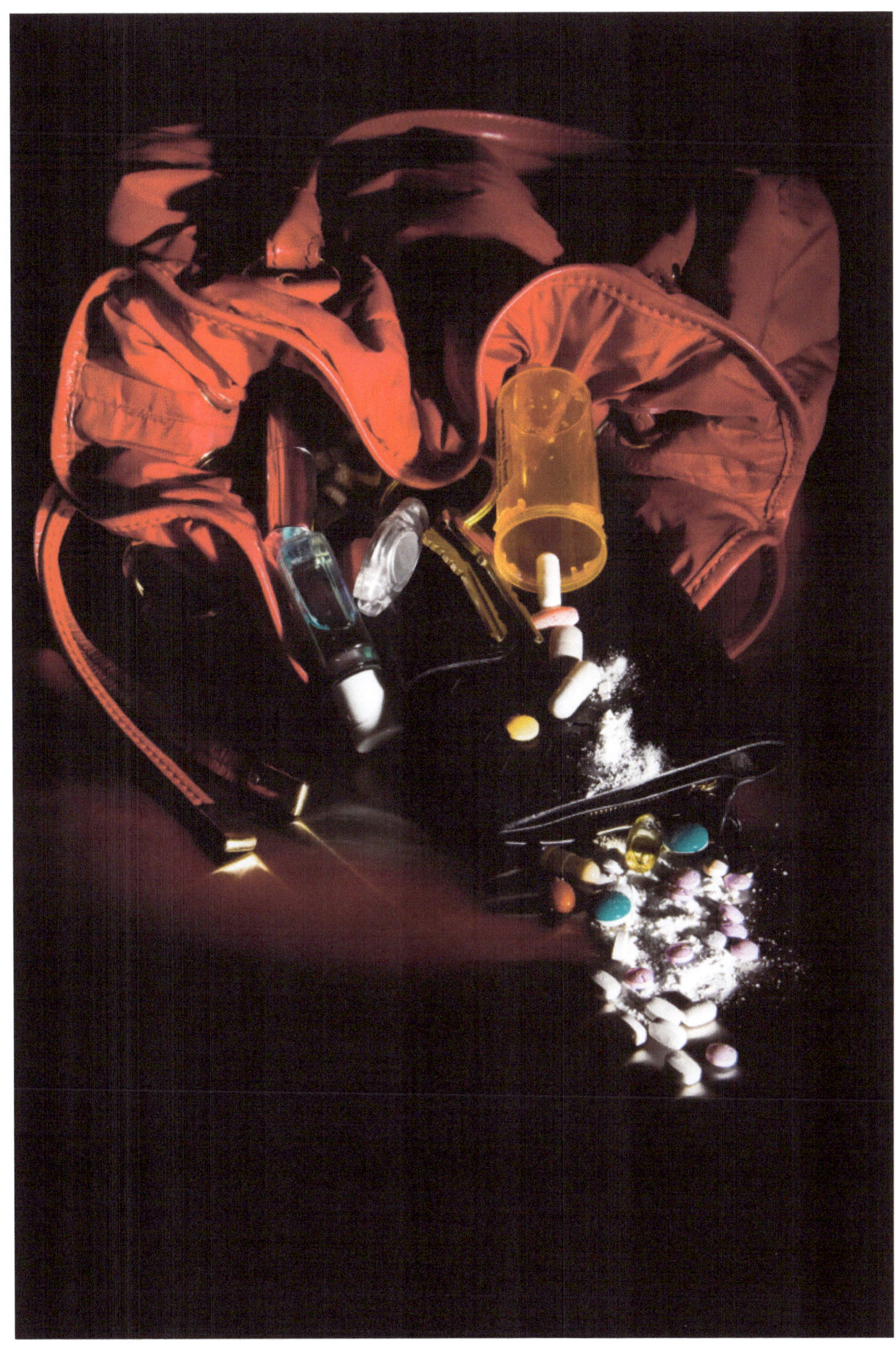

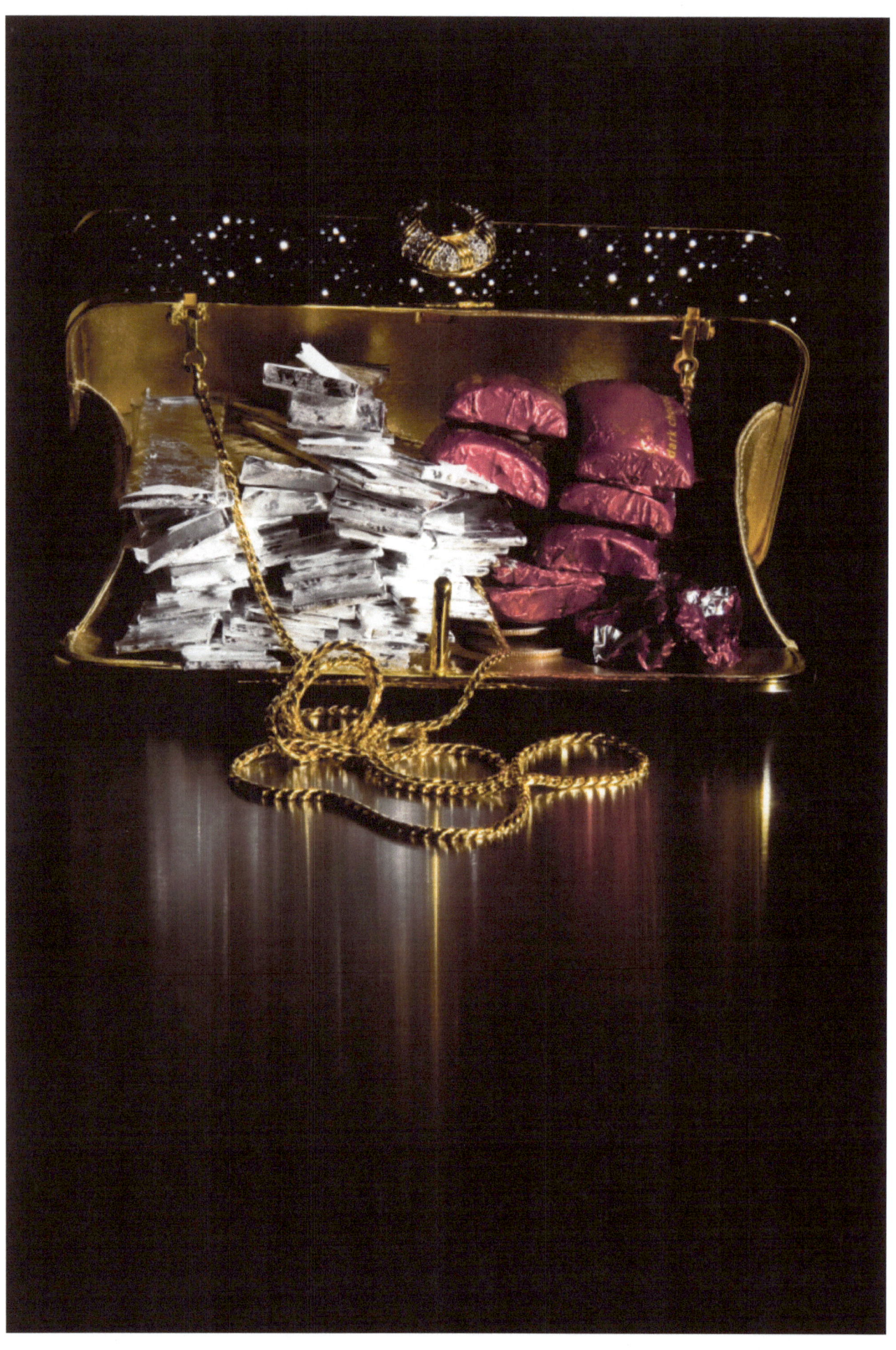

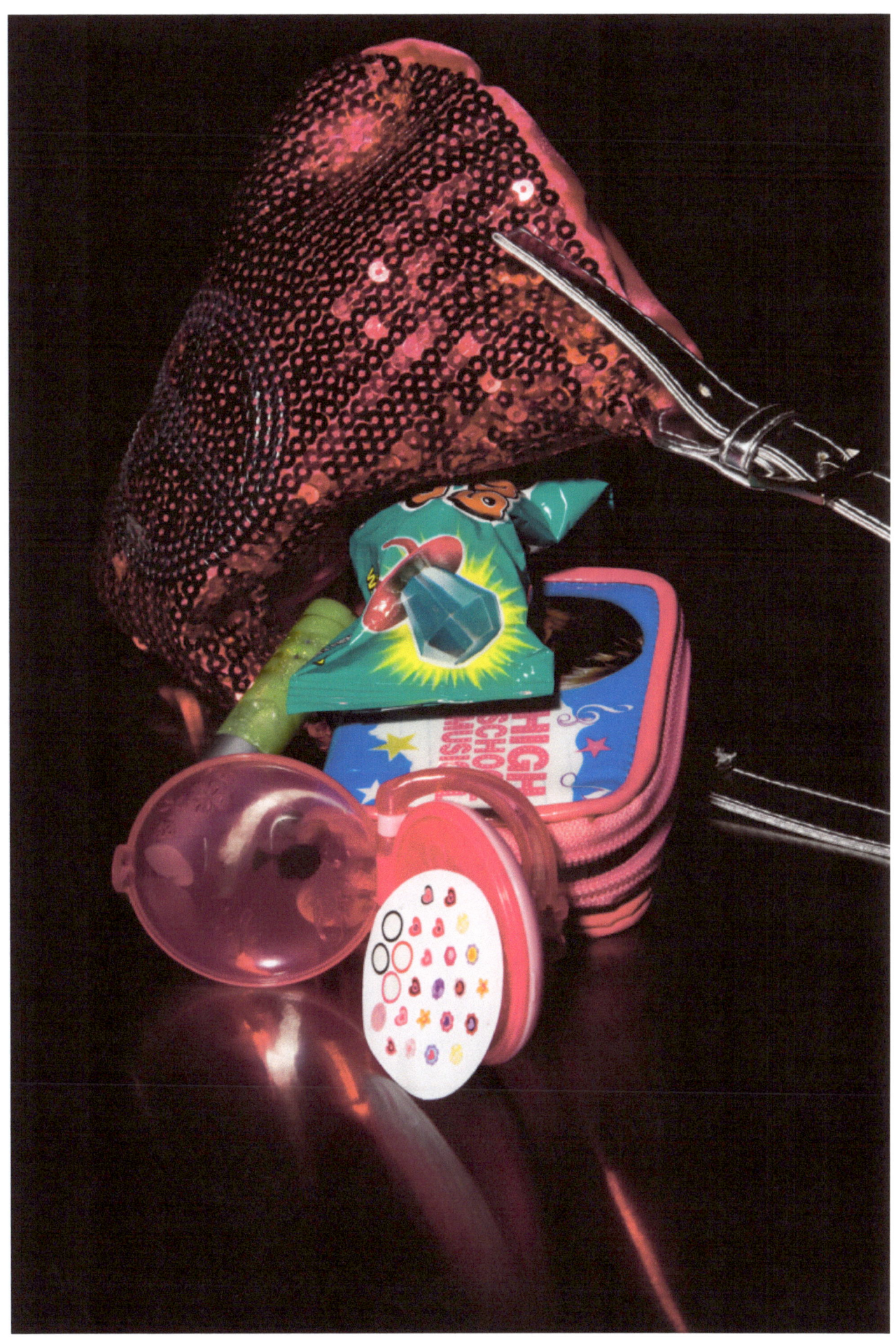

Her Case #6 (size 16 inches × 24 inches) 🔖 **31**

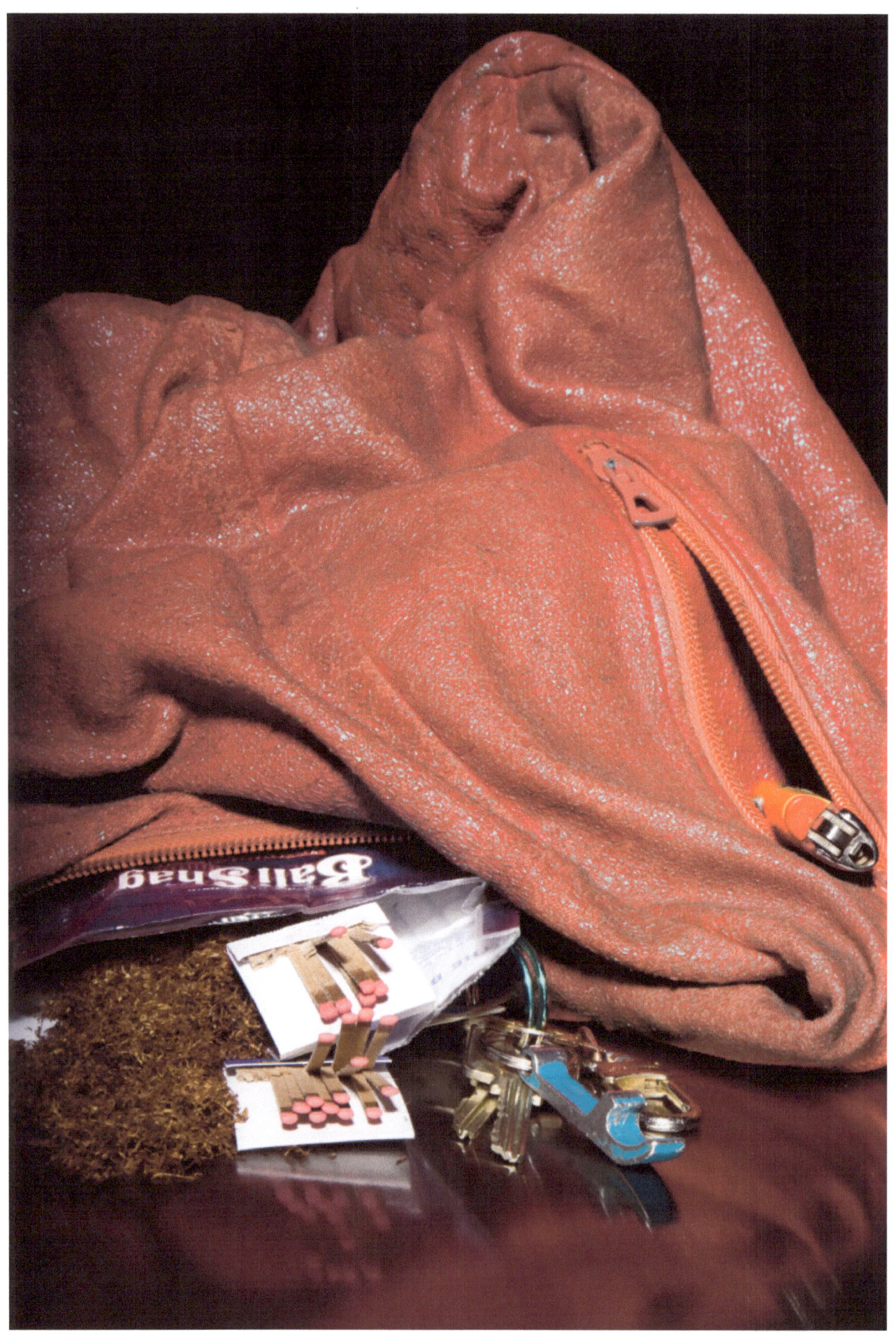

∽ Her Case #5 (size 16 inches × 24 inches)

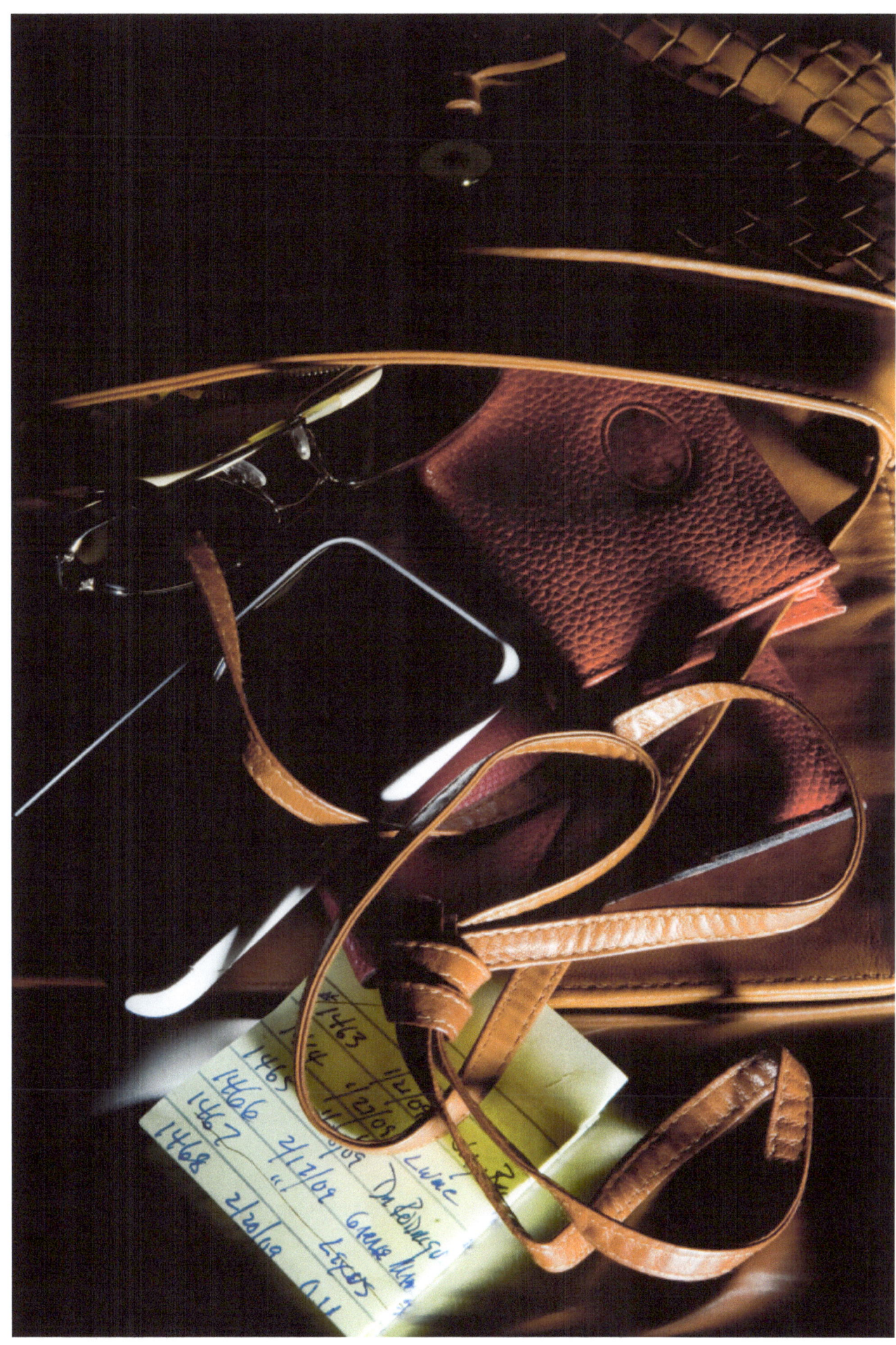

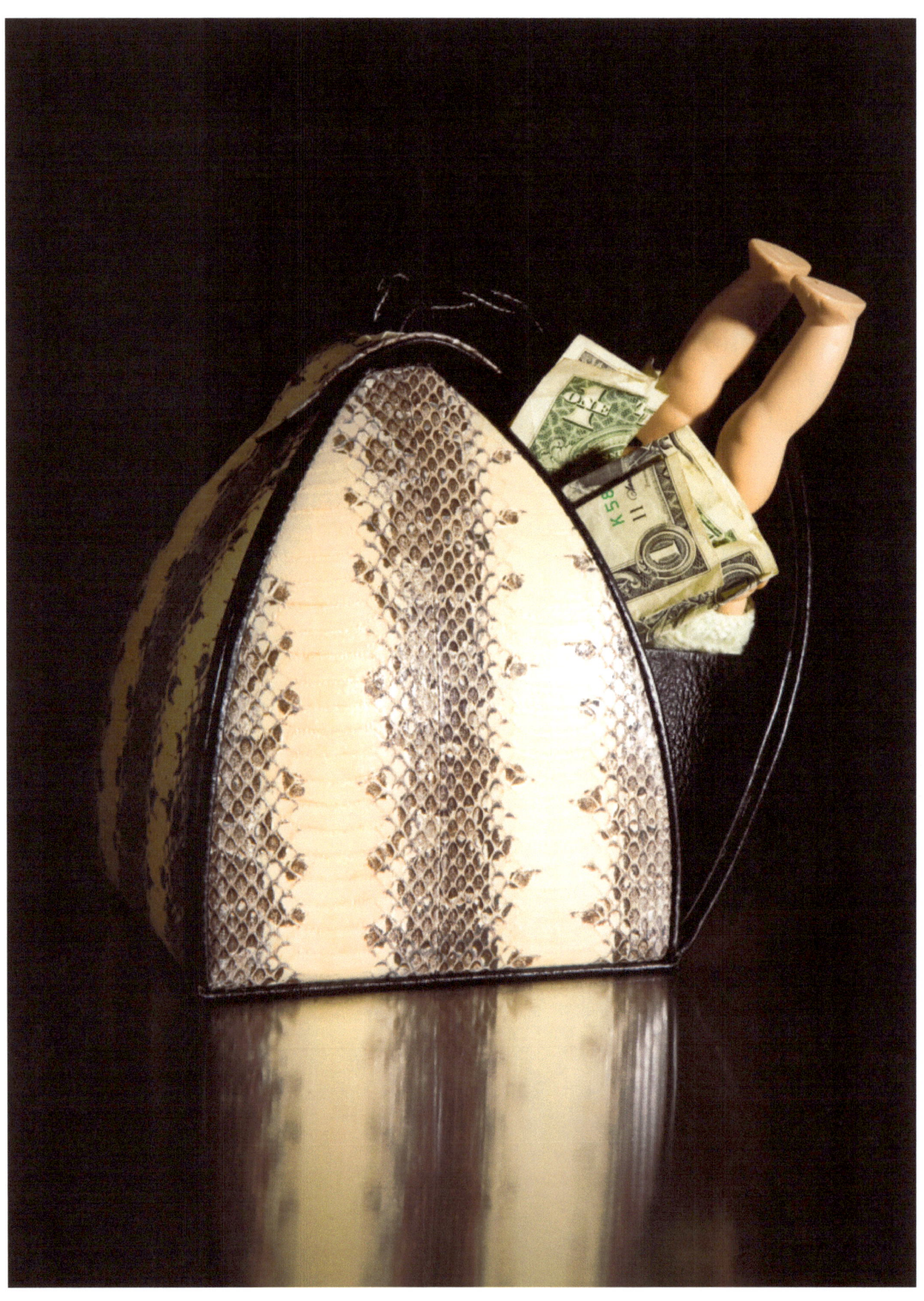

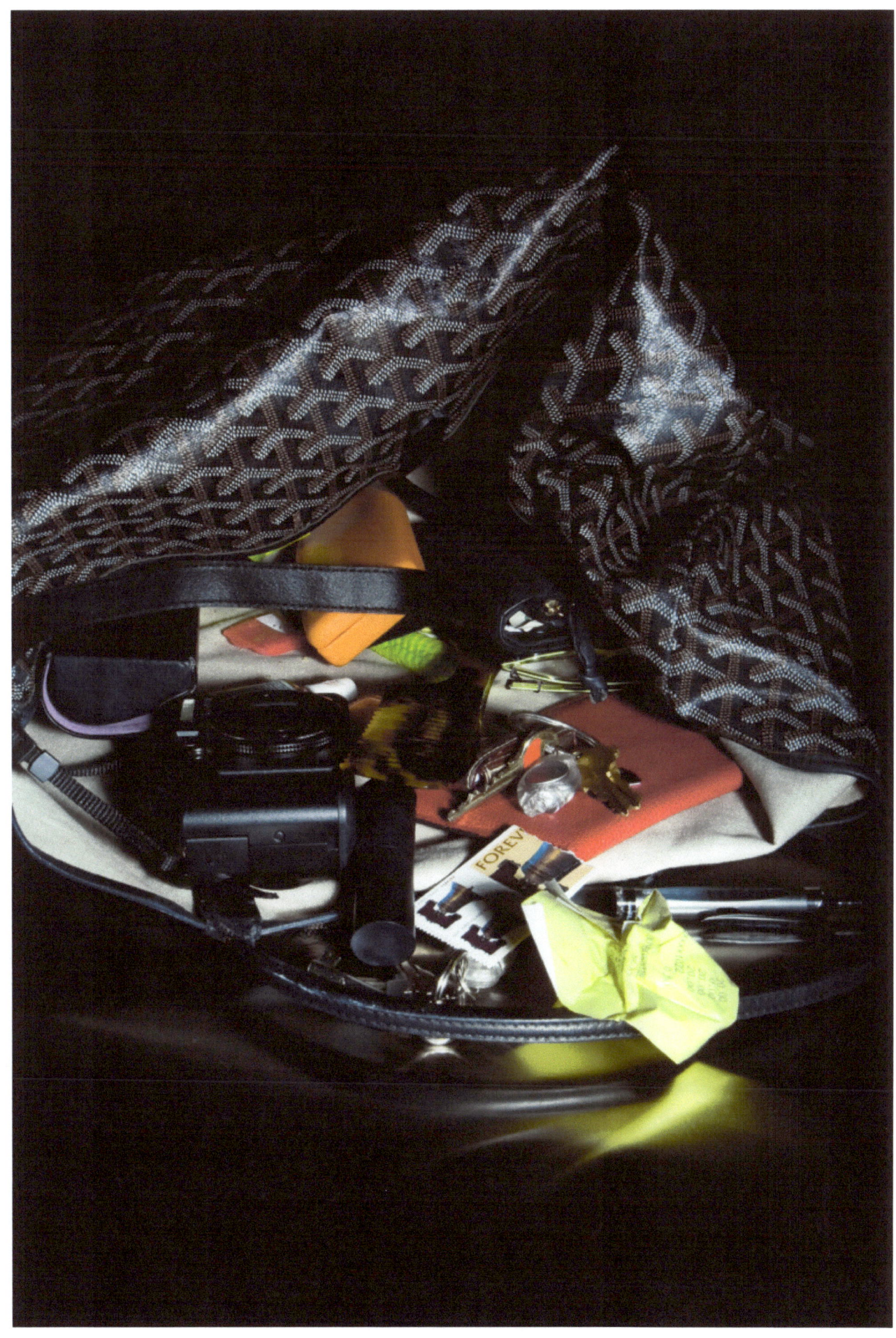

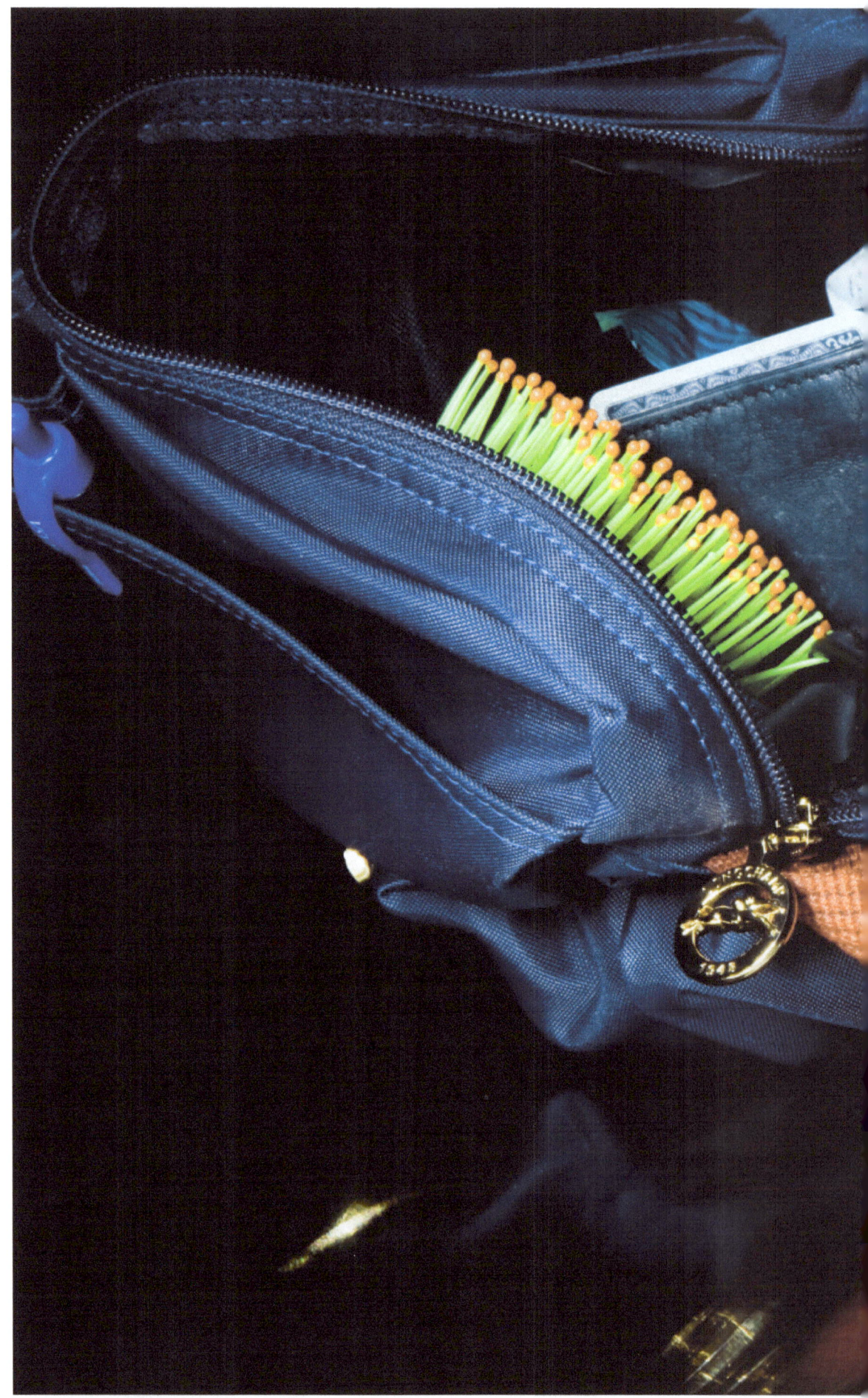

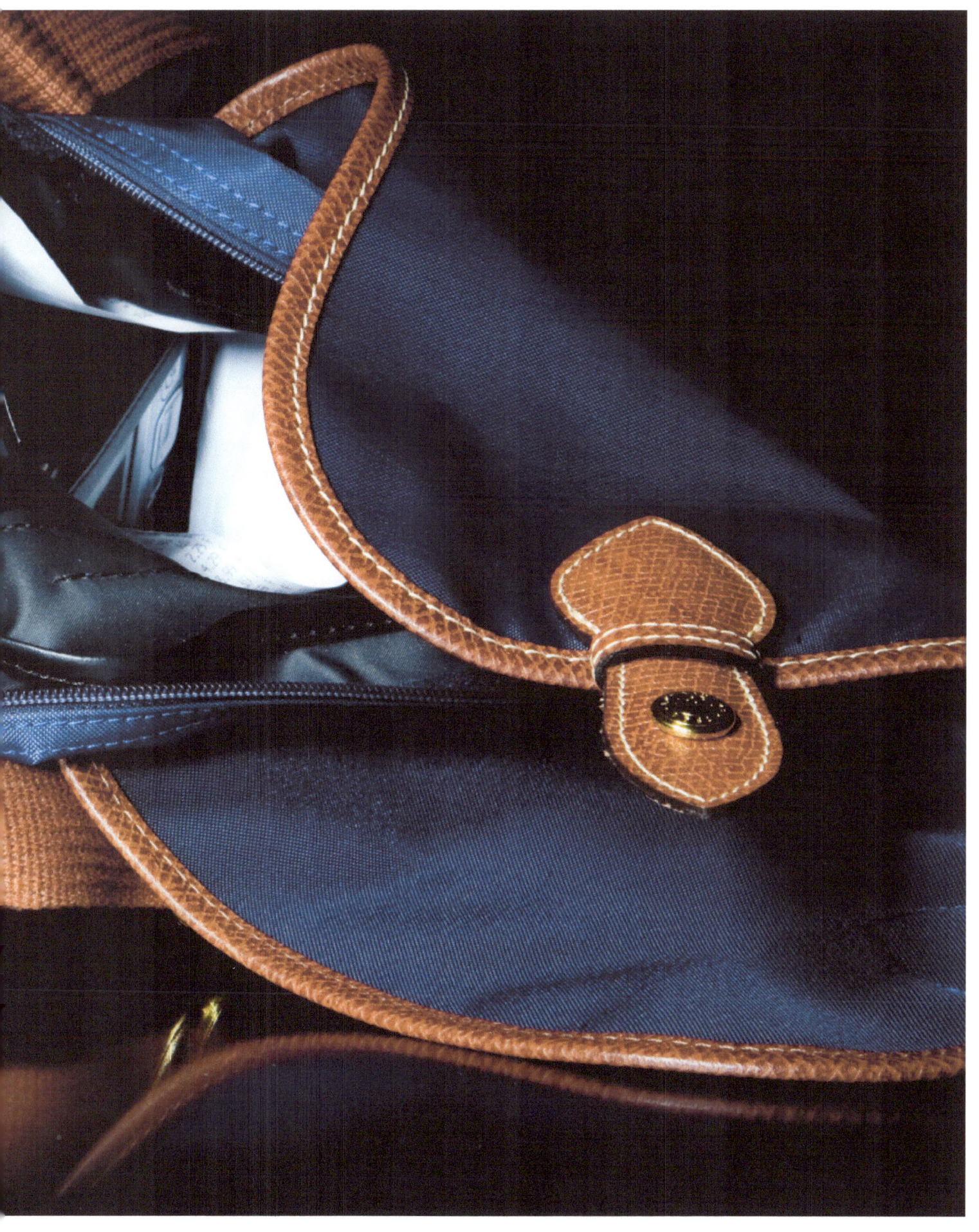

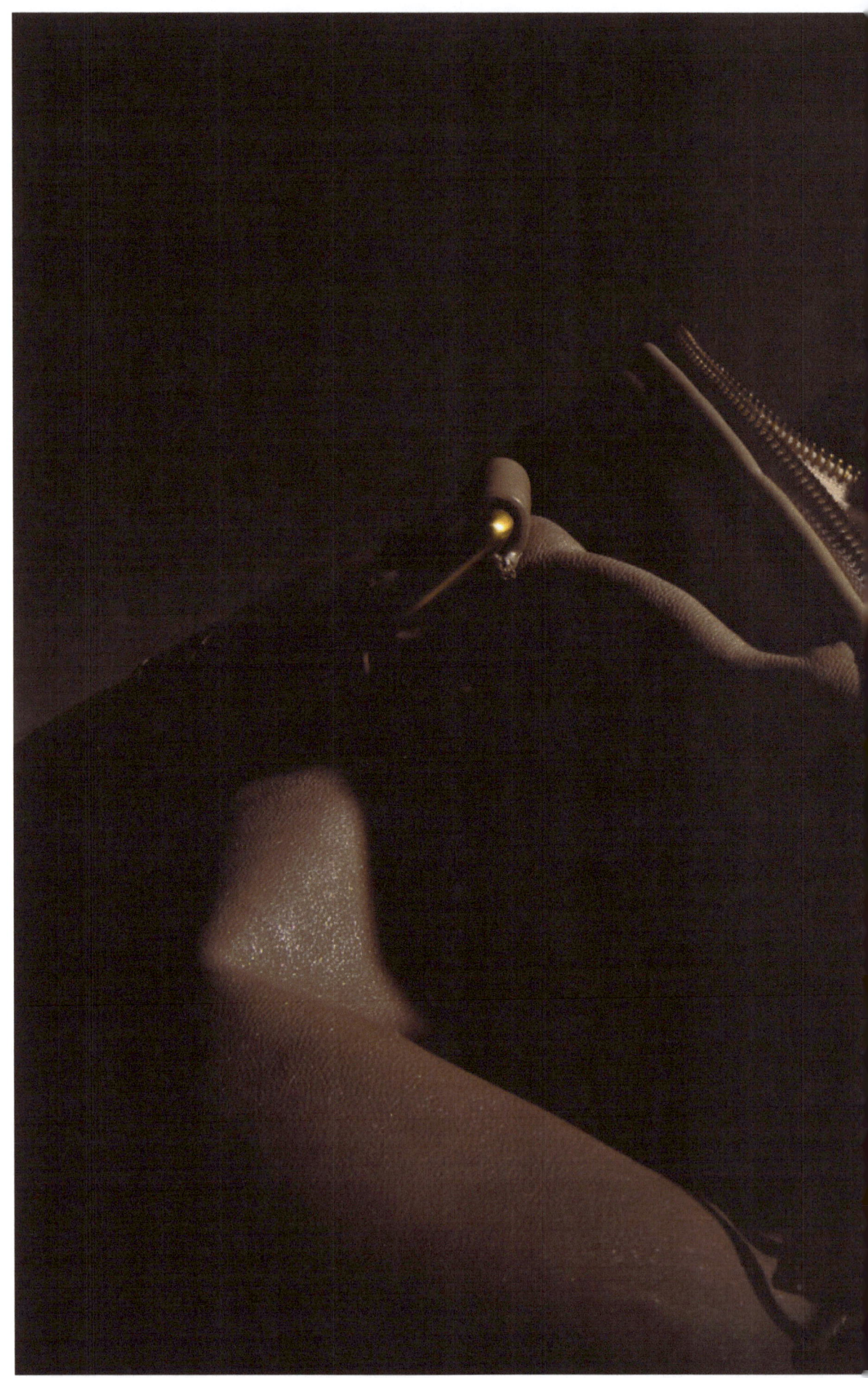

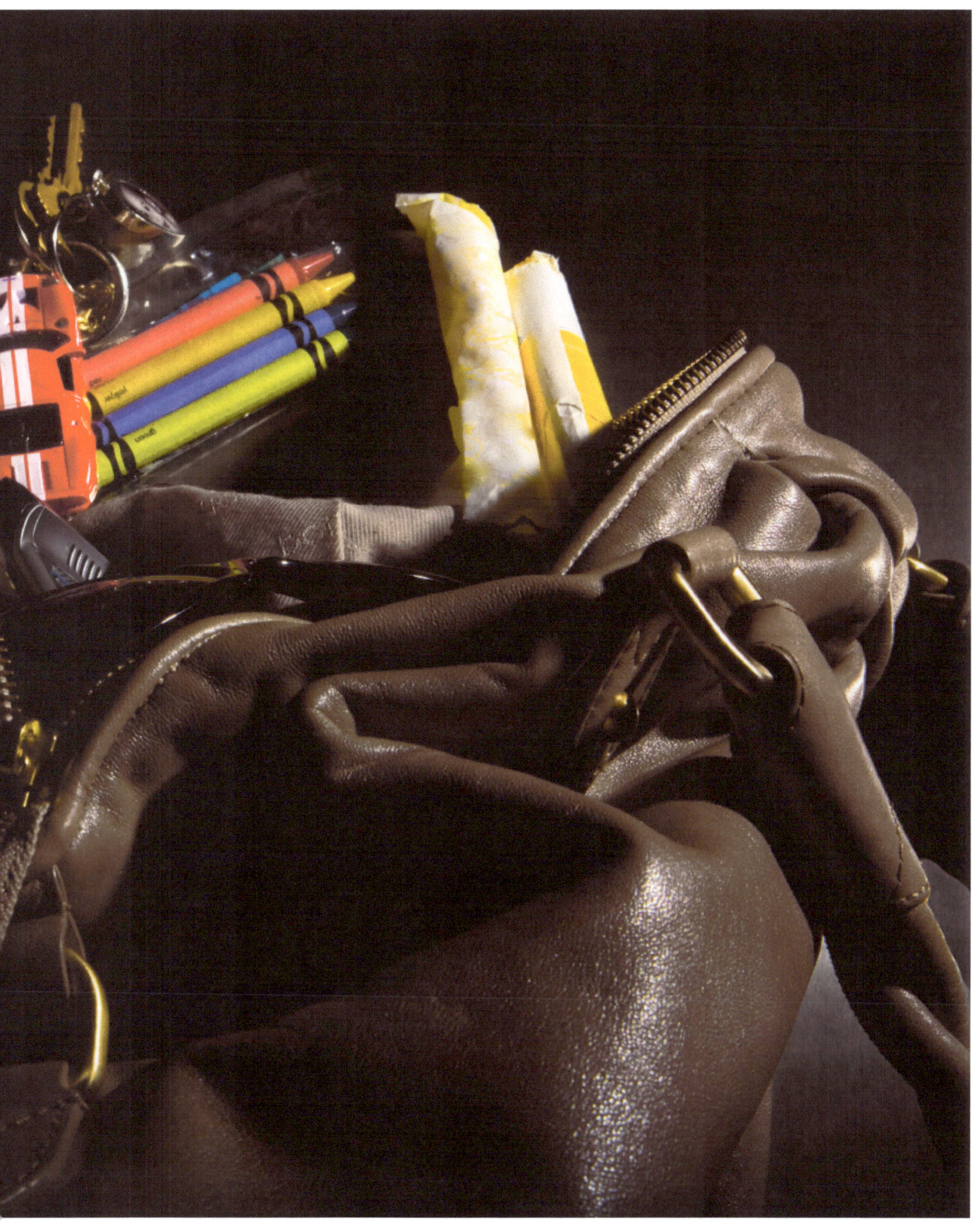

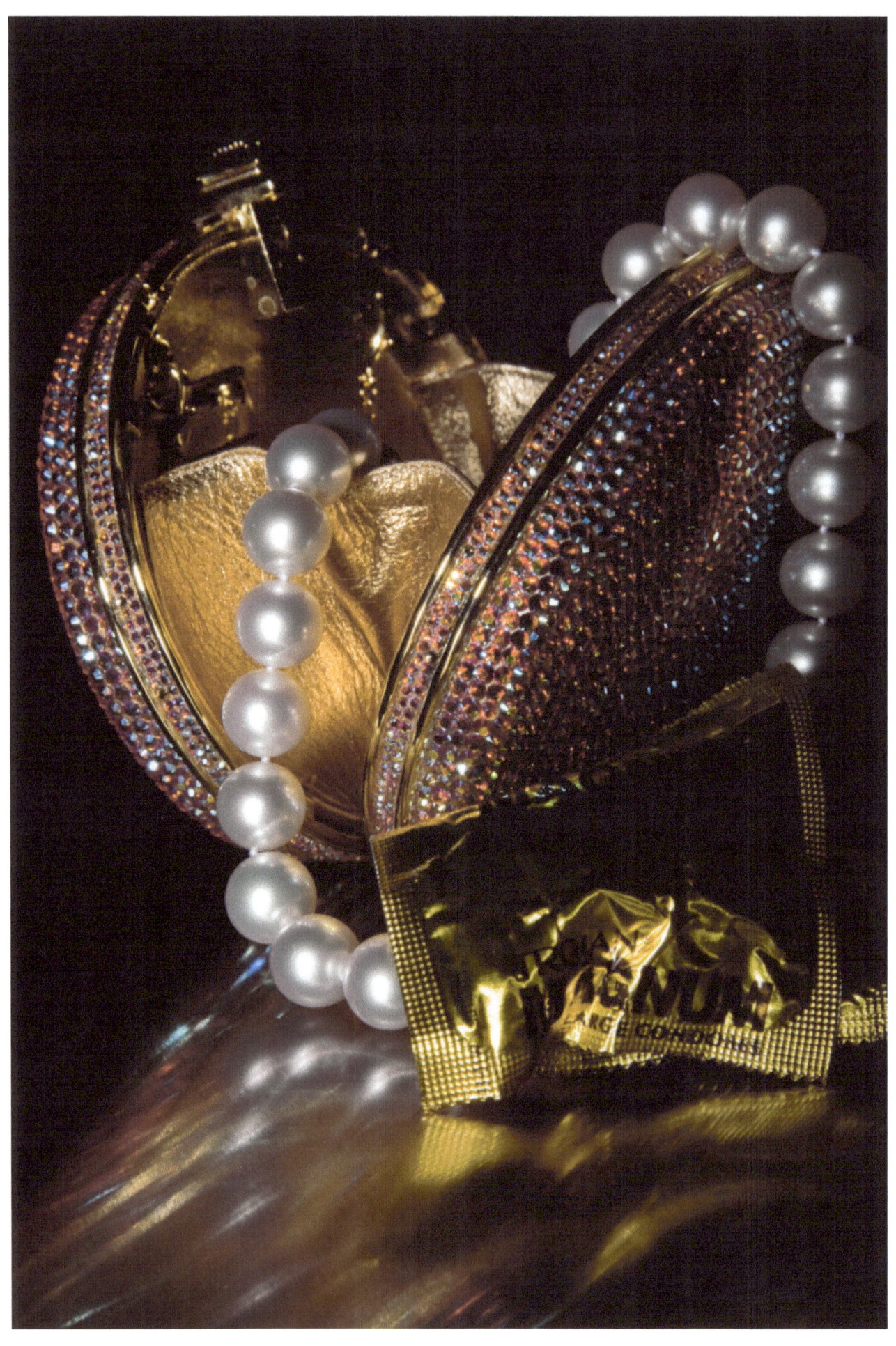

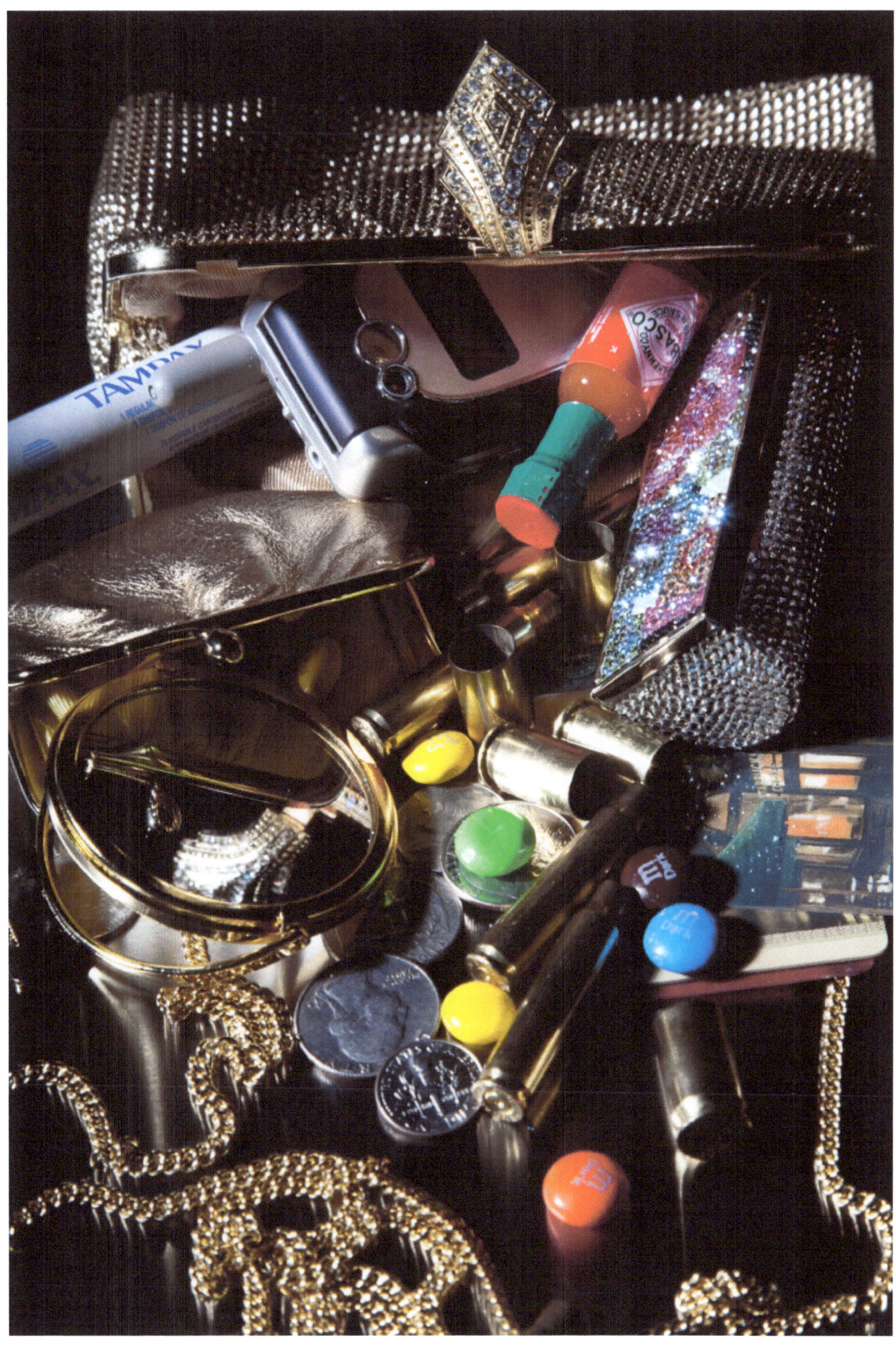

Her Case #9 (size 16 inches × 24 inches) ✦ **41**

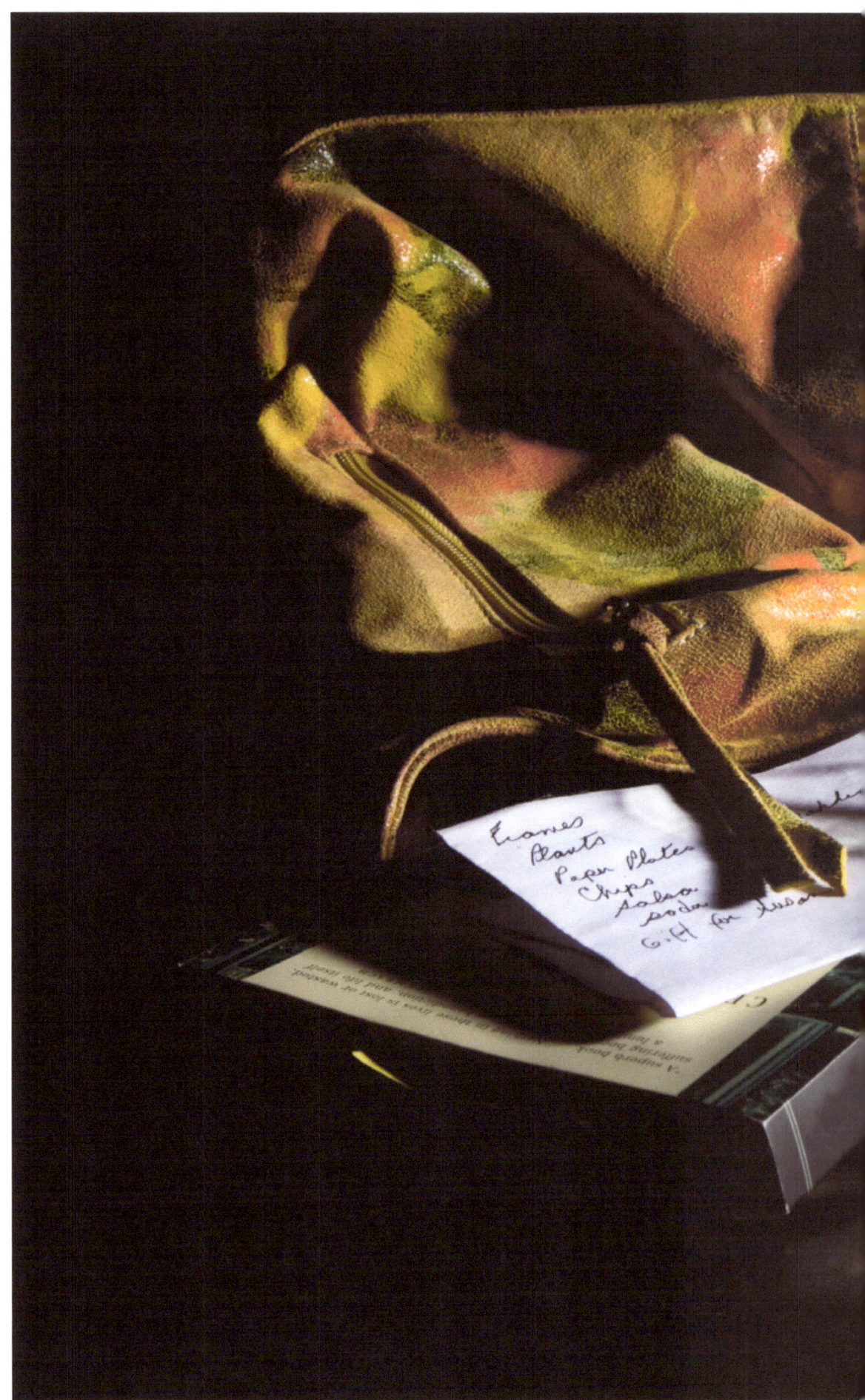

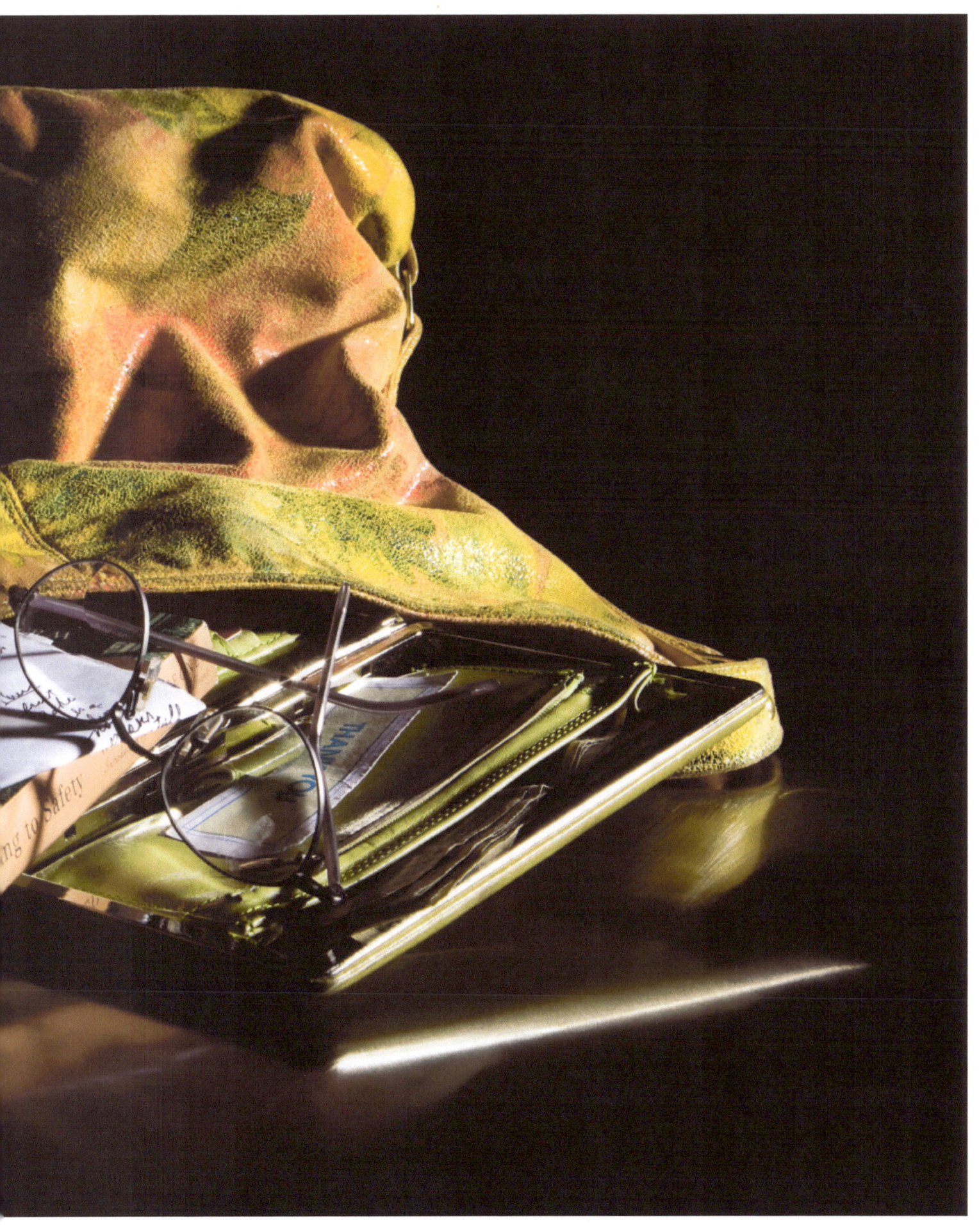

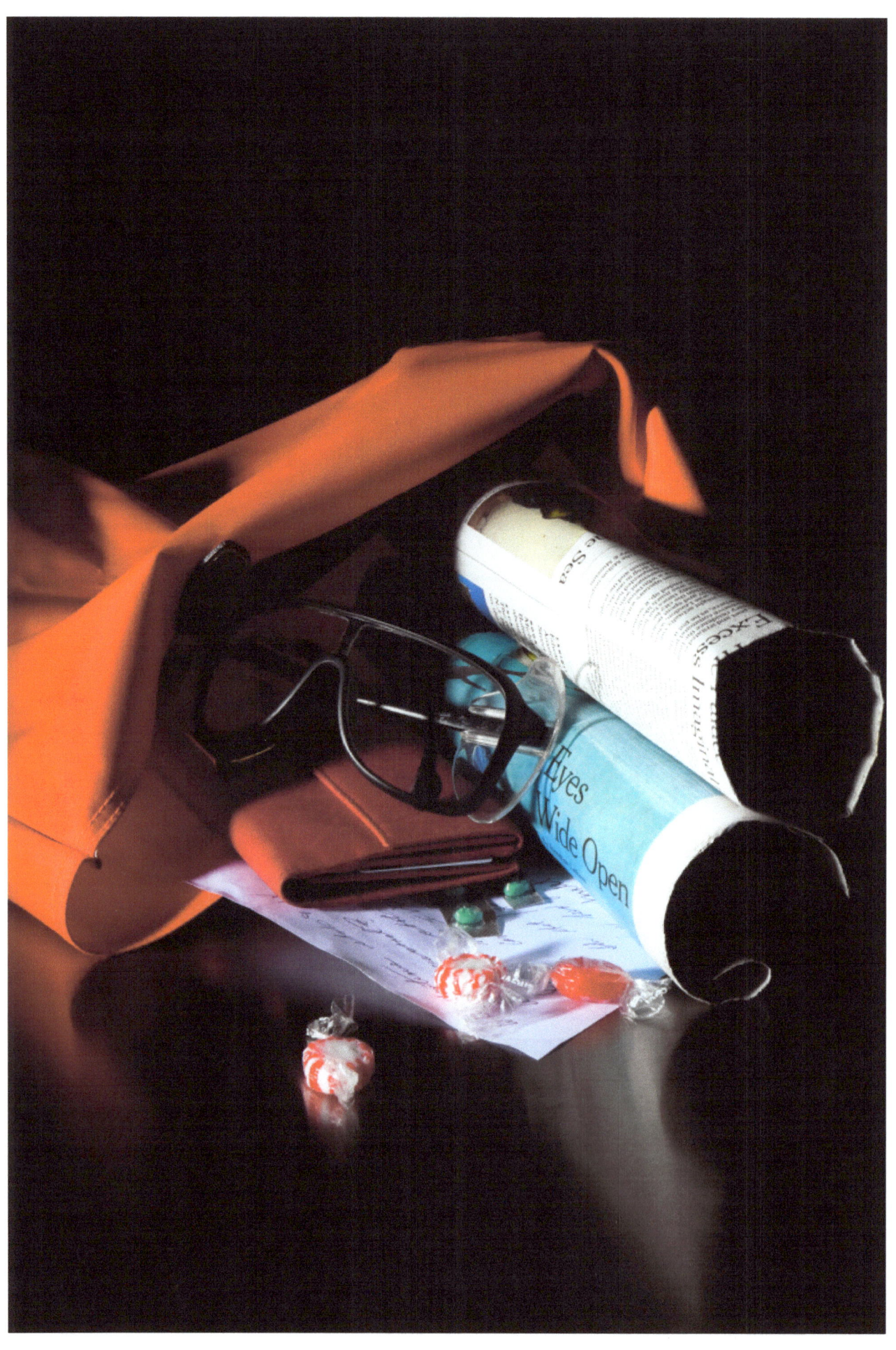

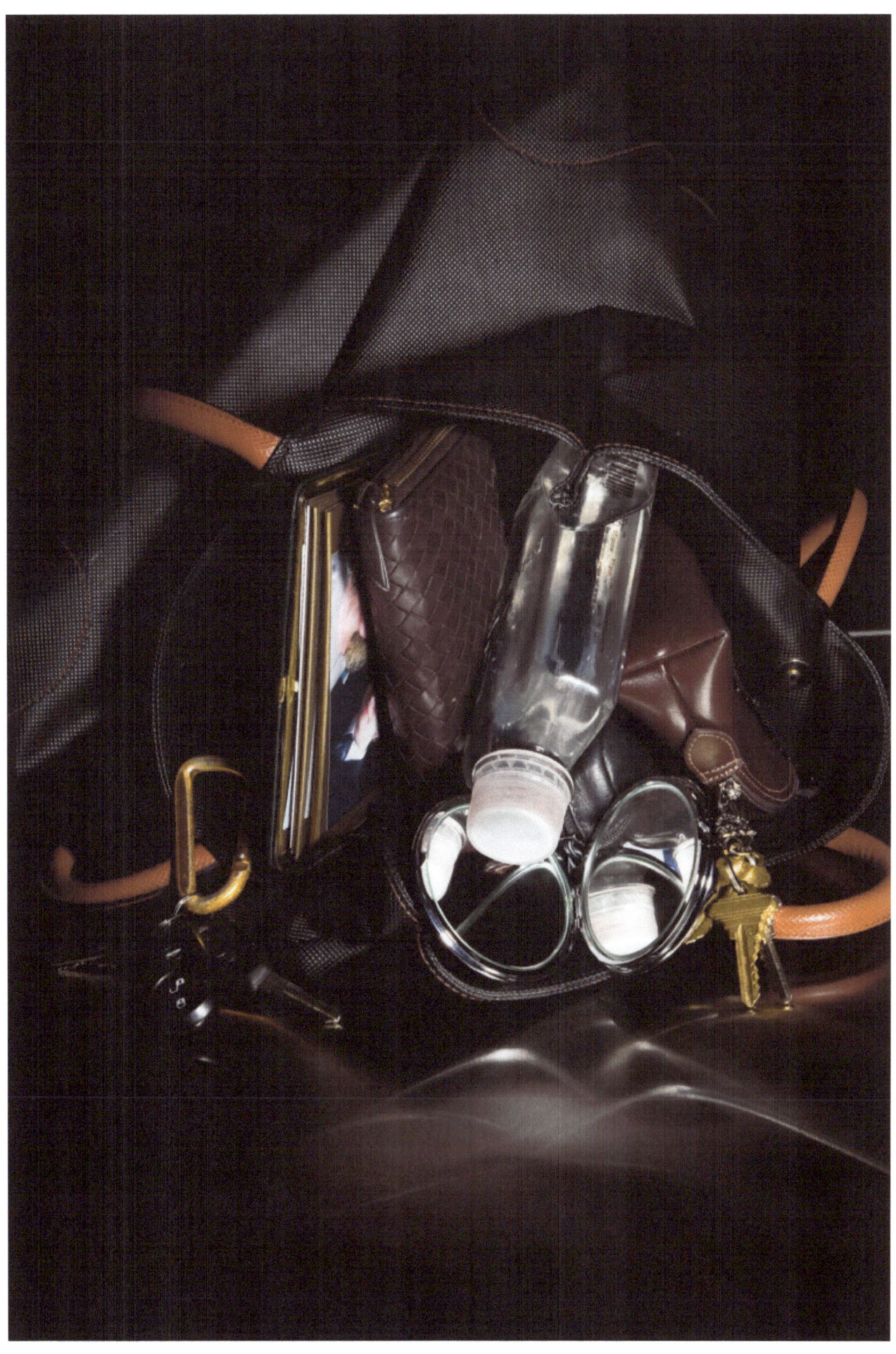

Her Case #14 (size 16 inches × 24 inches) ✦ **45**

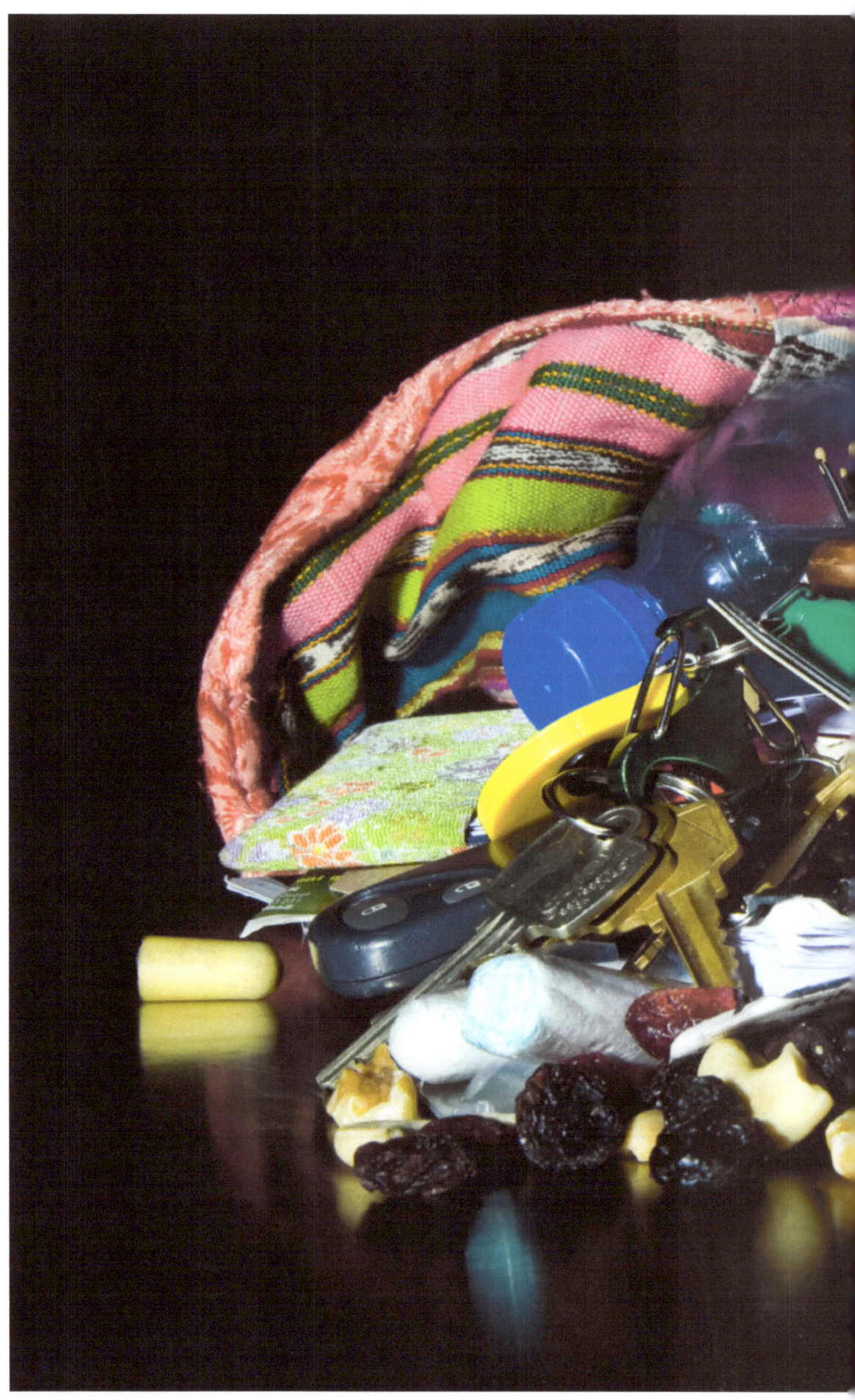

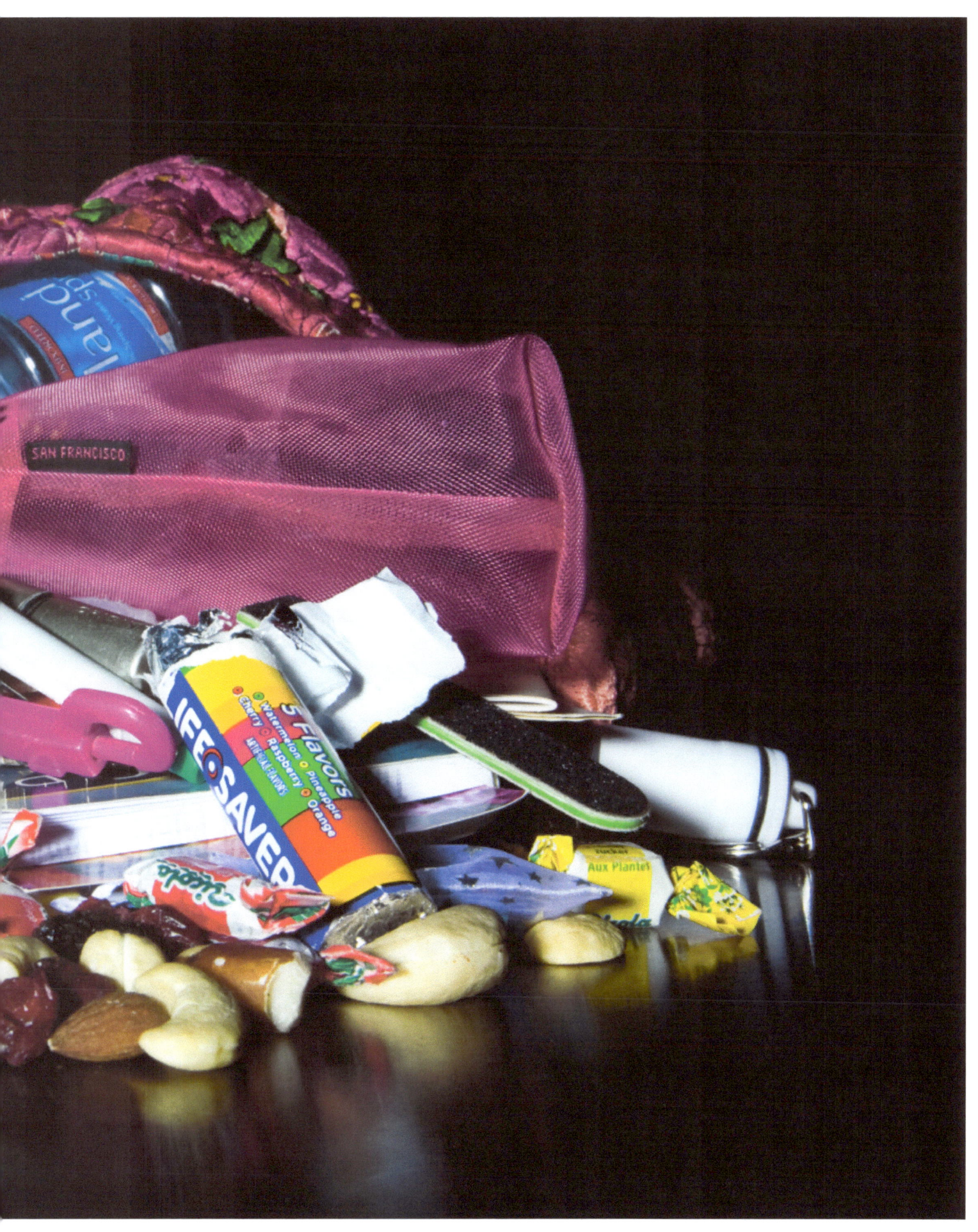

Under the Surface

"Under the Surface" explores how women feel about their bodies, as suggested by the undergarments they choose to wear.

The project began after one of my favorite sculpting models showed up at the studio covering her huge torso with delicate lace undies and a sheer tank top.

The model explained that she loved her large body and had accepted her size after years of near starvation in an attempt to be part of a ballet company. Years later, the model died and I decided it was time to expose what women of different ages, nationalities, walks of life, and sexual orientation wore "under the surface."

I find beauty in every individual and was delighted with the positive self-images that most of the women who posed for this project possessed, but noted that the younger women were more self-critical. My hope for the future is that women accept the beauty of their inner and outer selves.

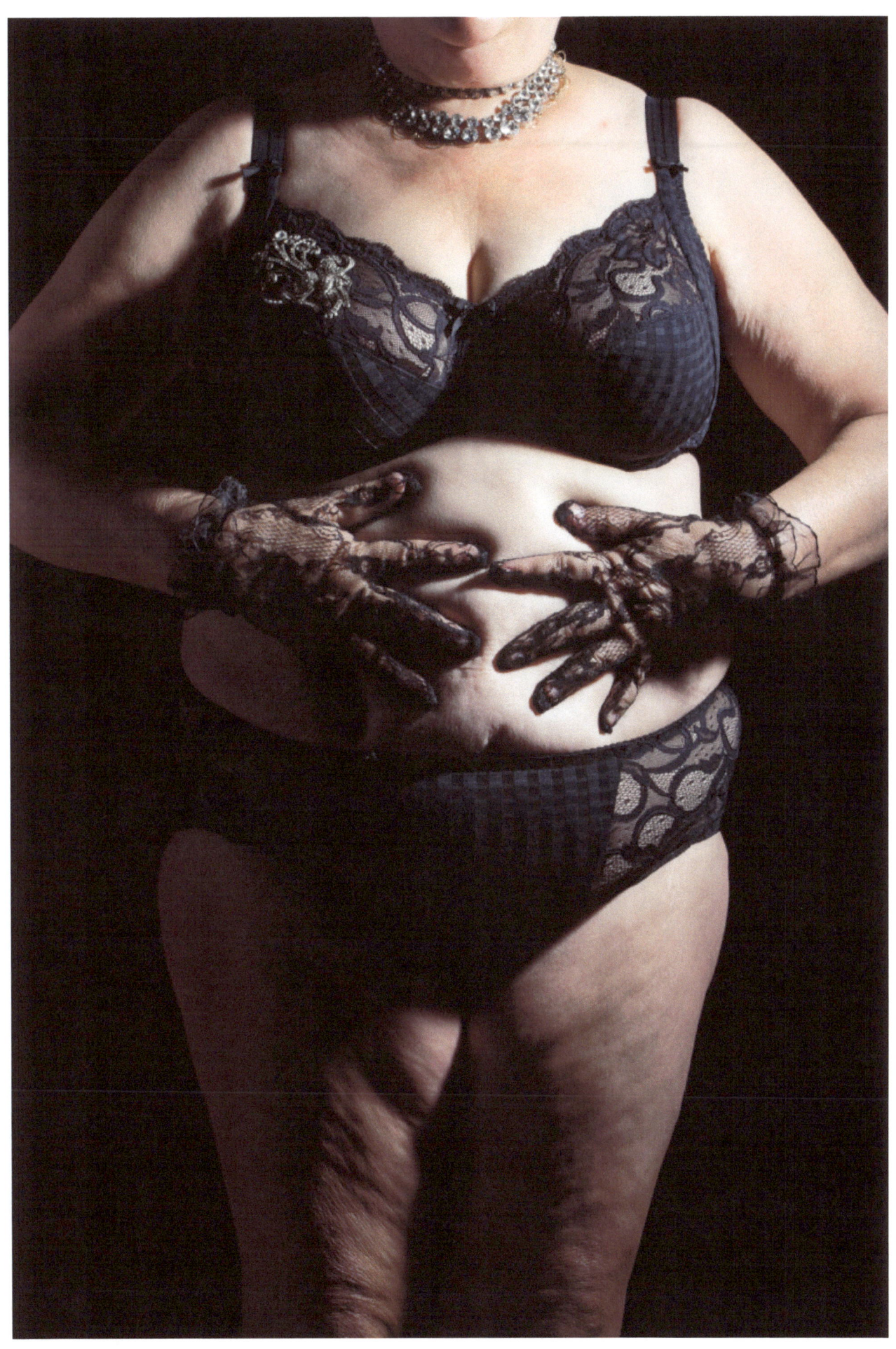

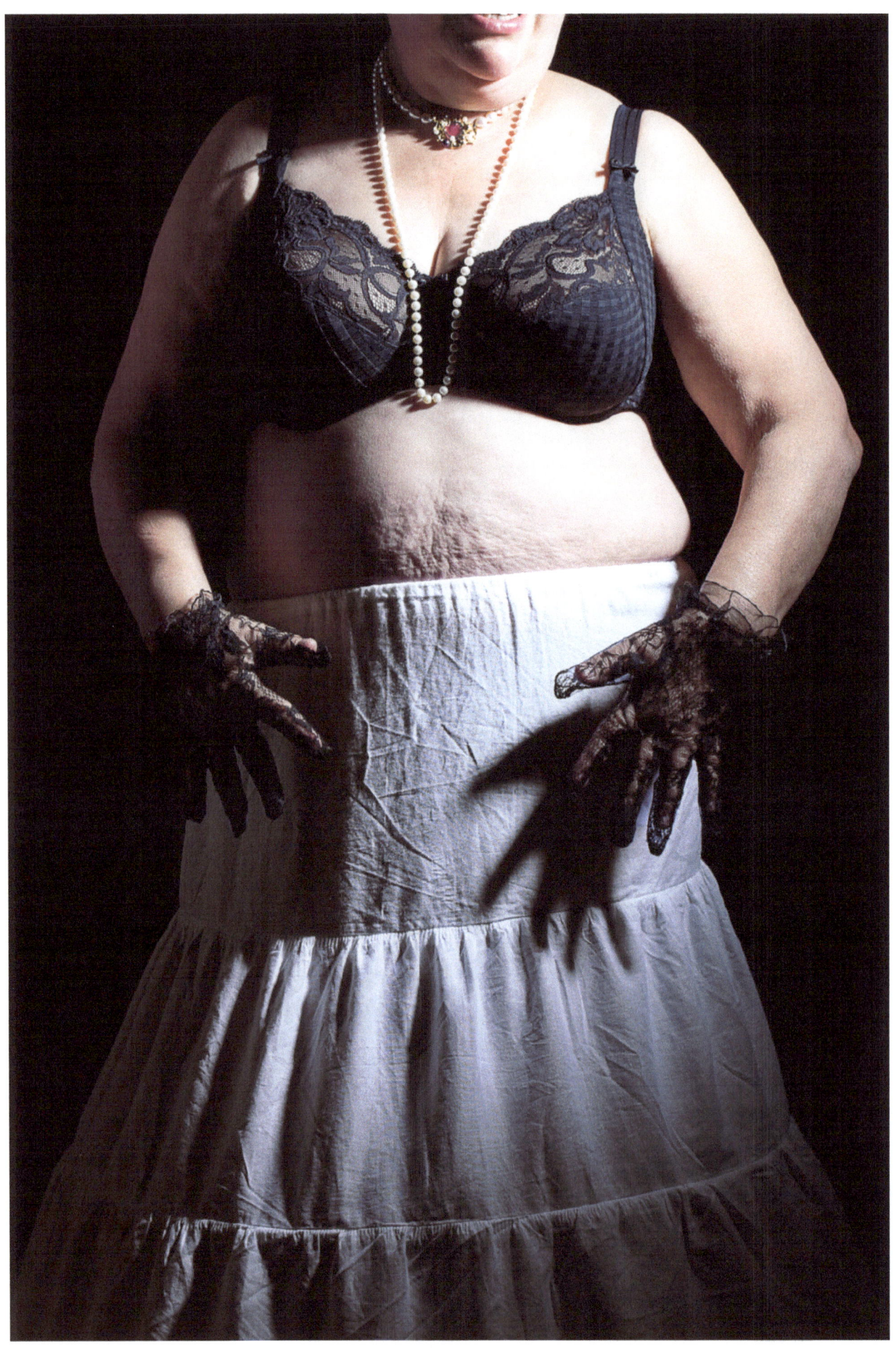

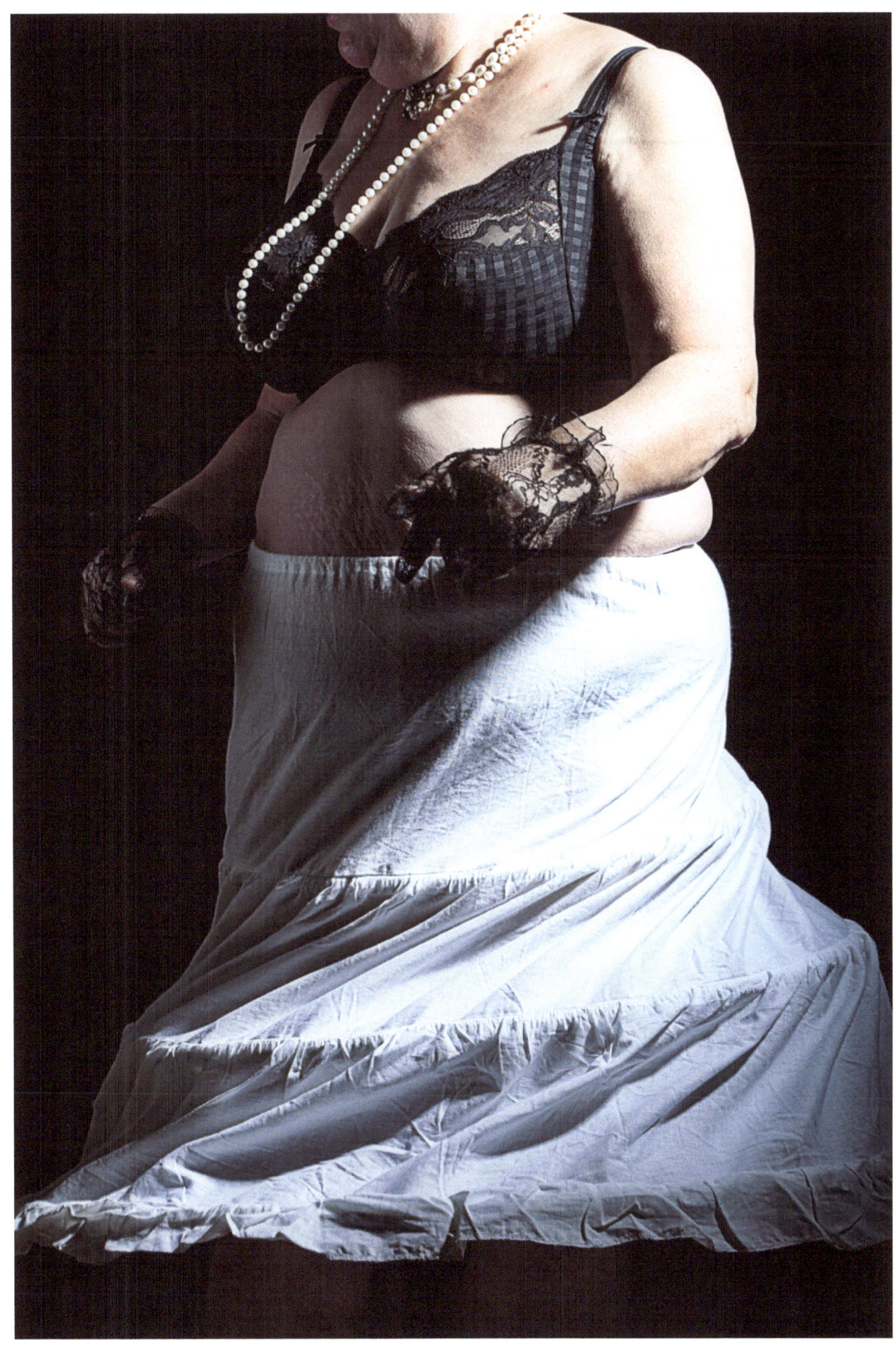

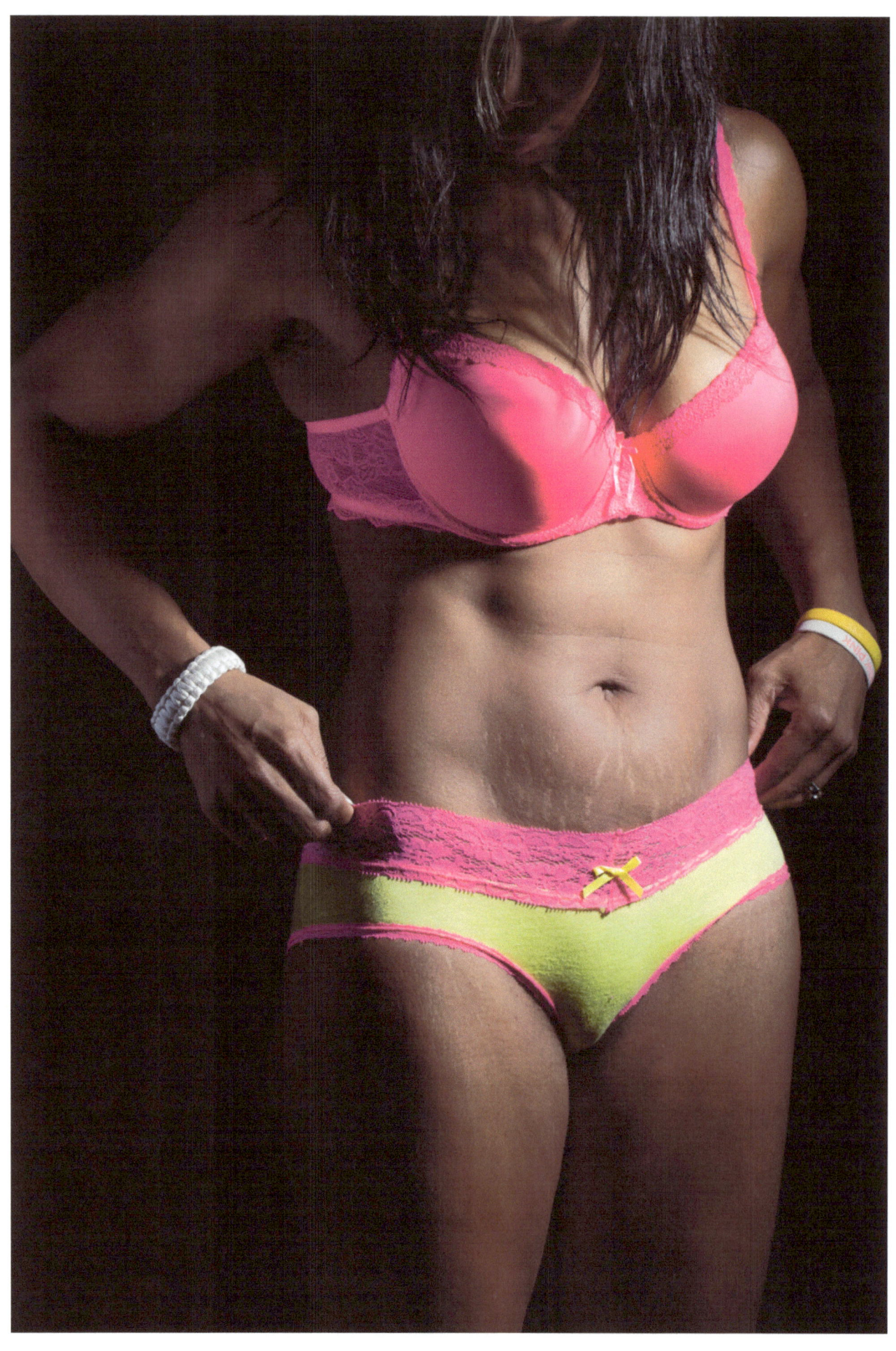

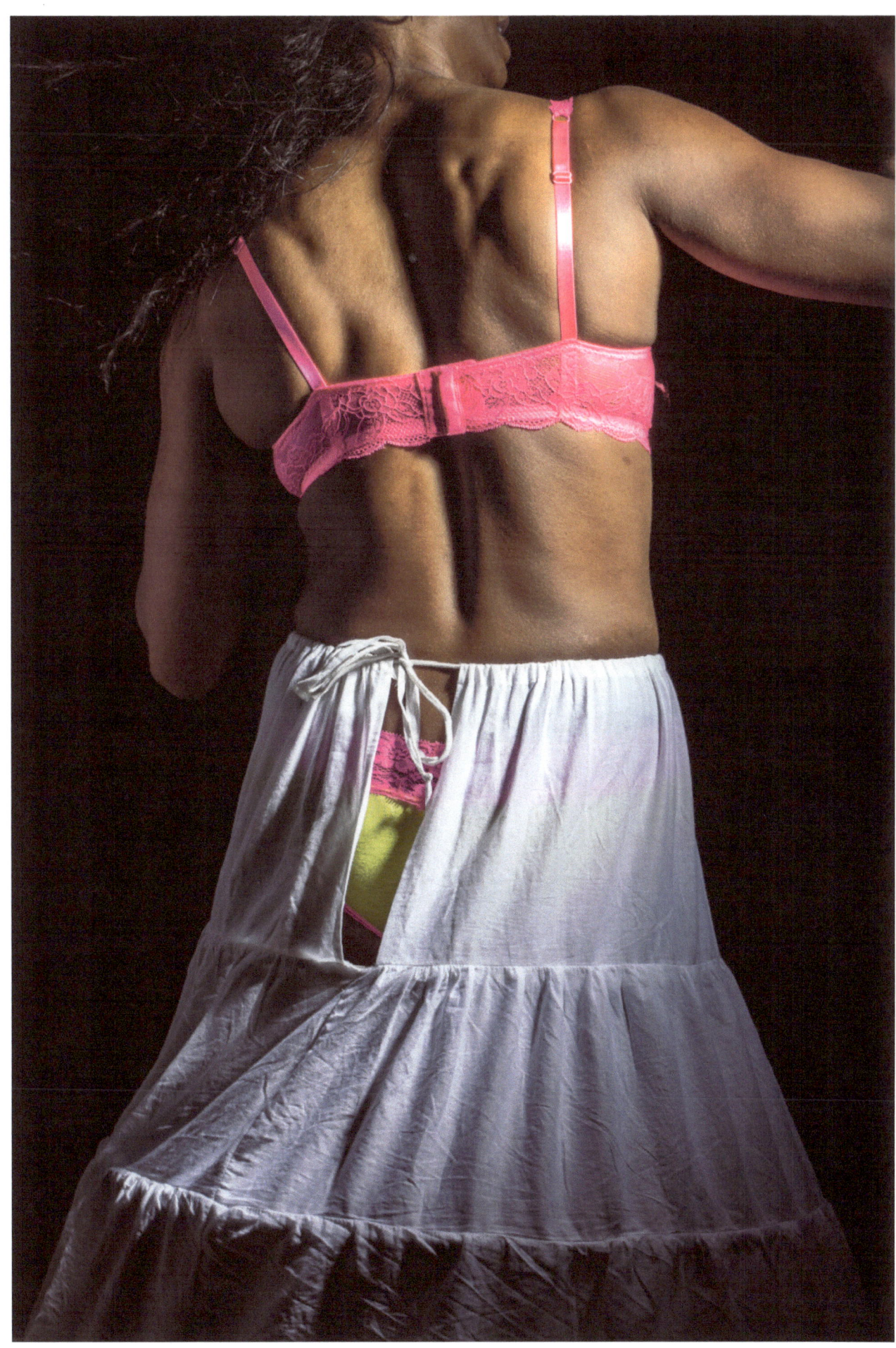

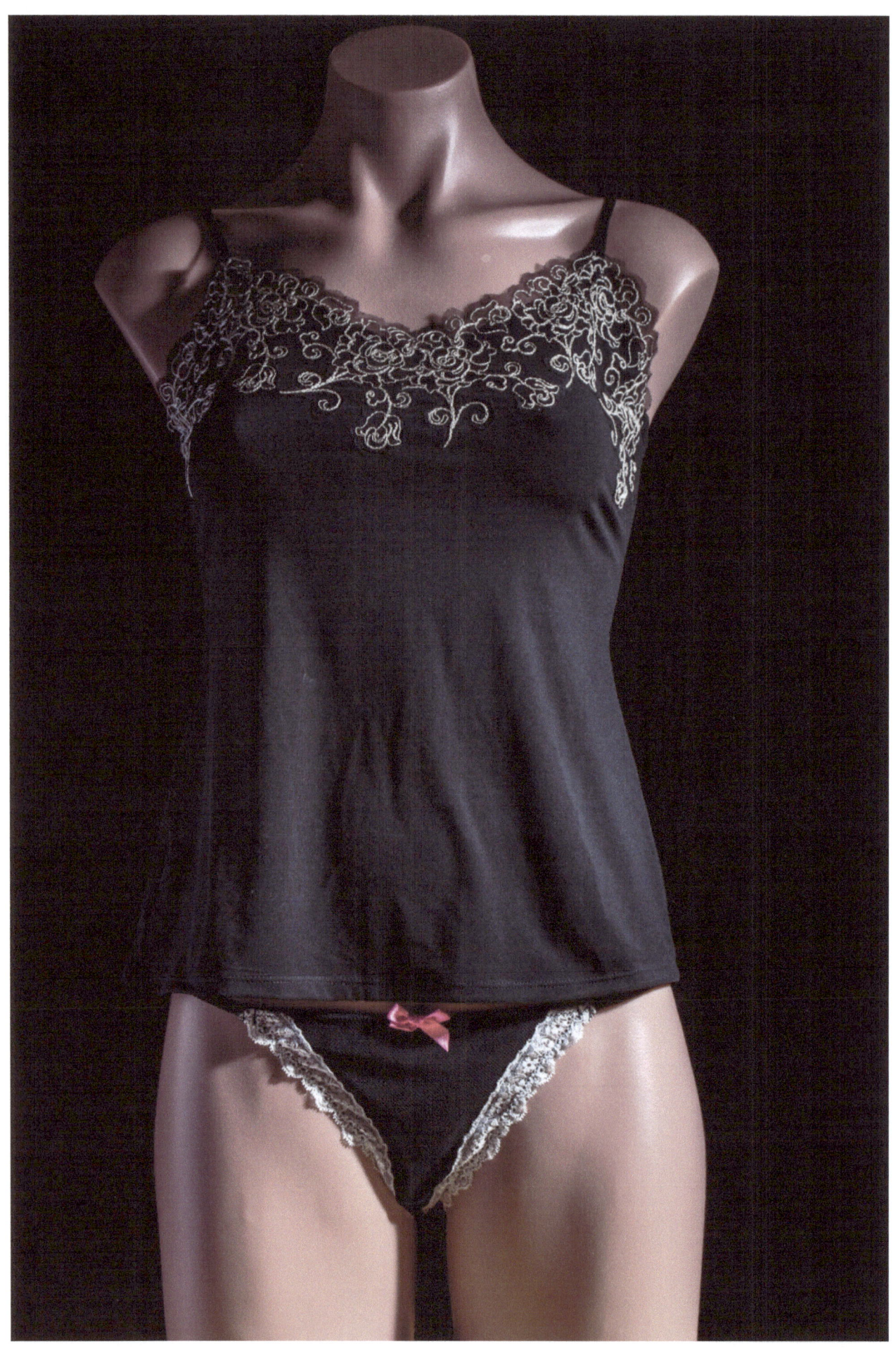

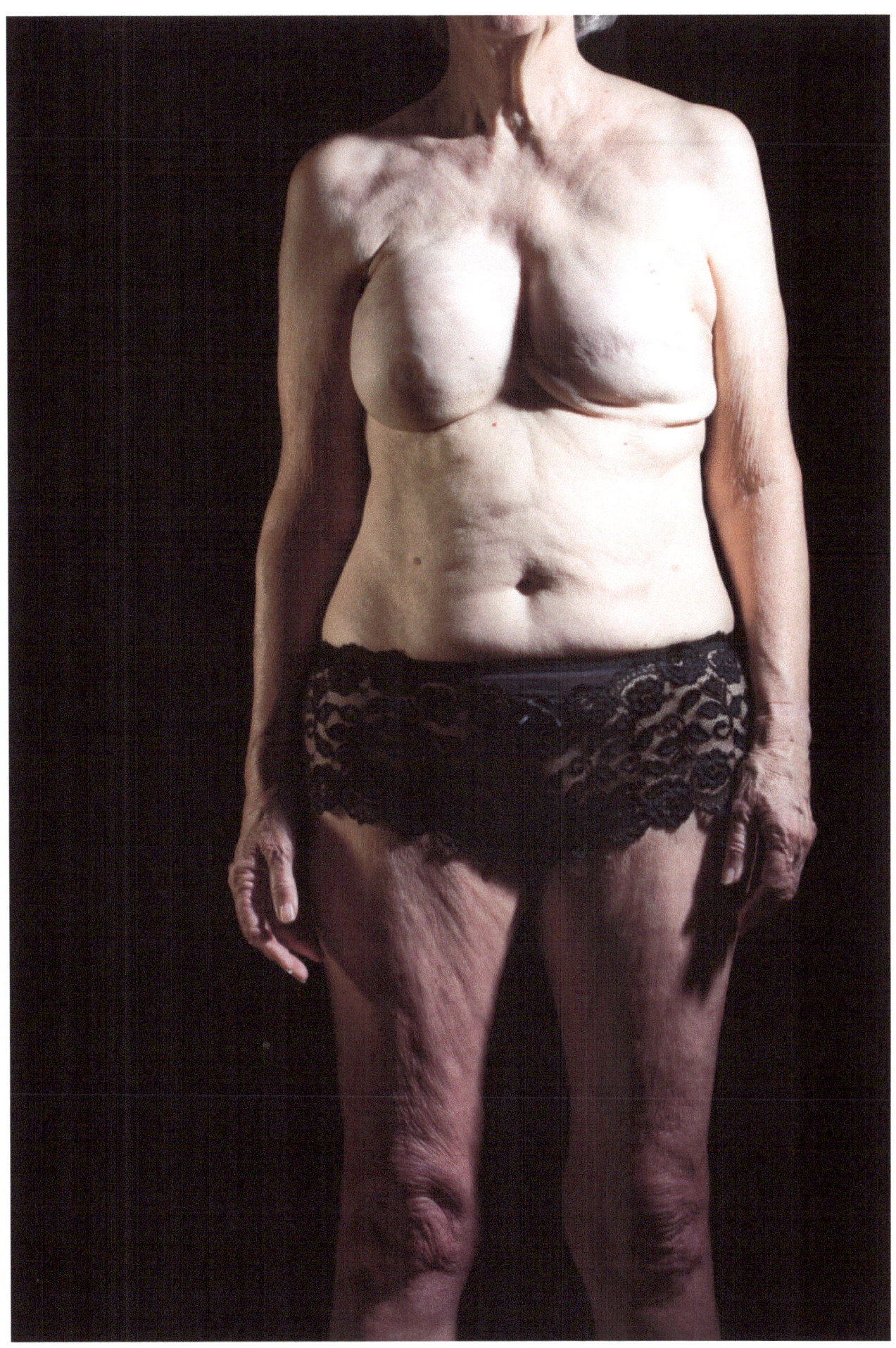

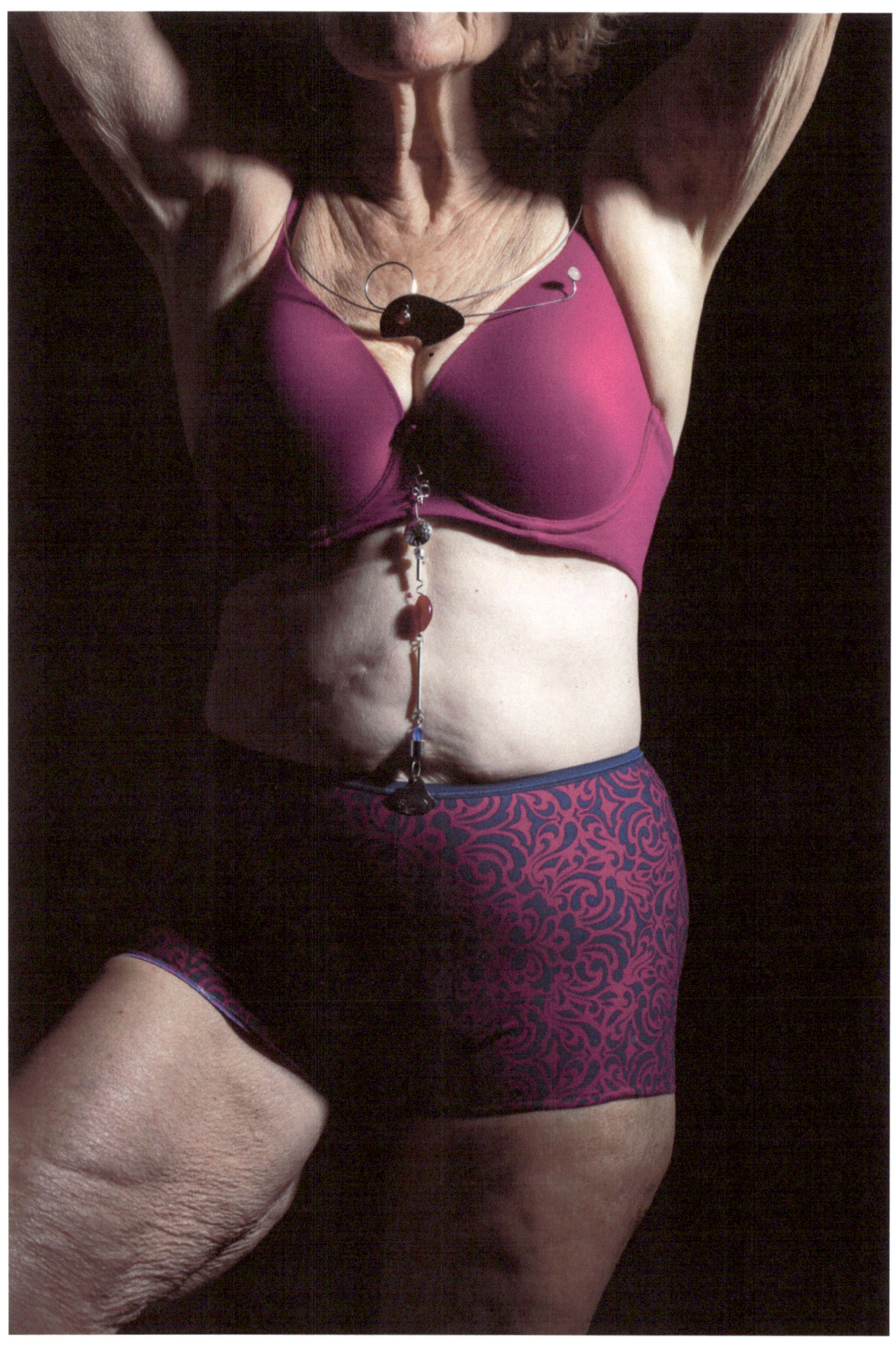

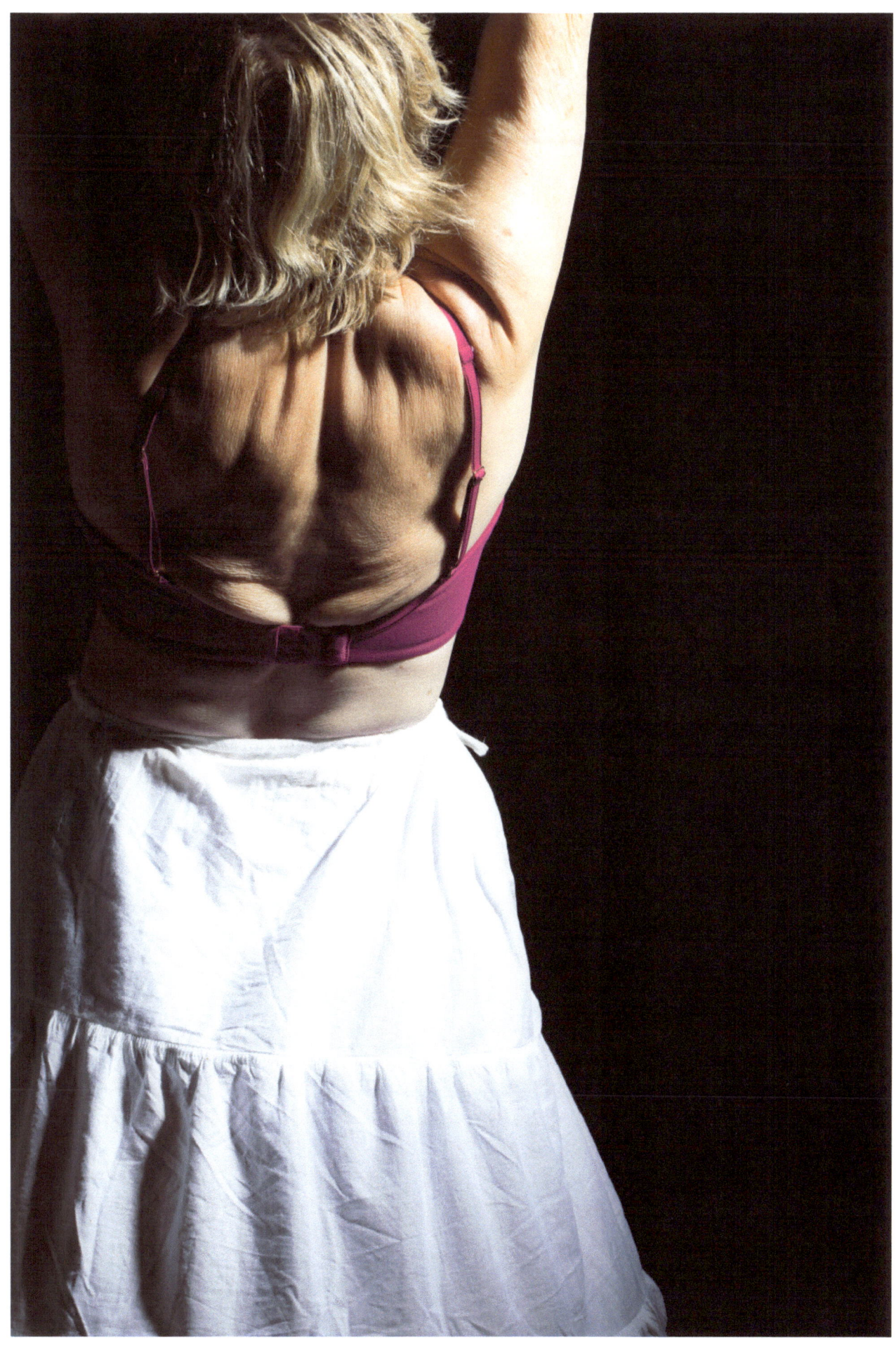

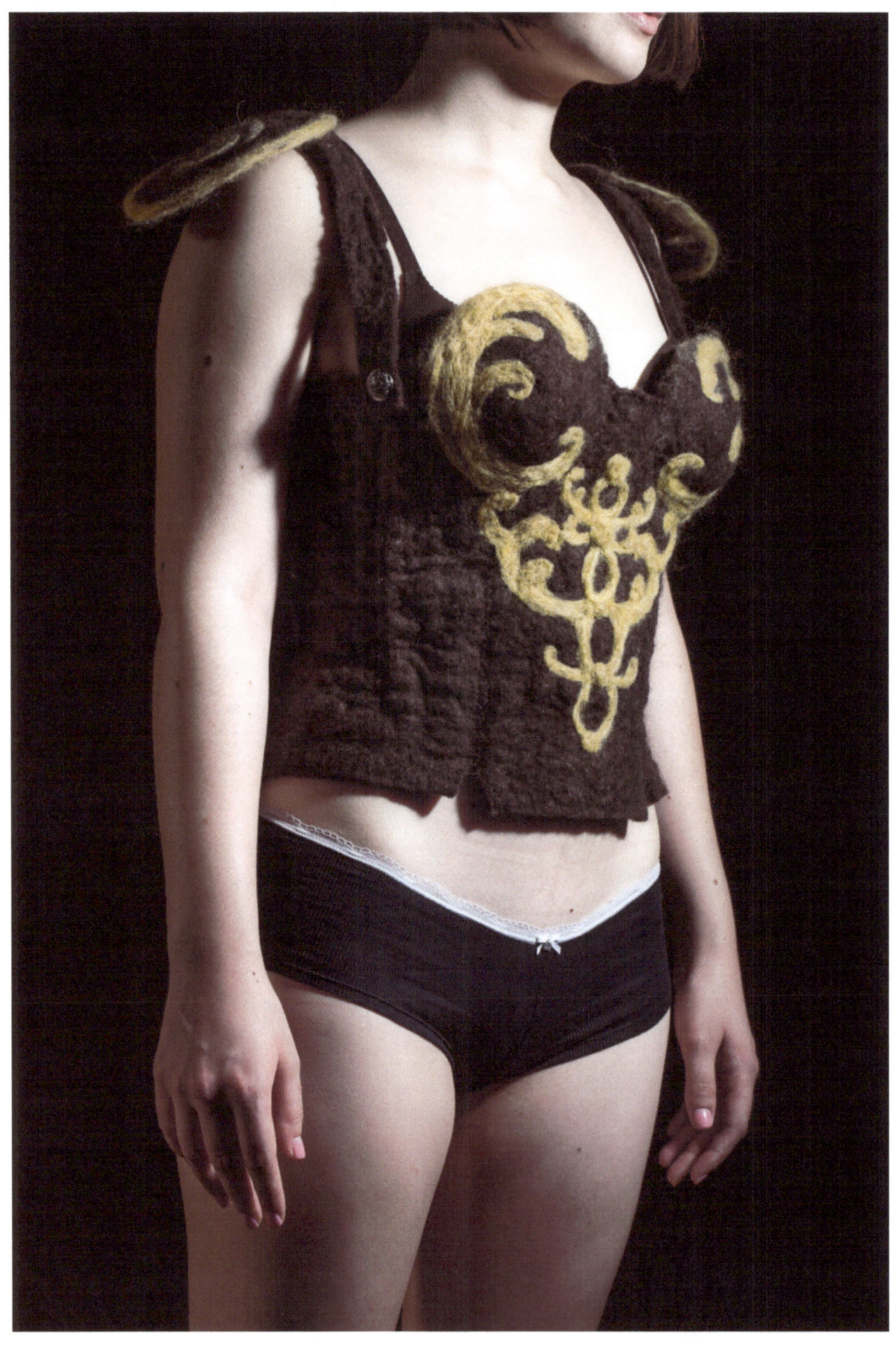

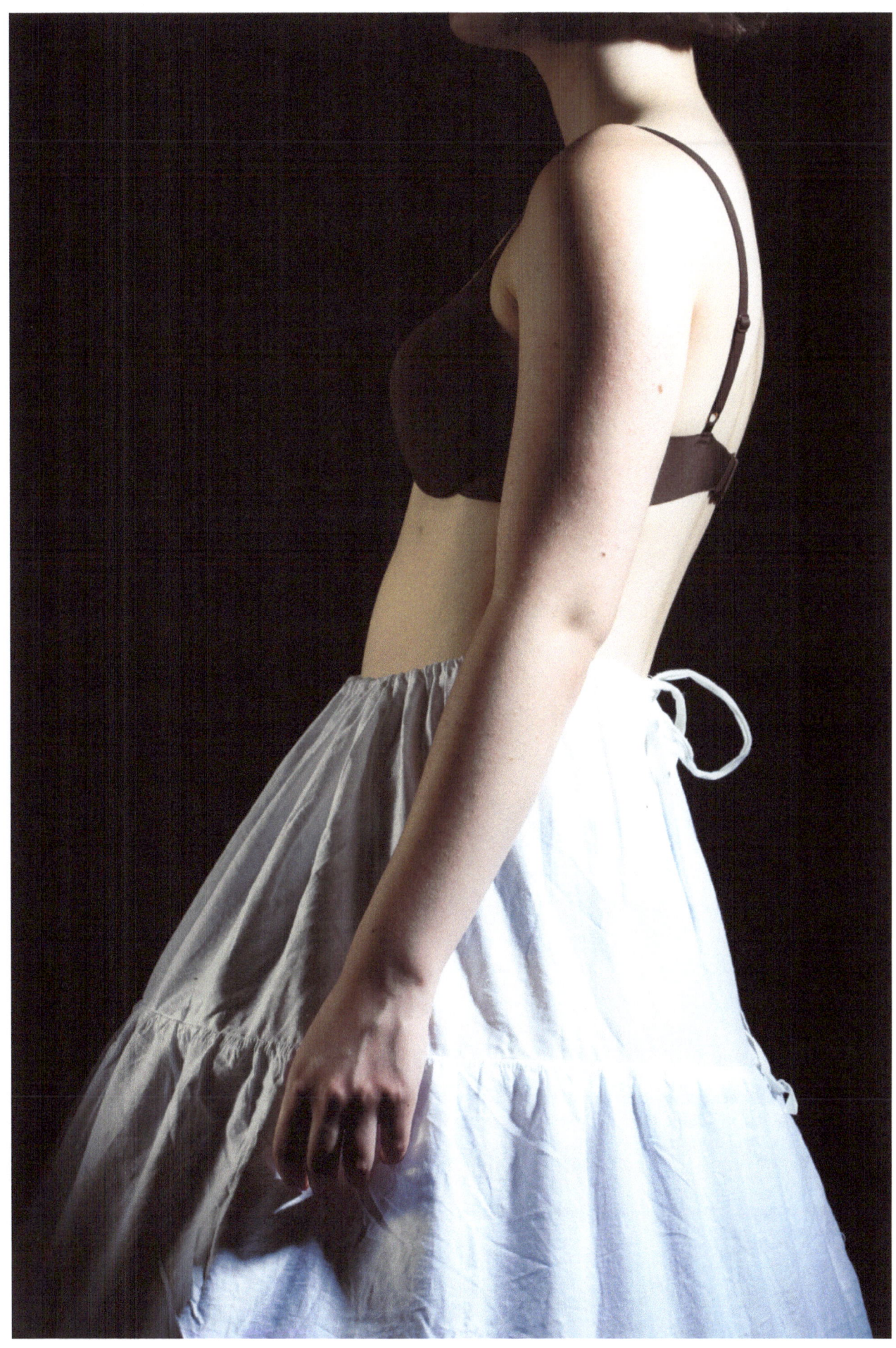

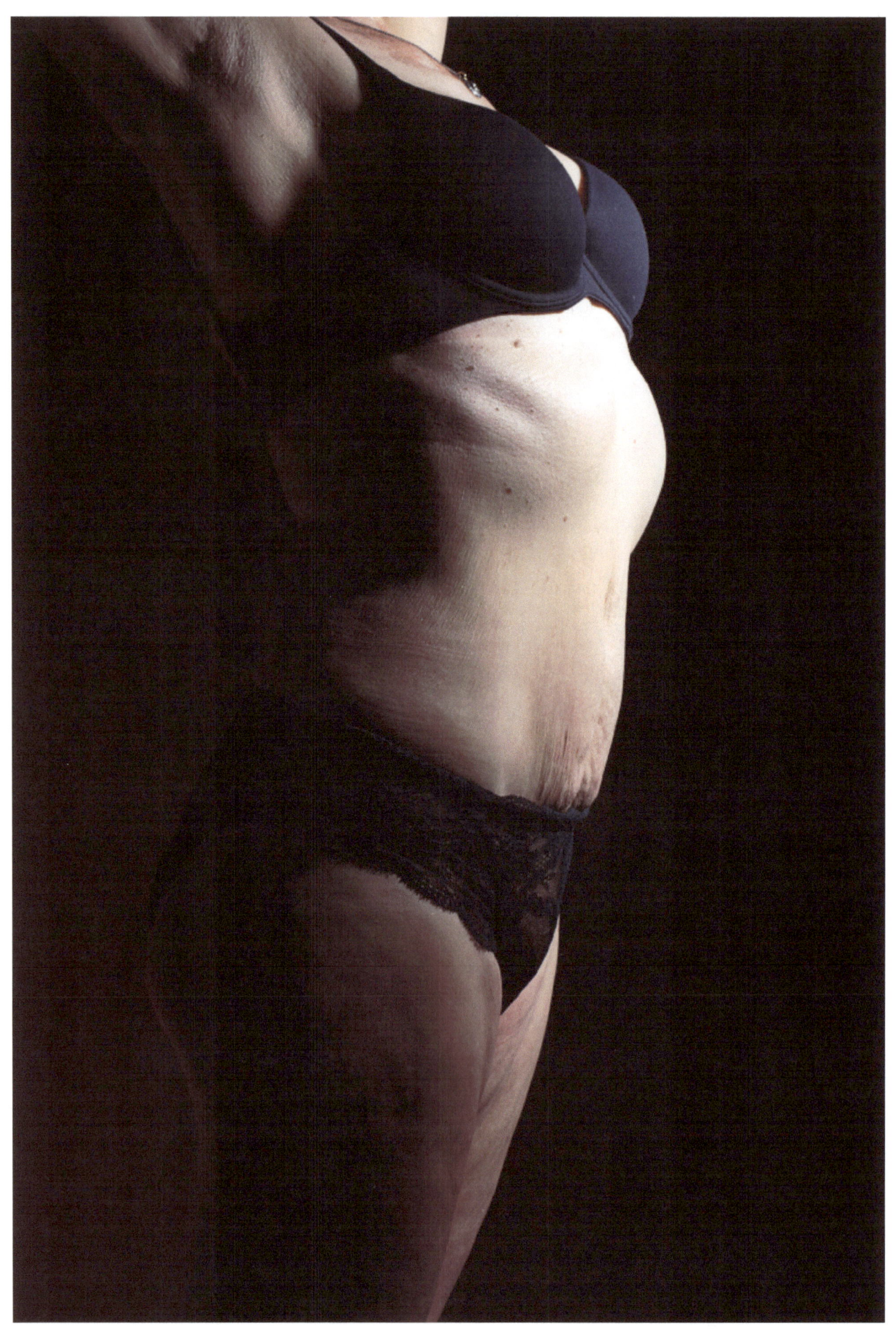

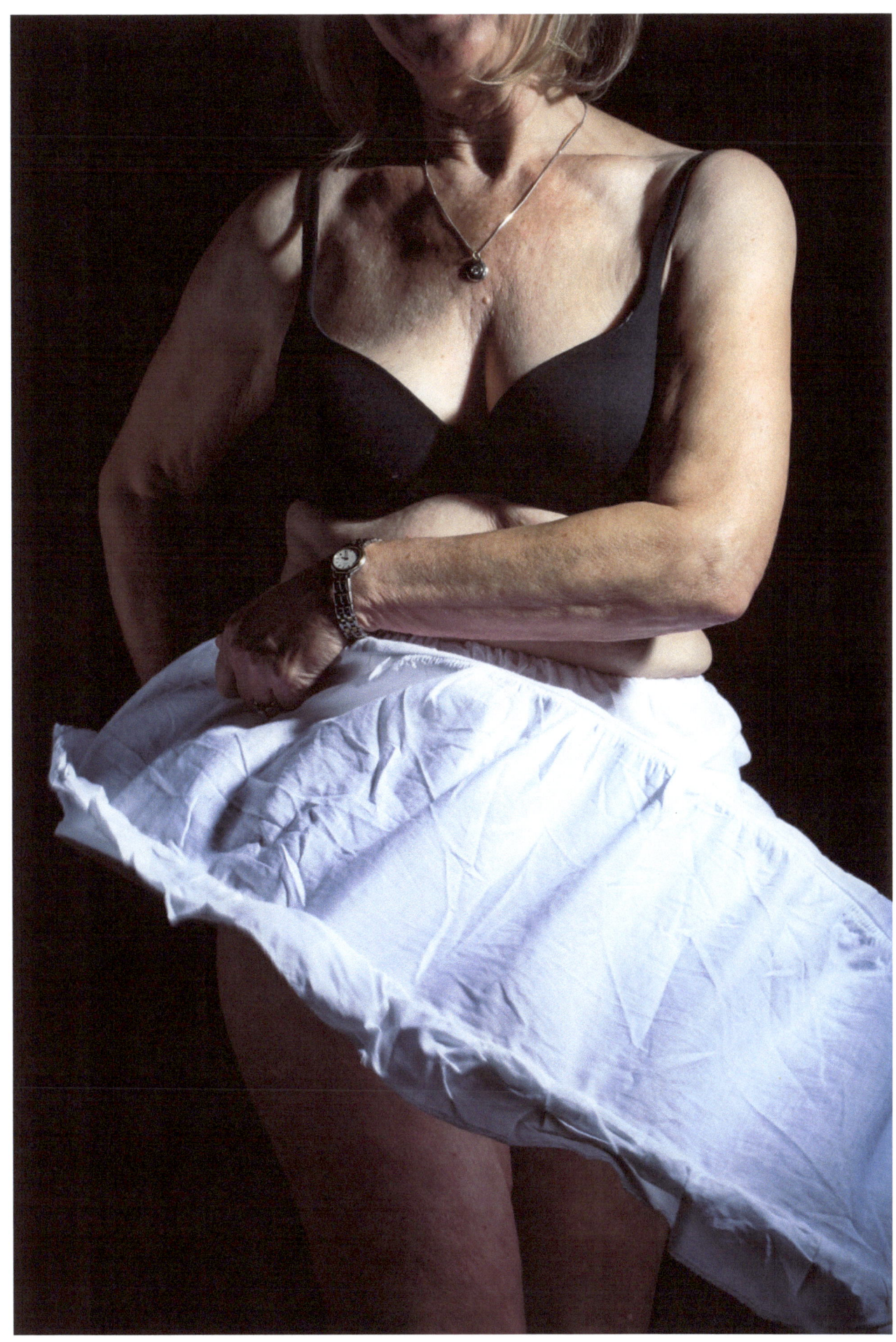

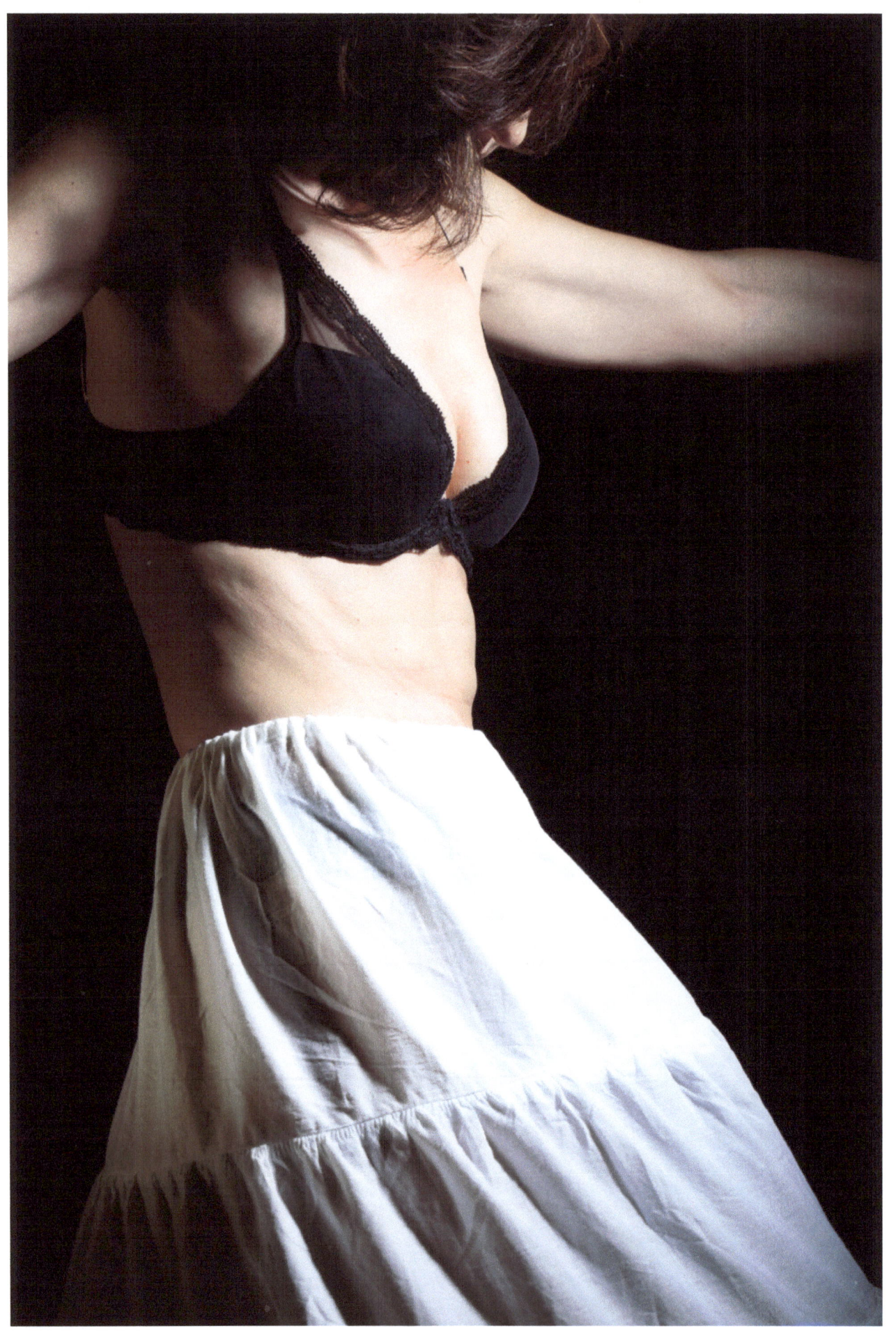

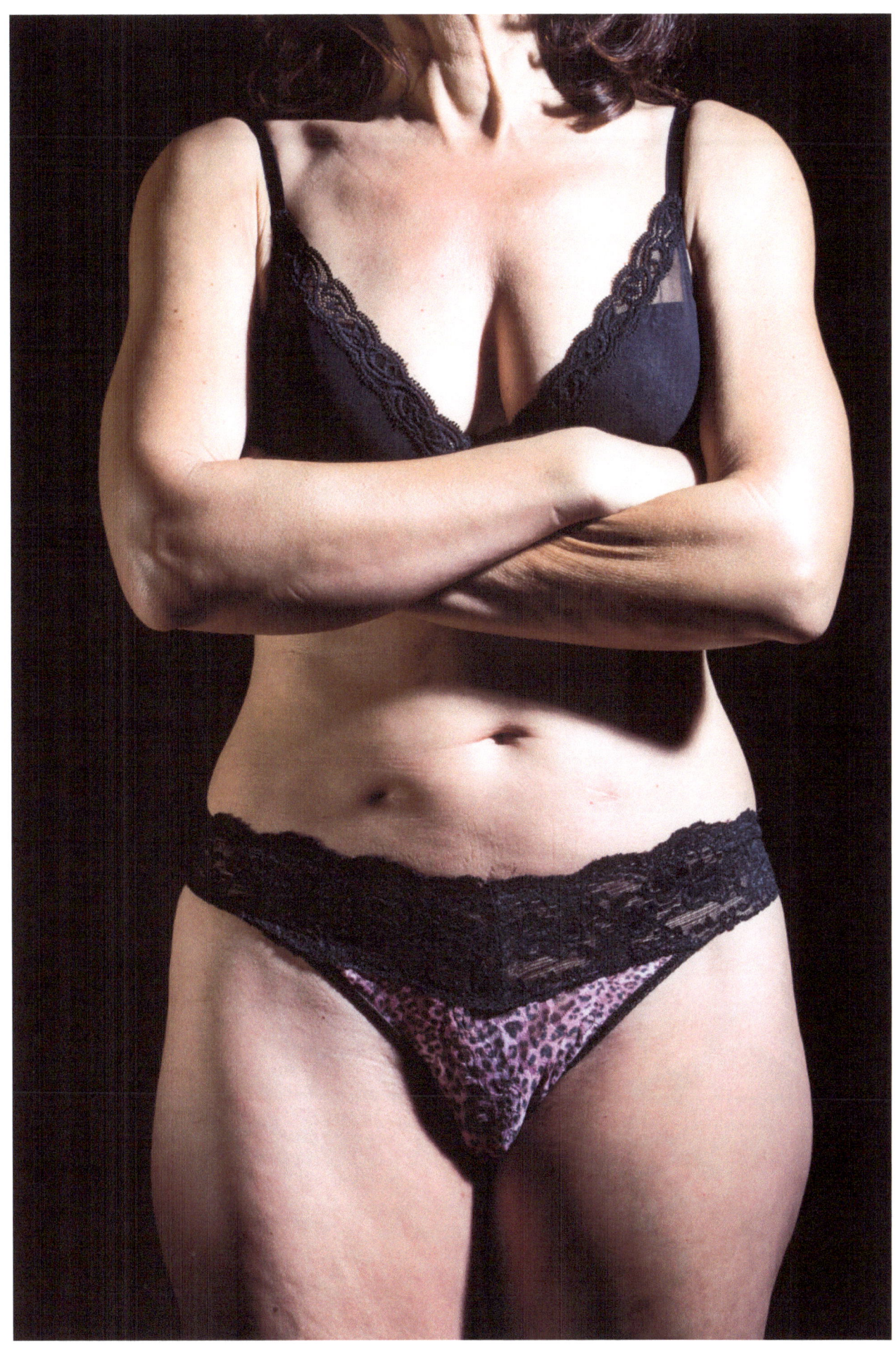

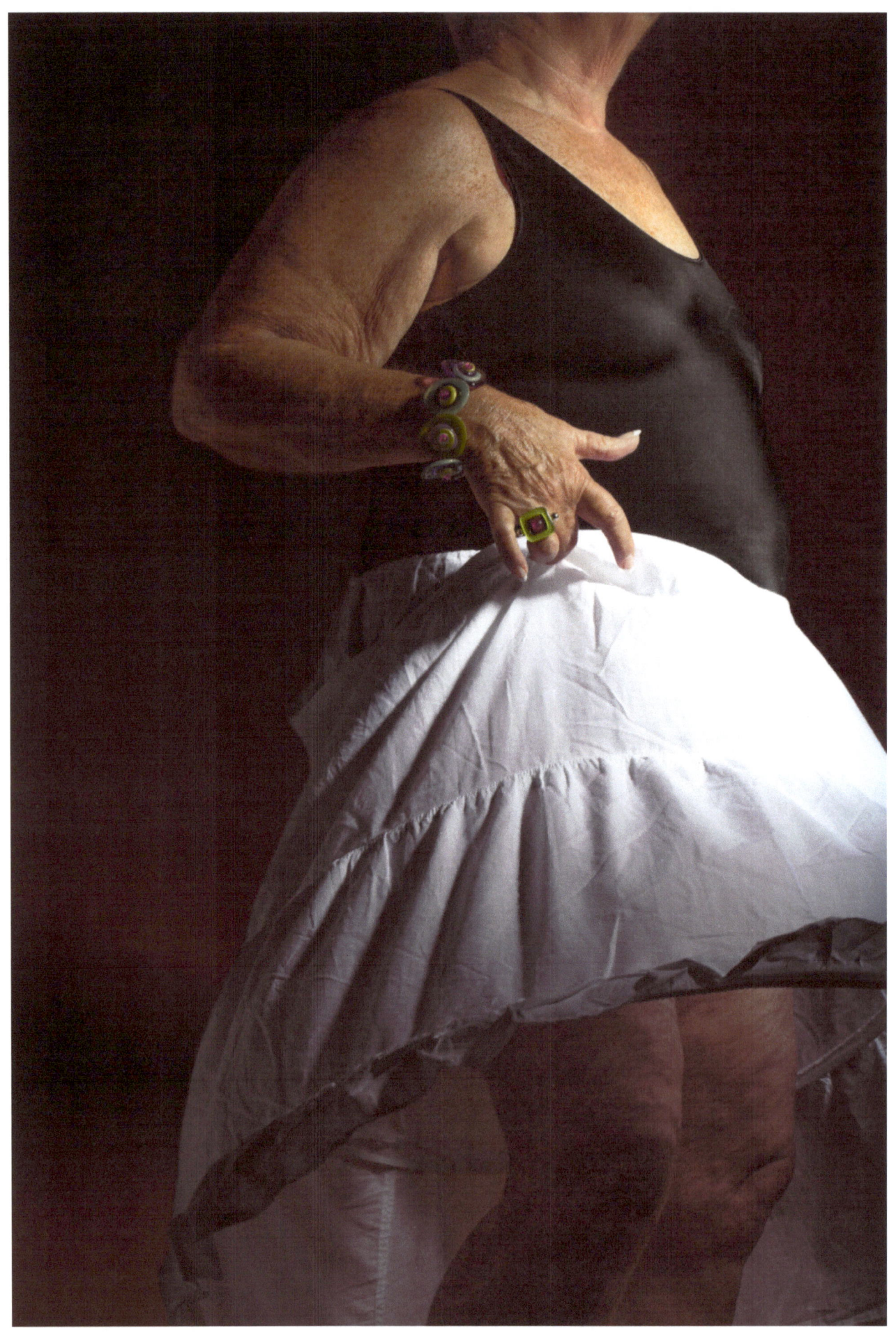

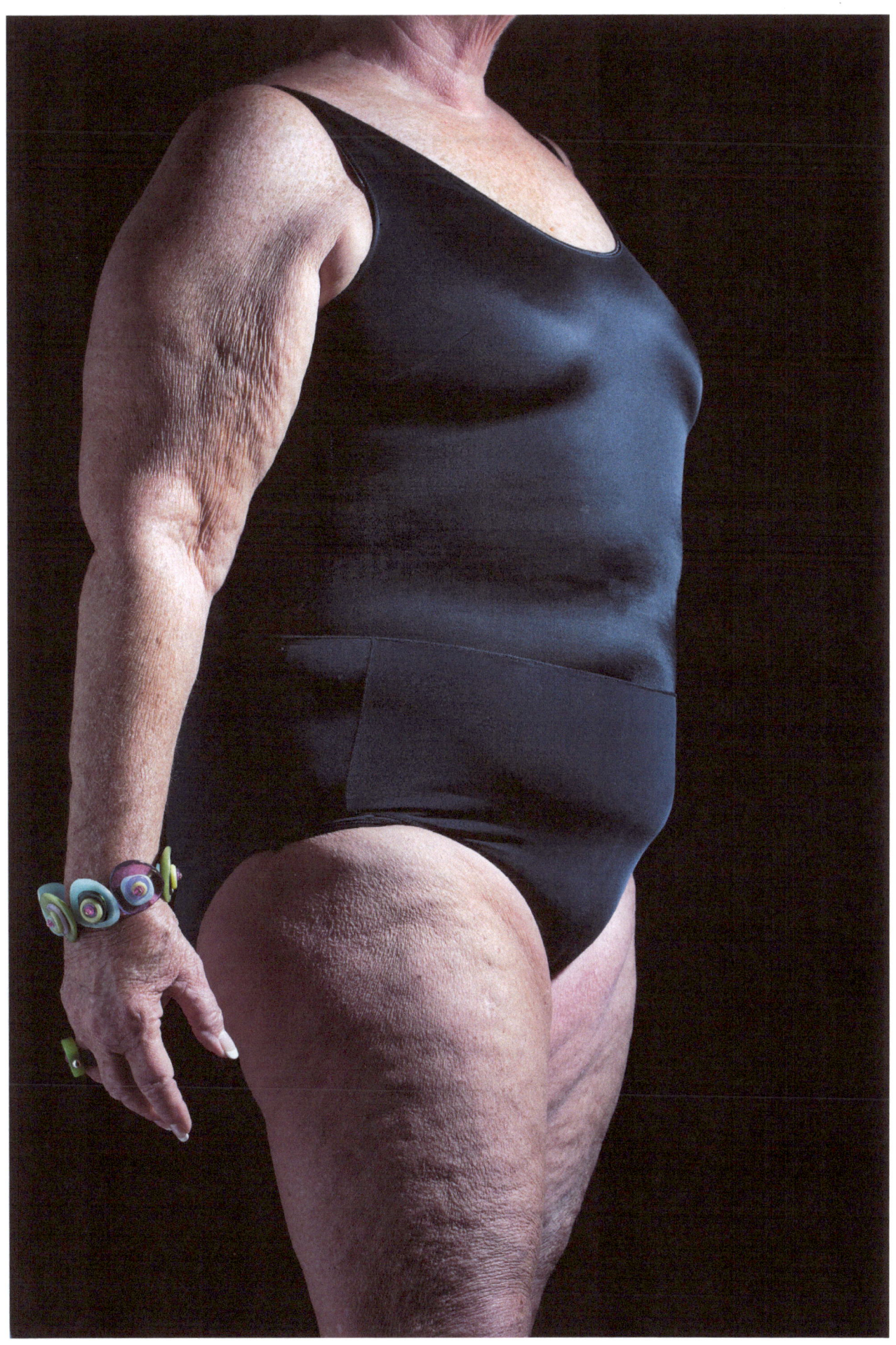

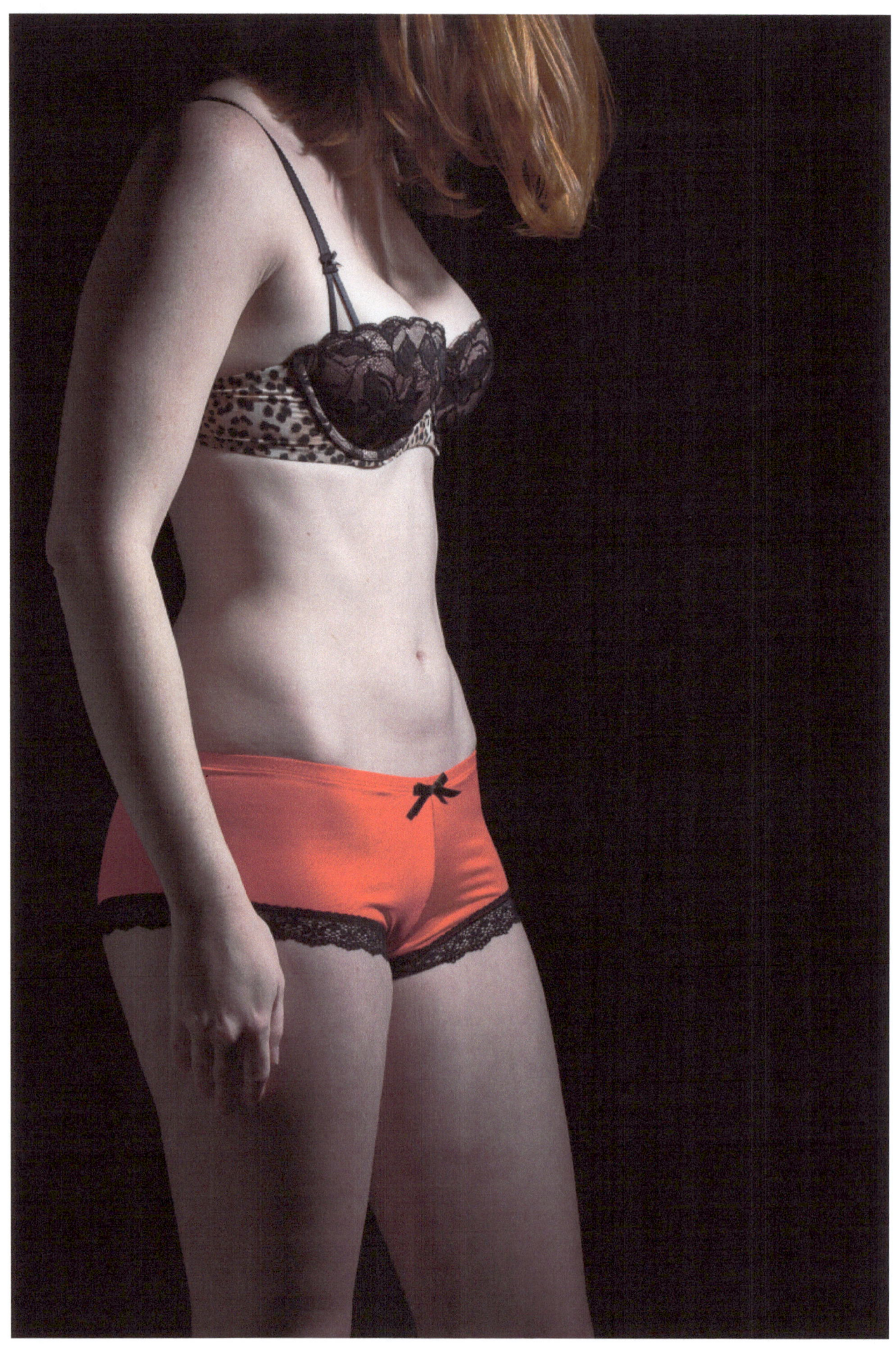

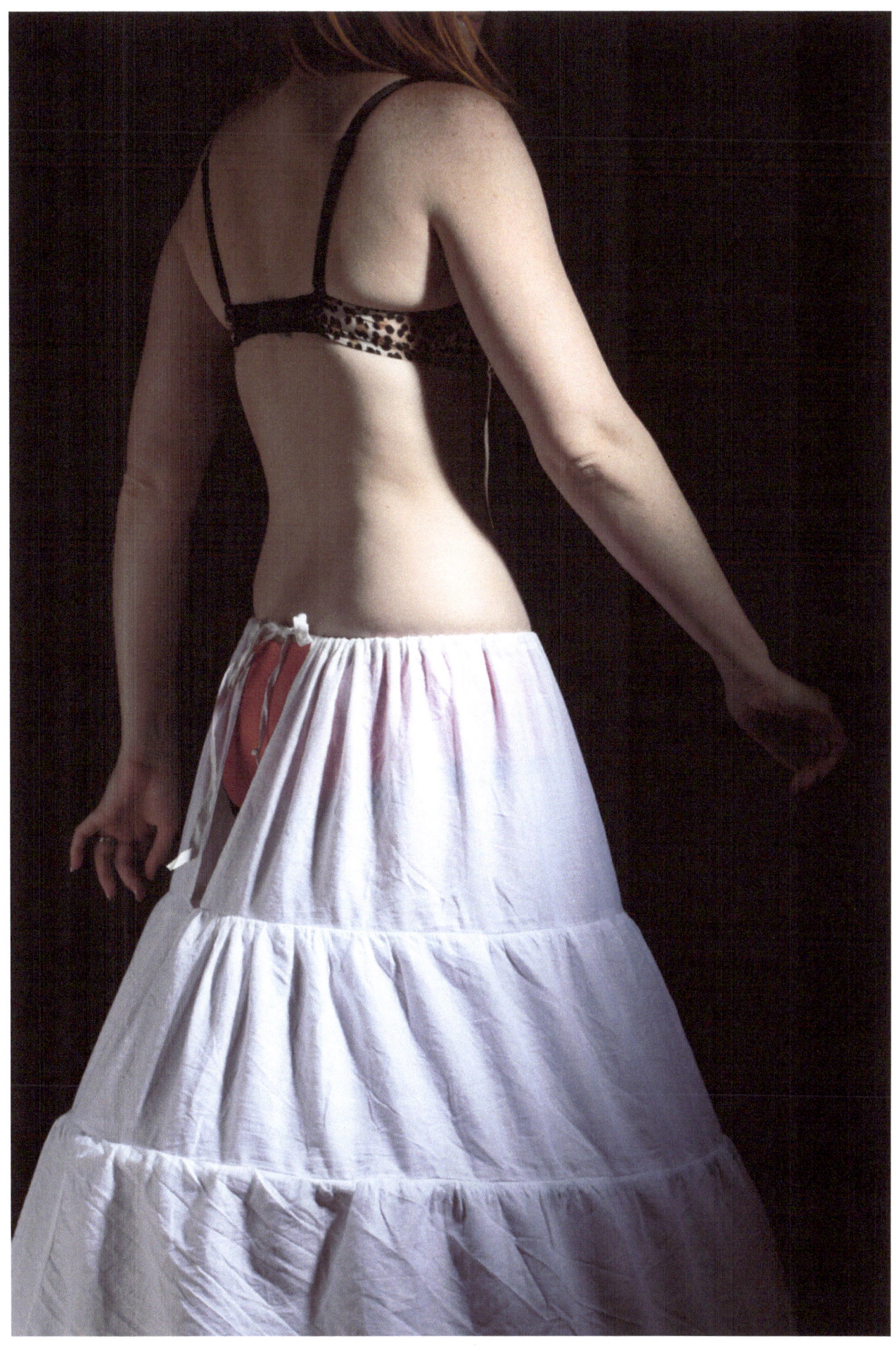

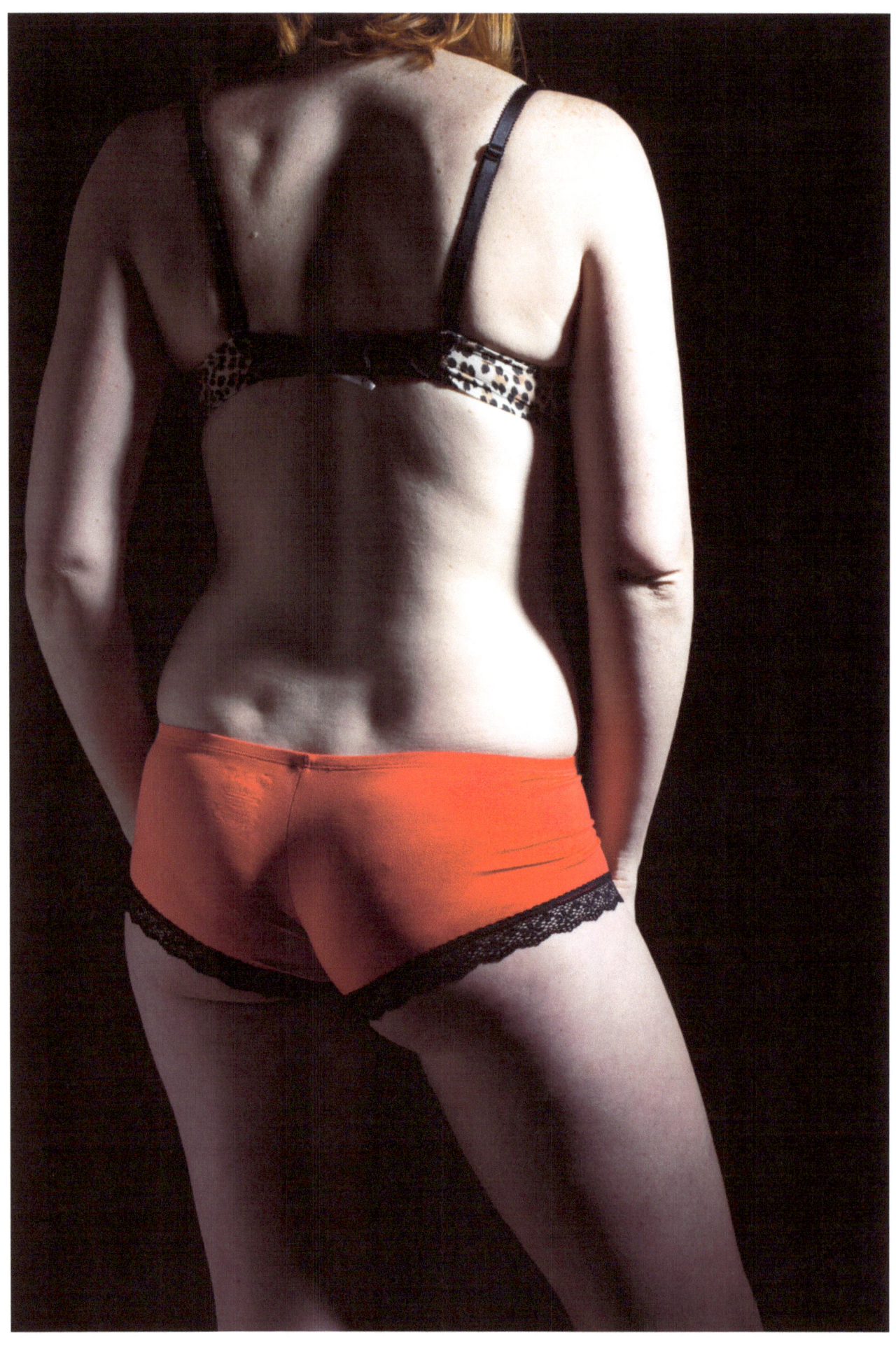

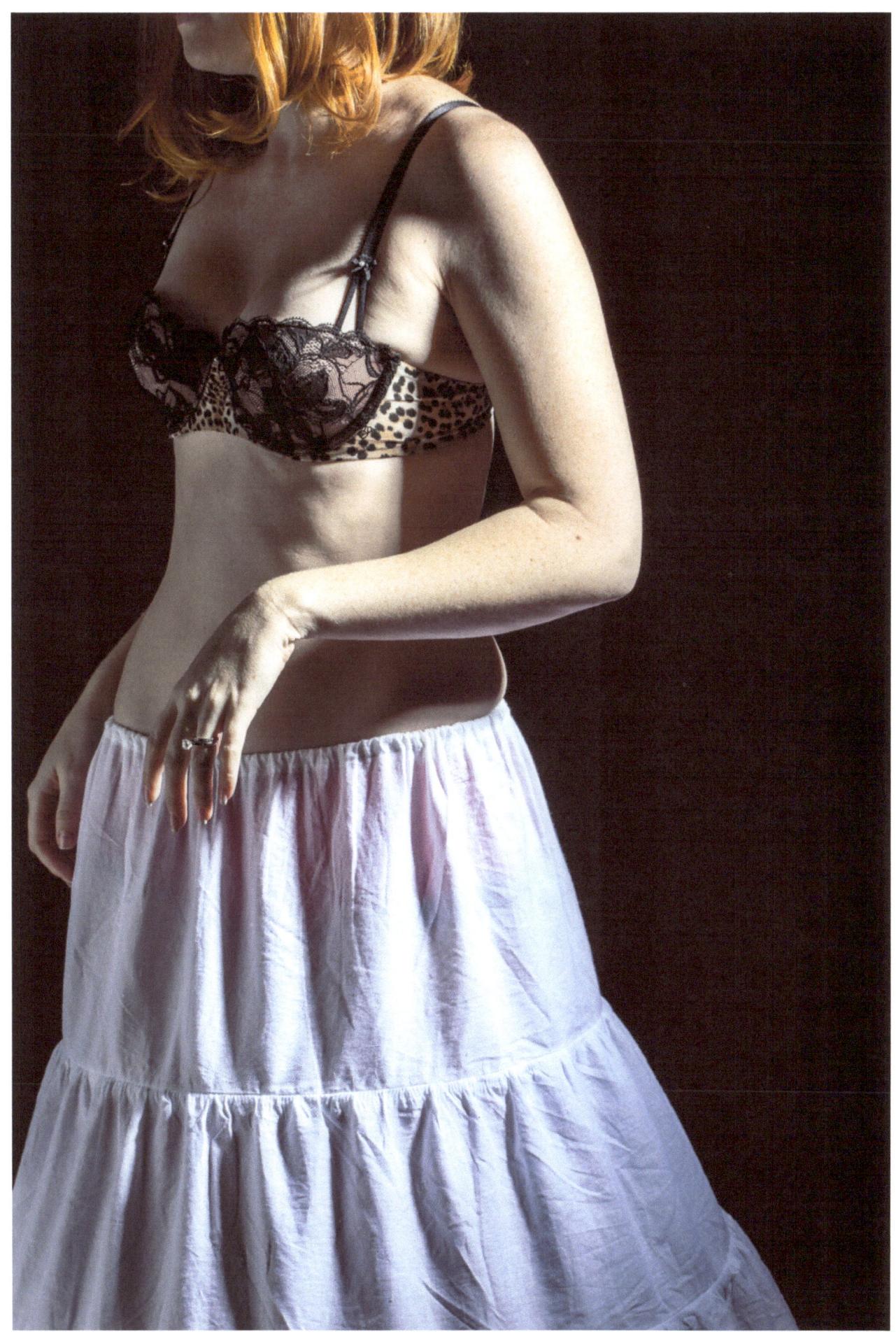

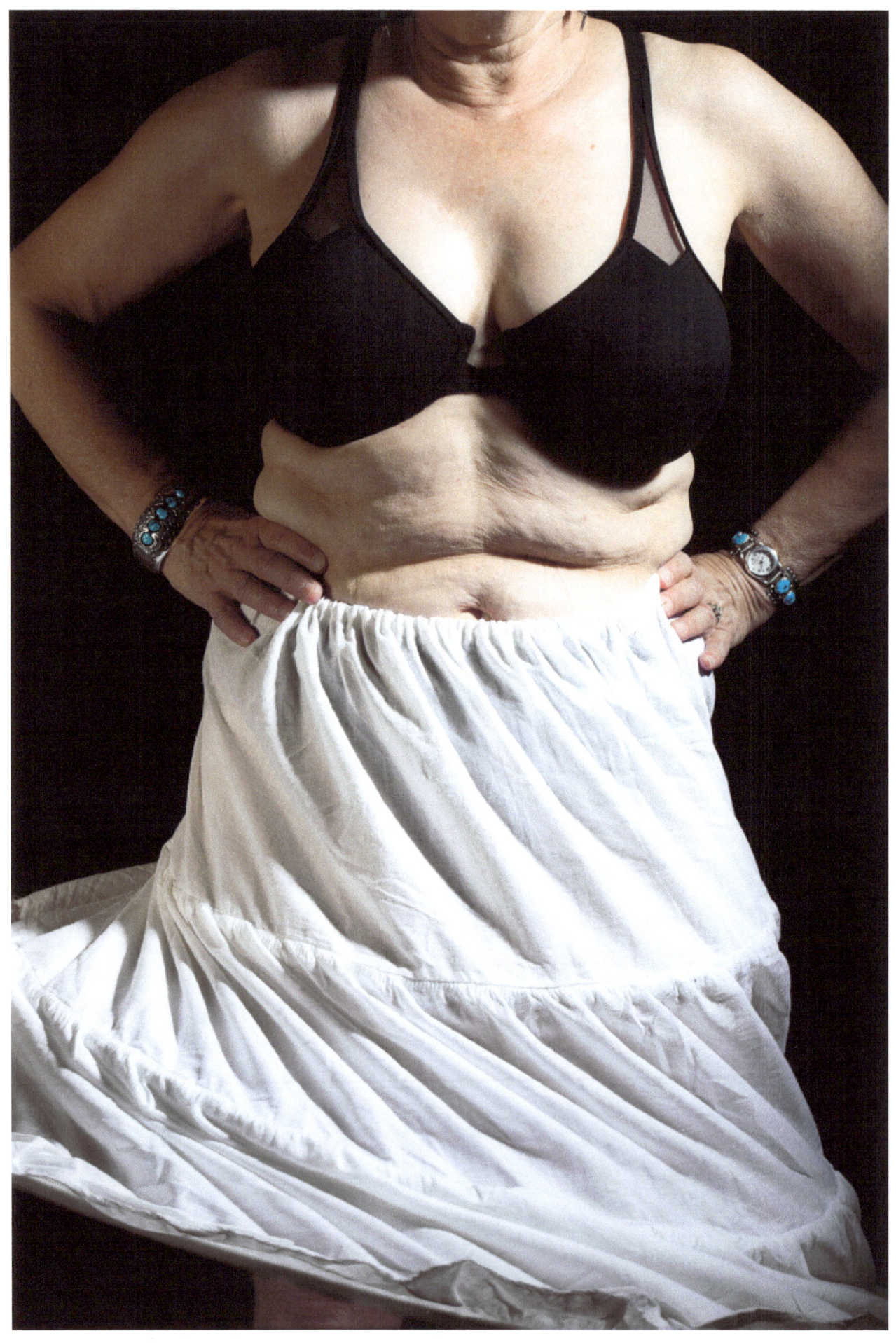

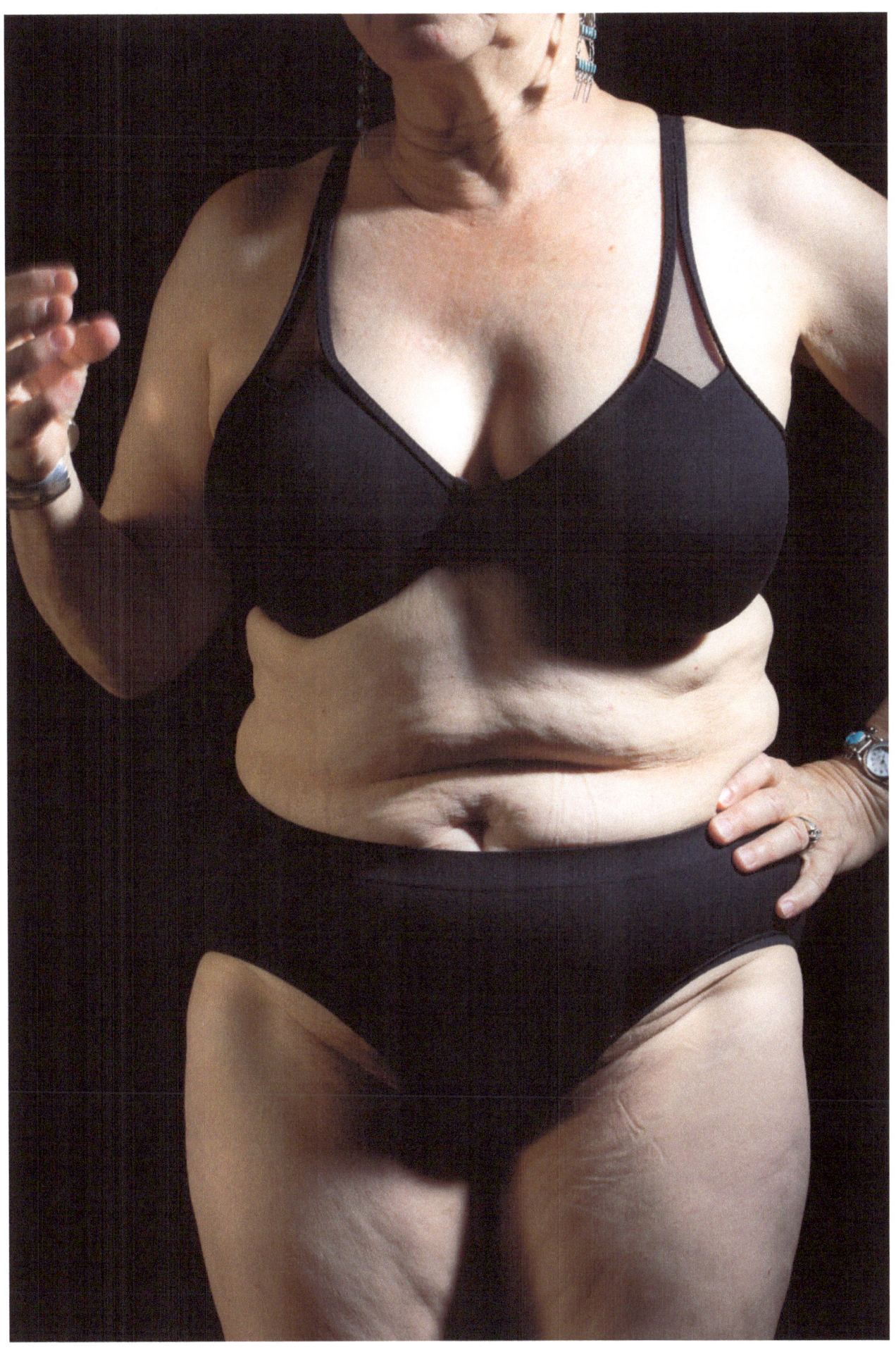

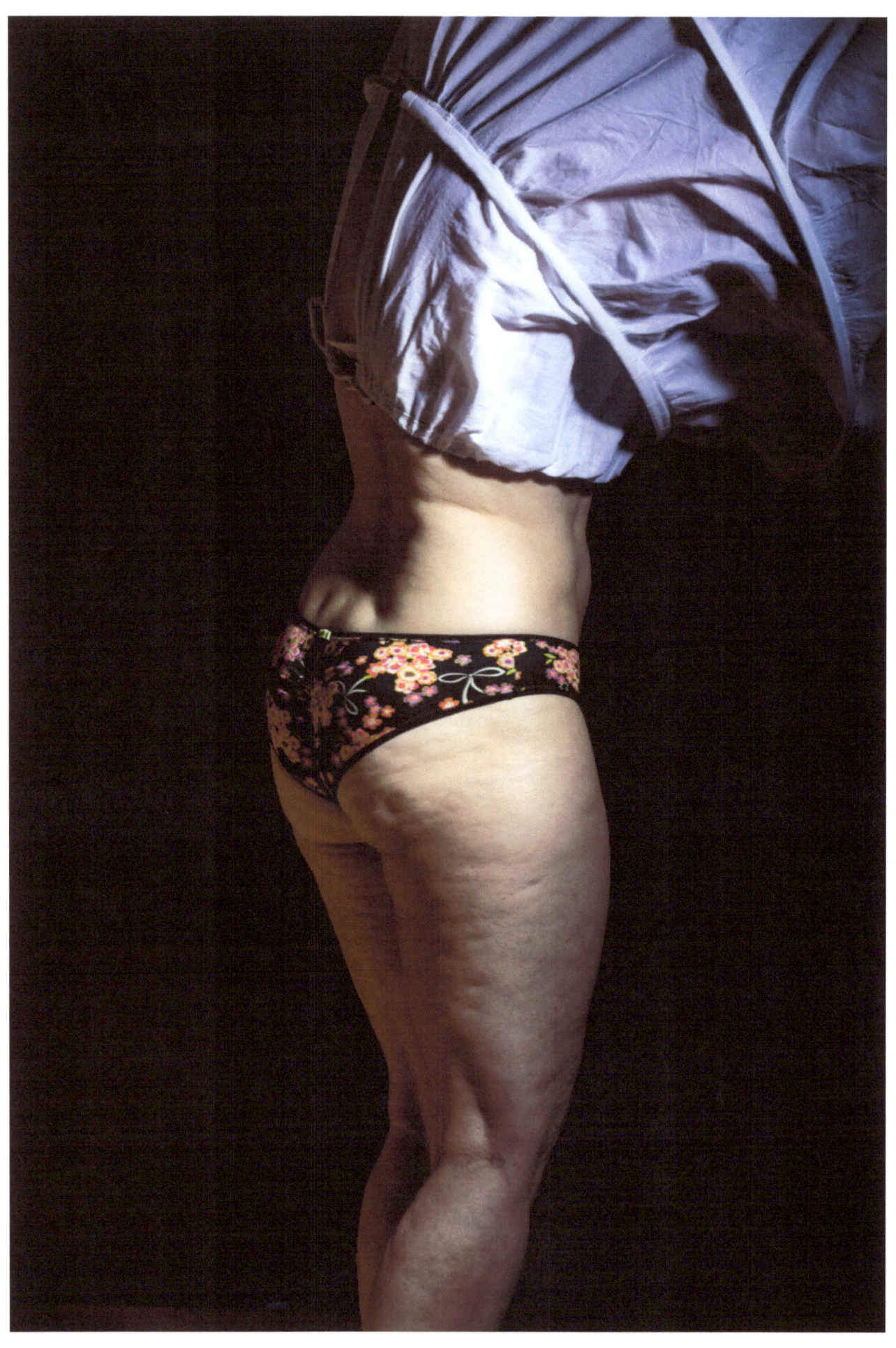

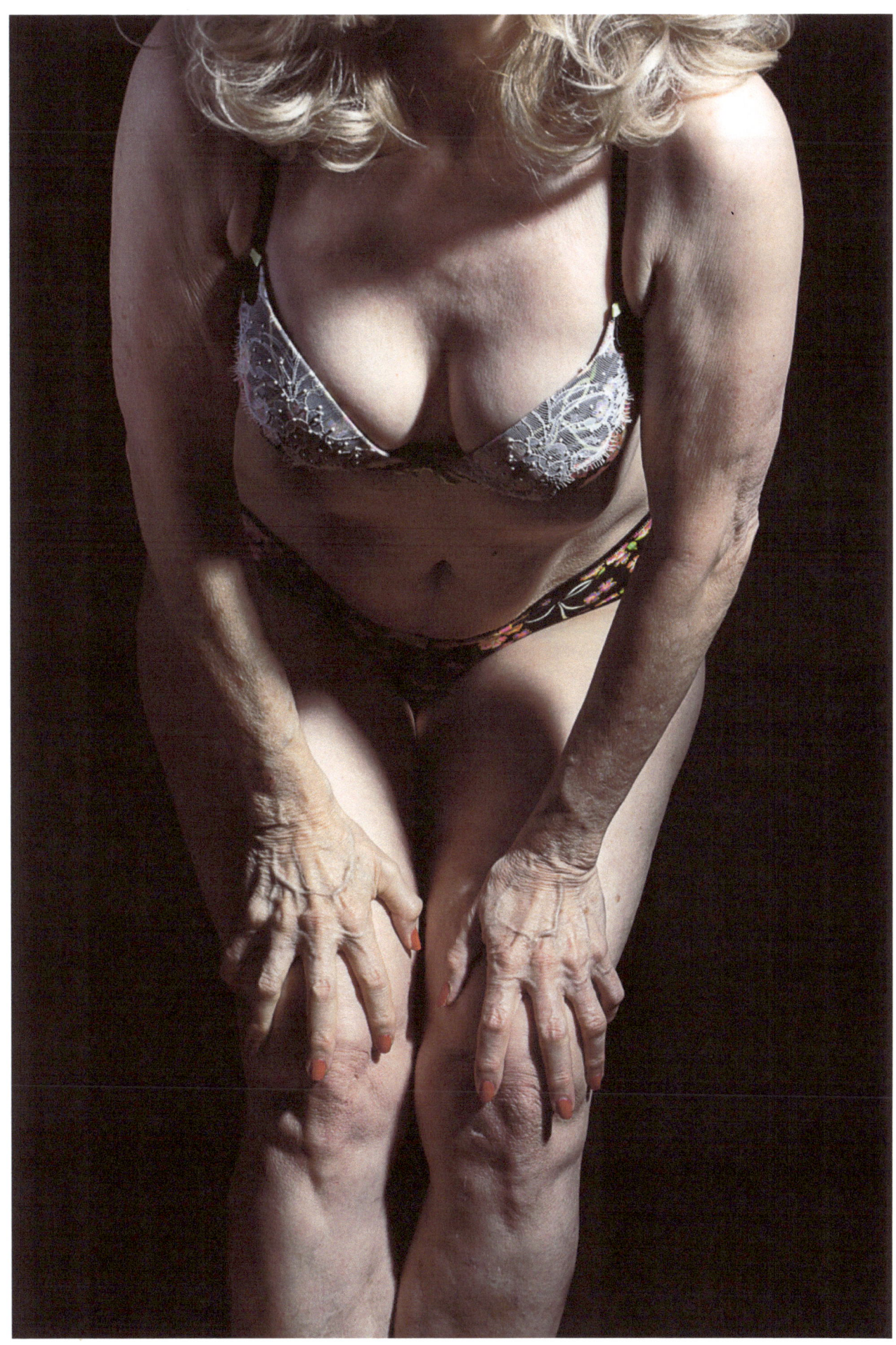

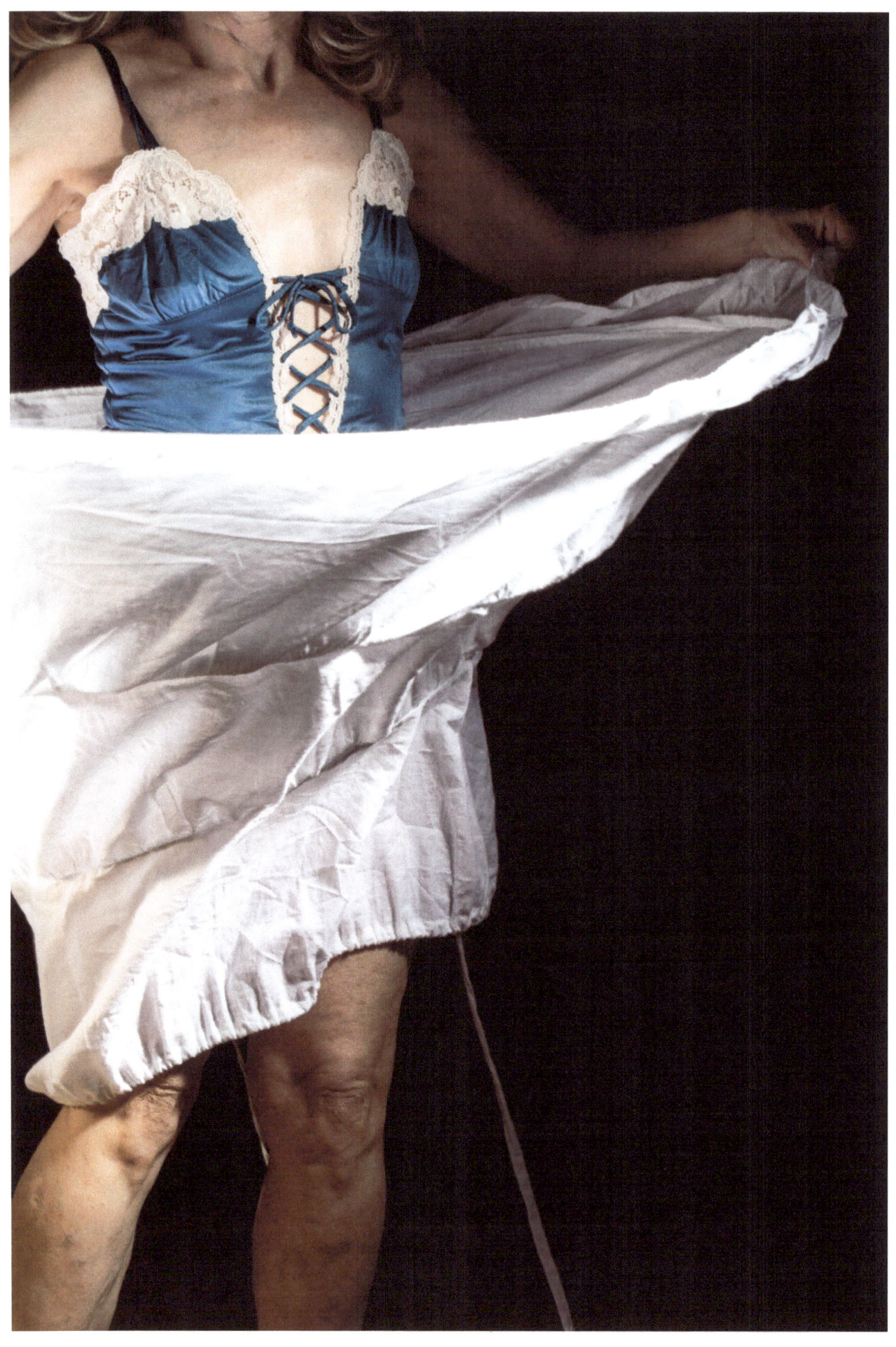

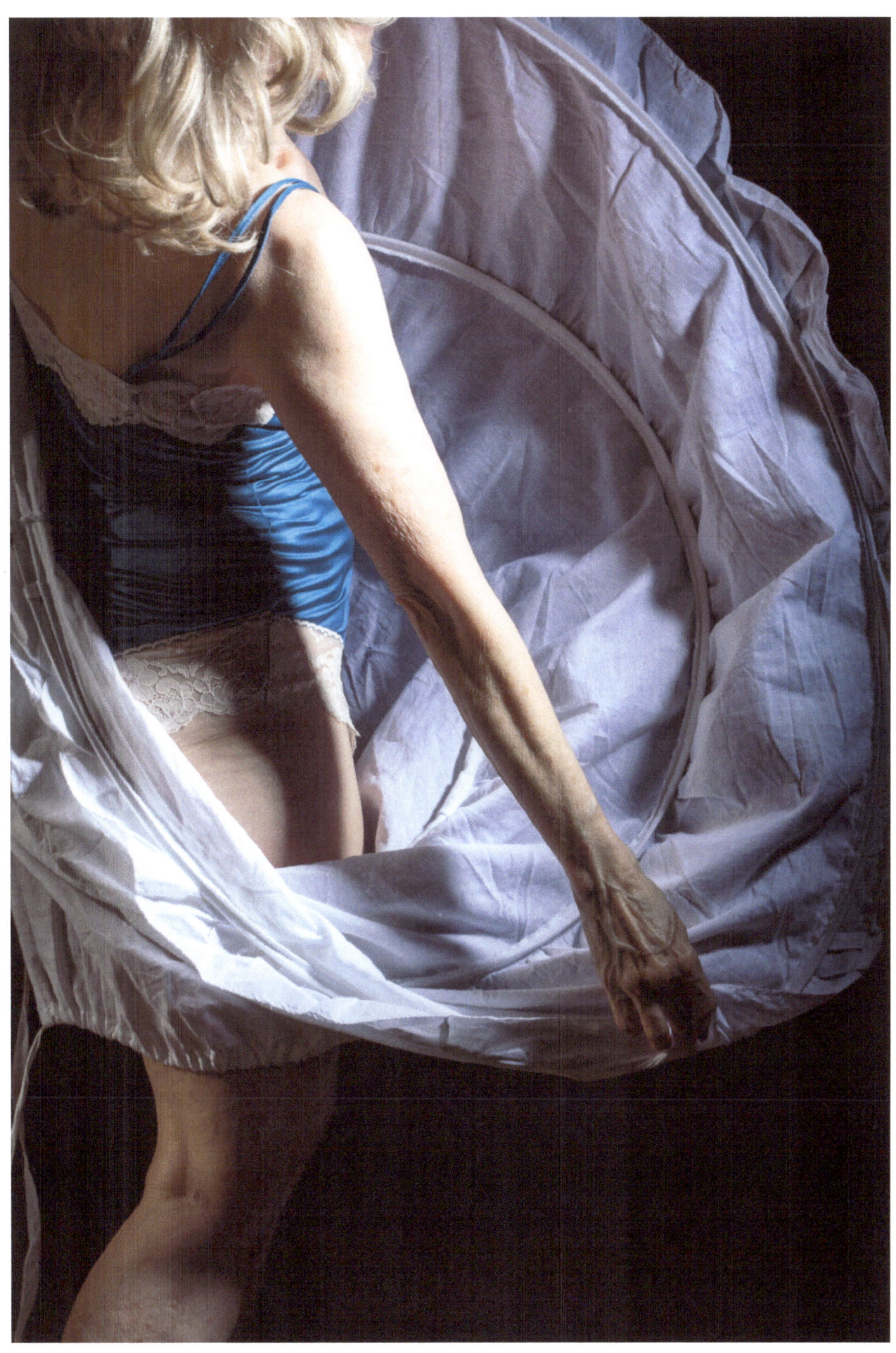

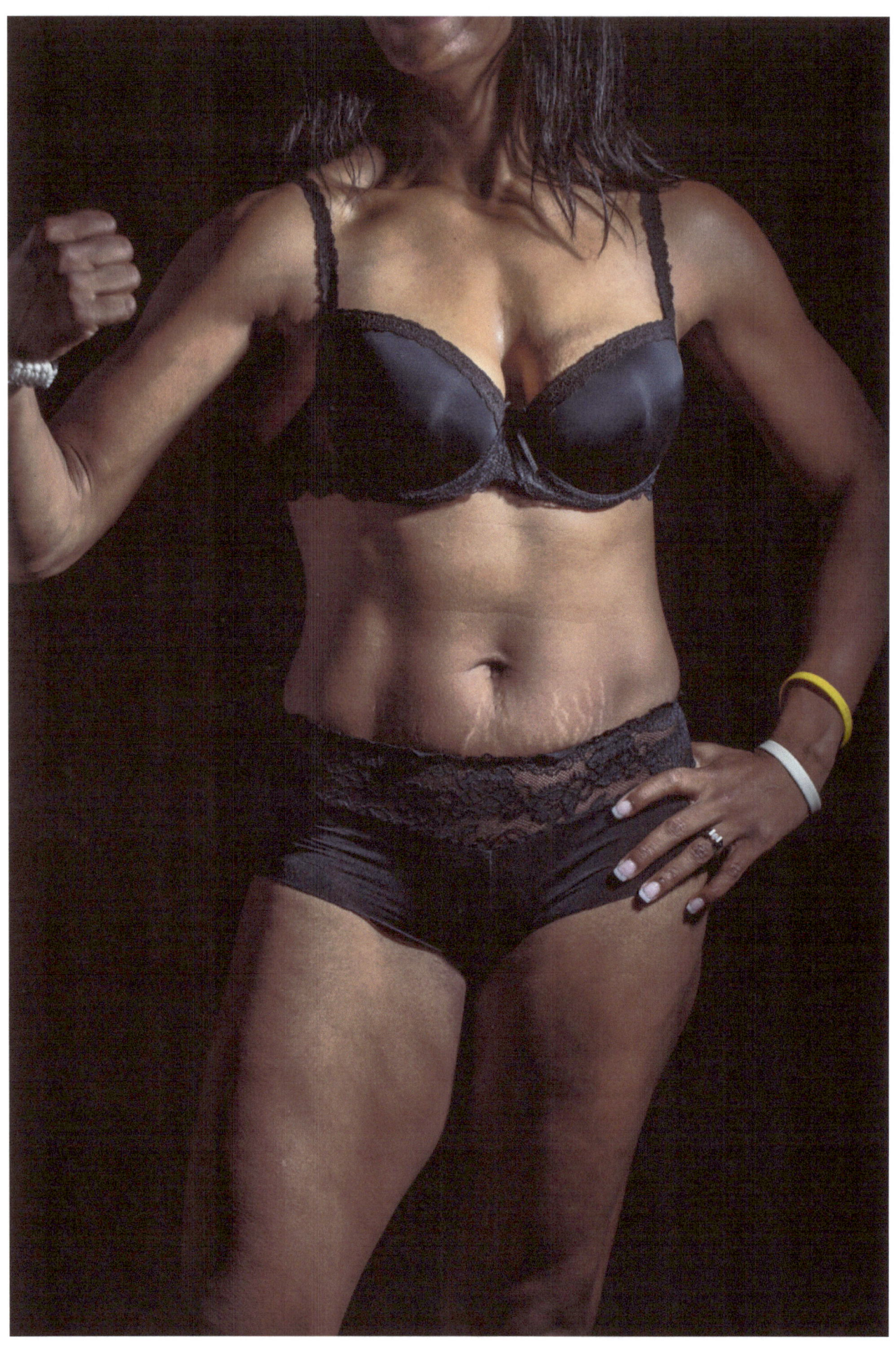

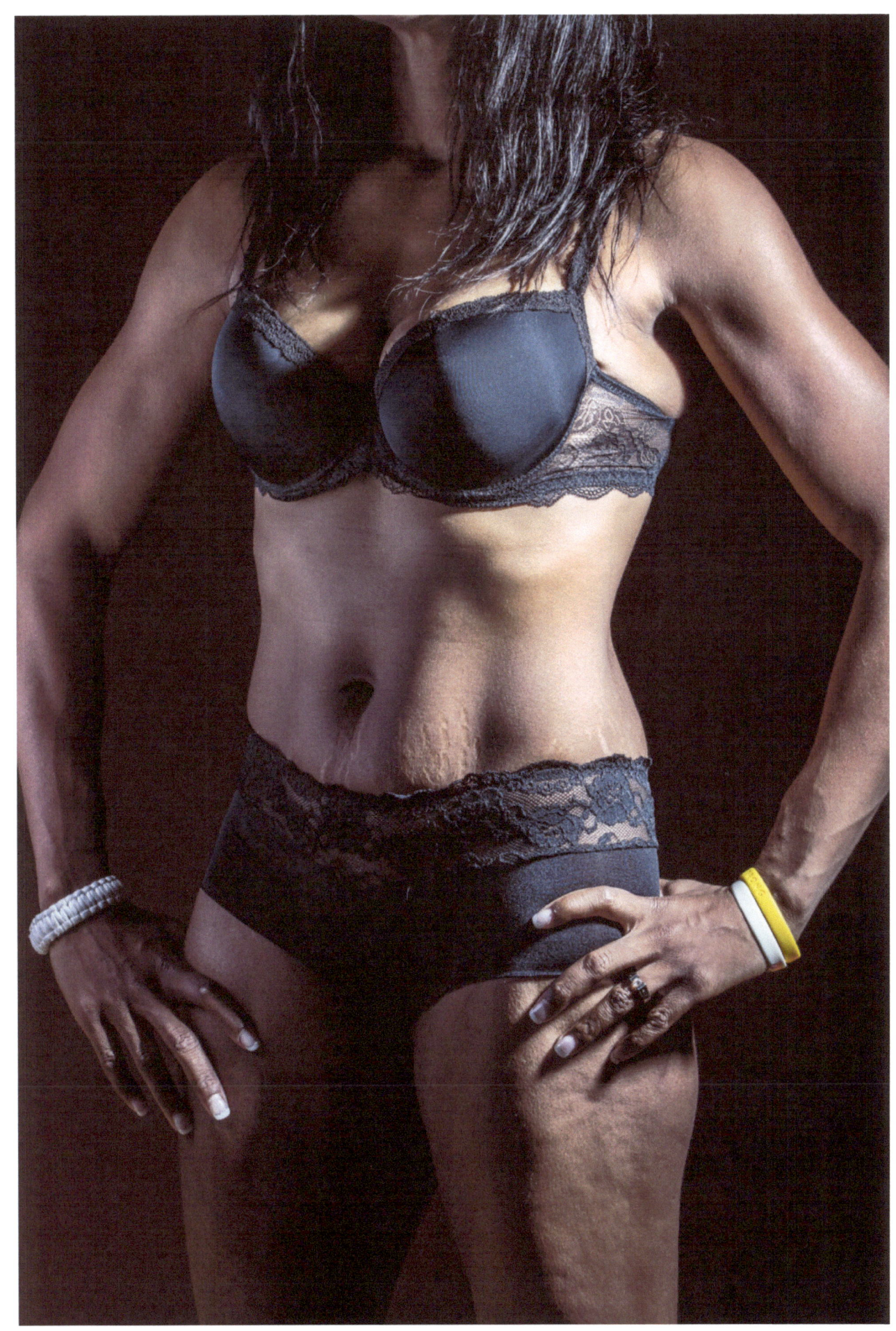

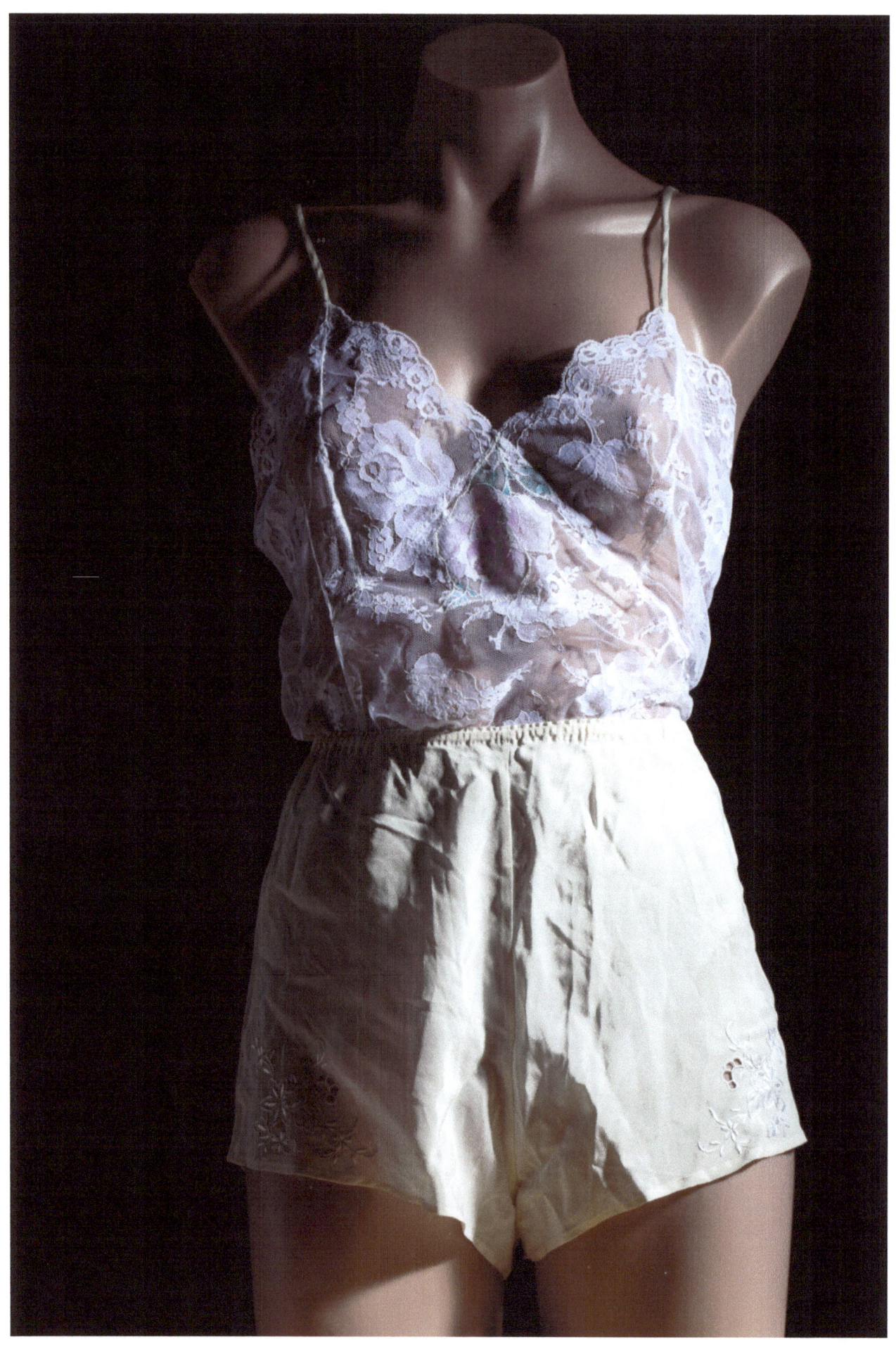

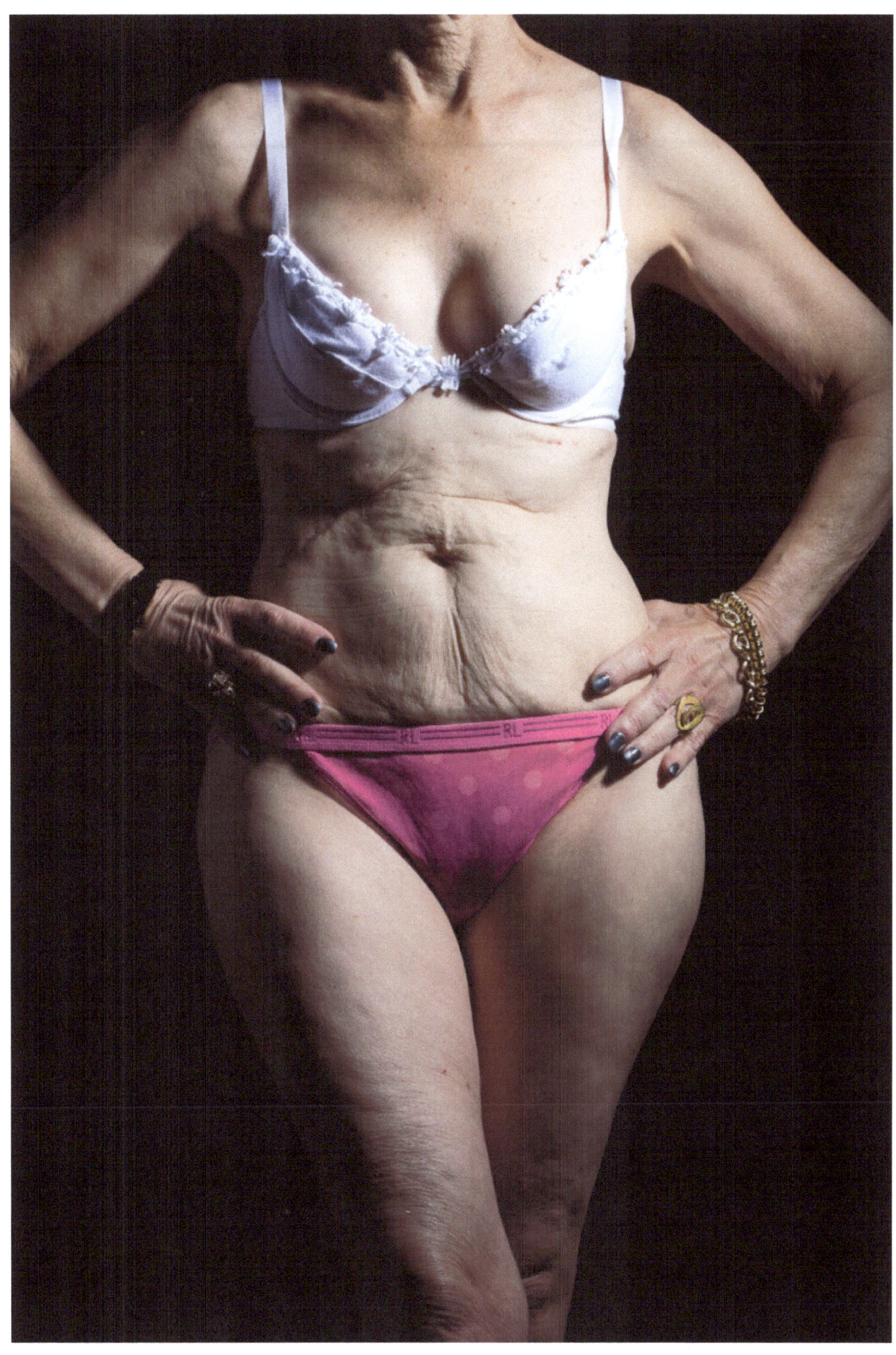

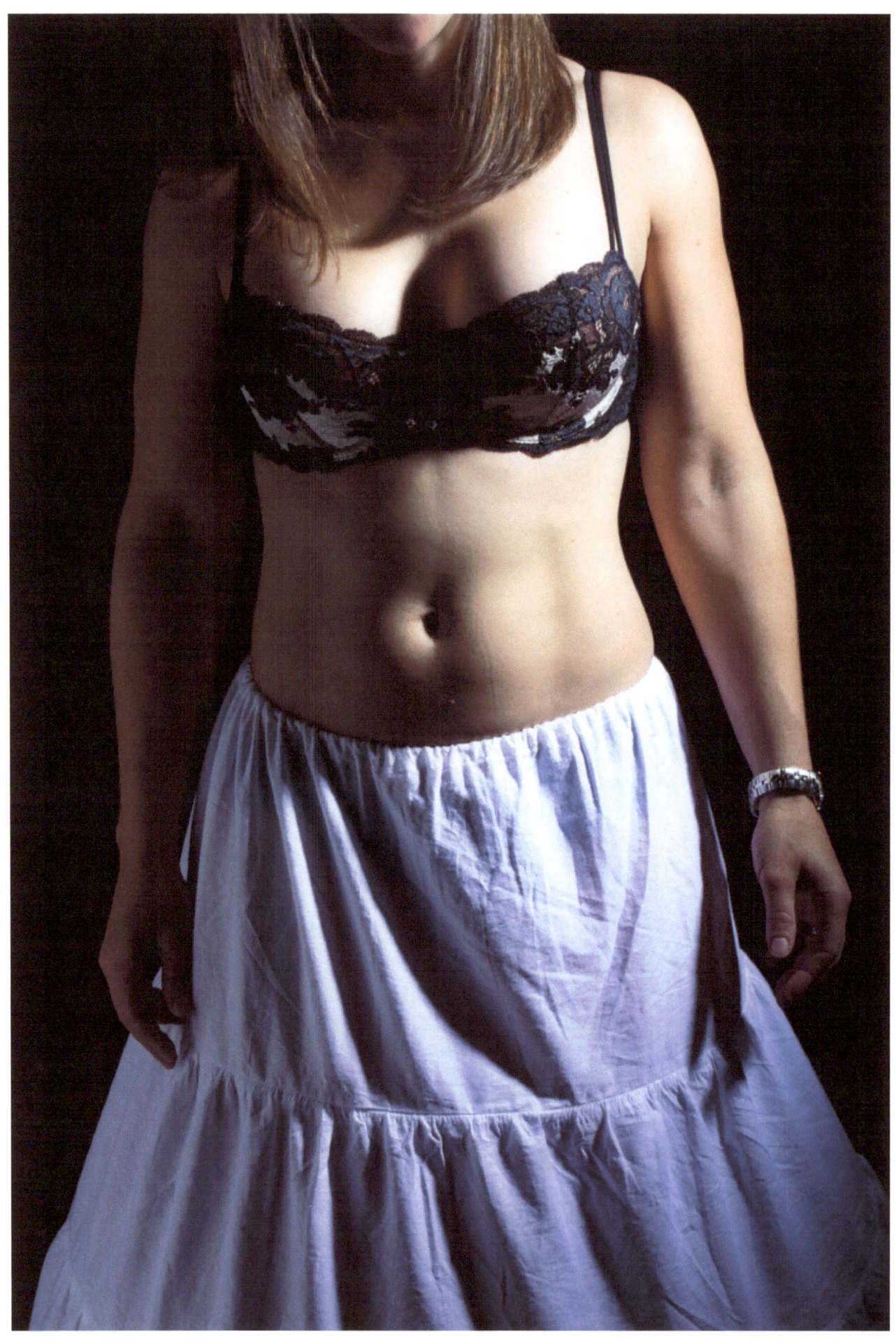

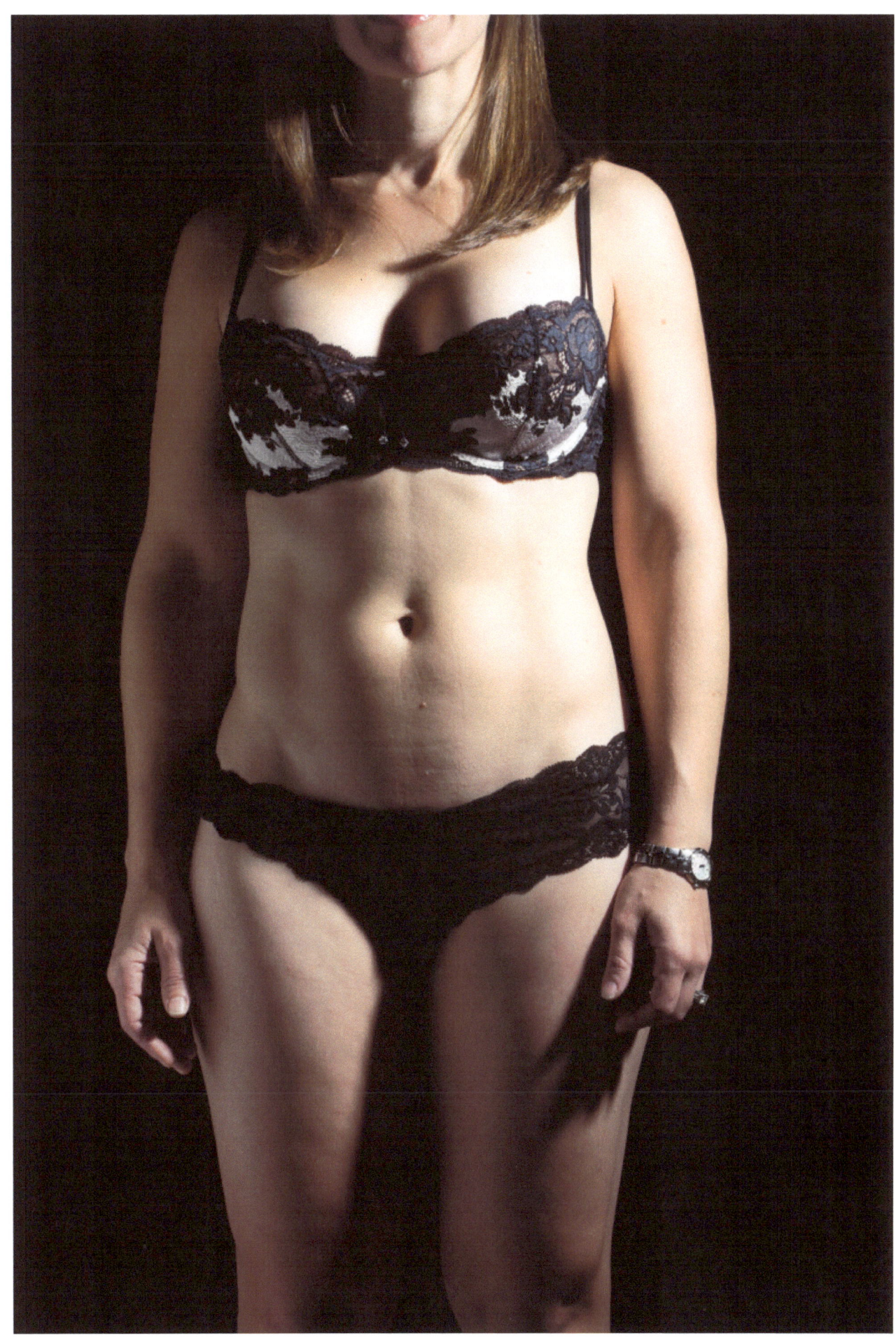

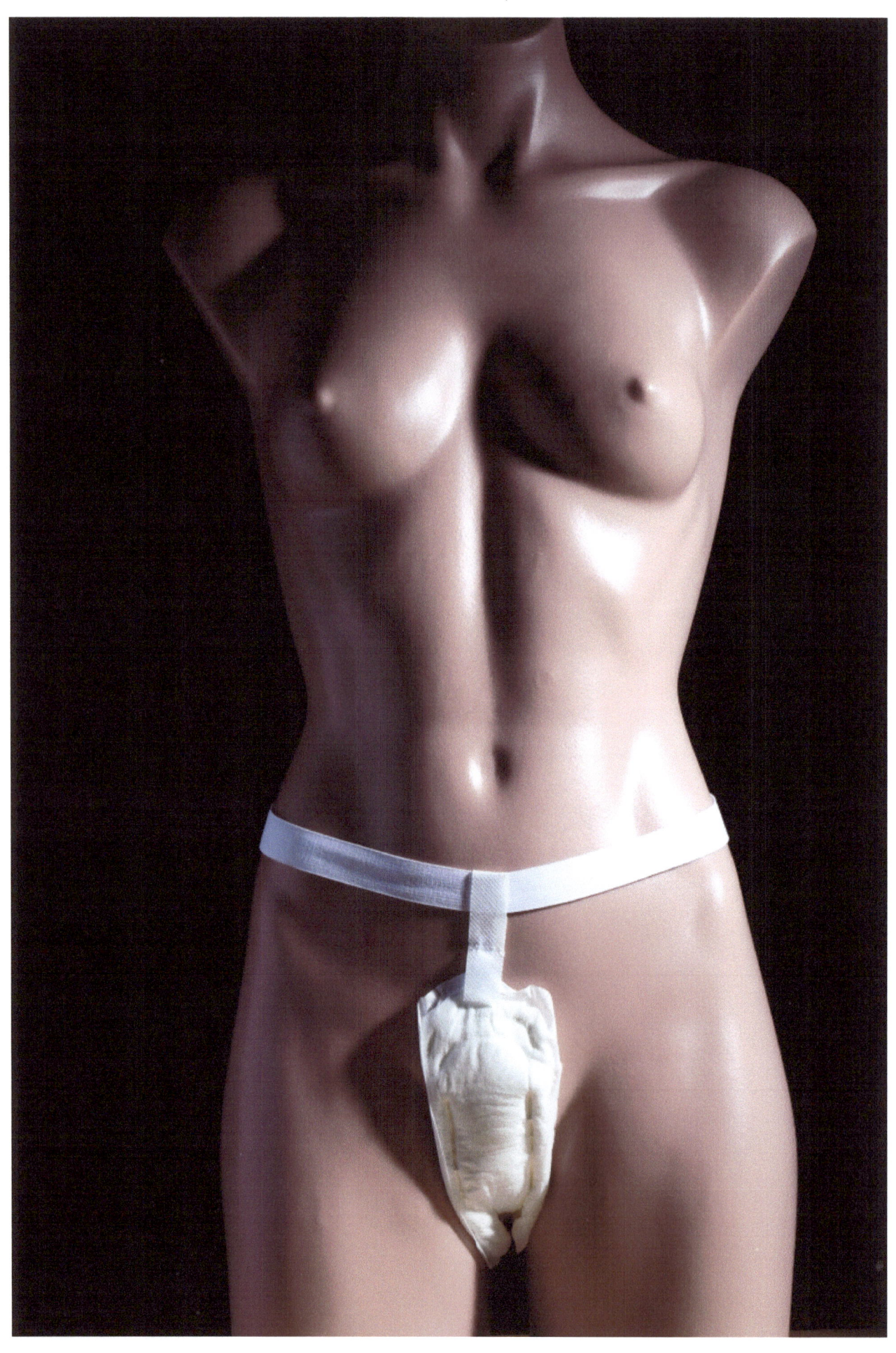

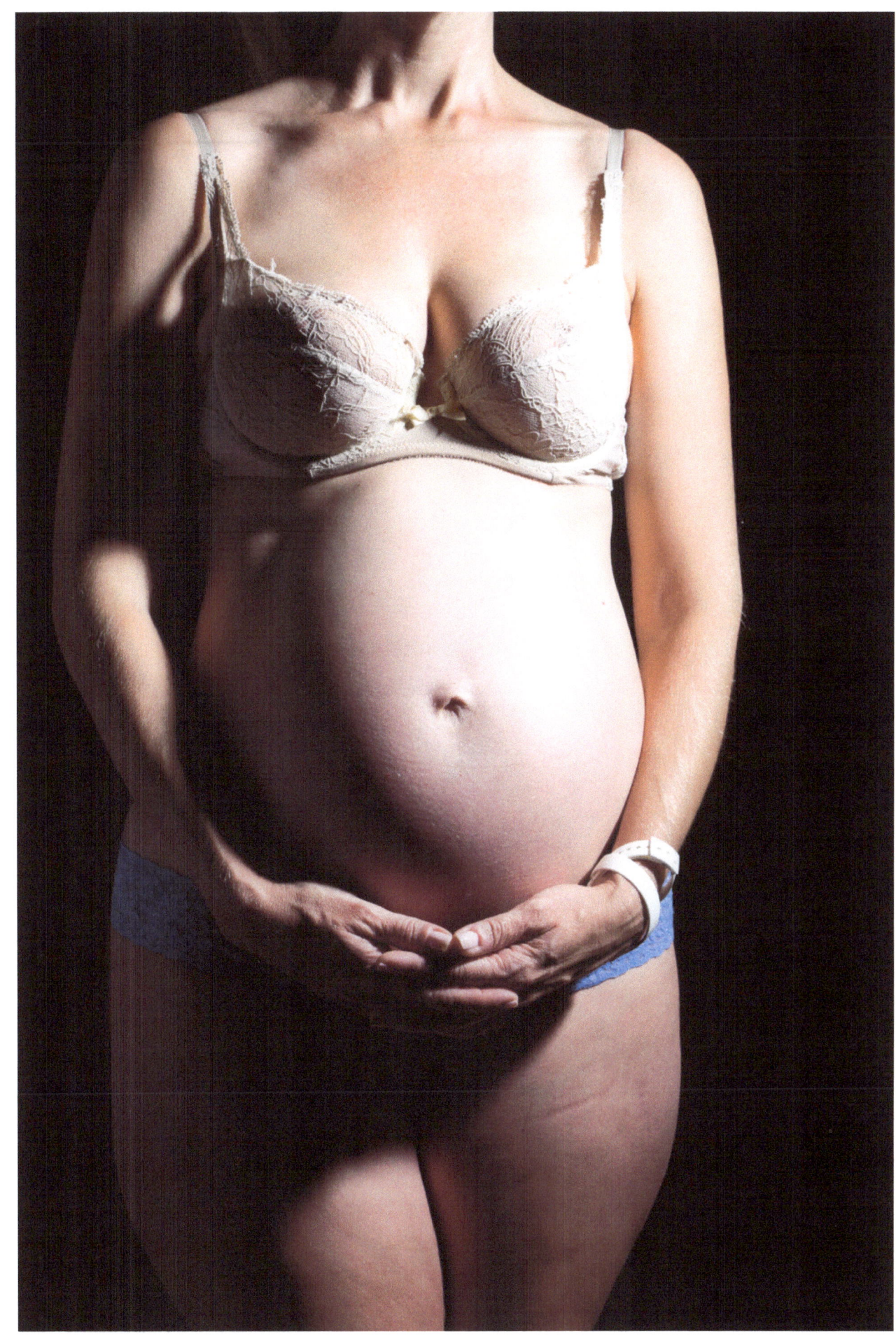

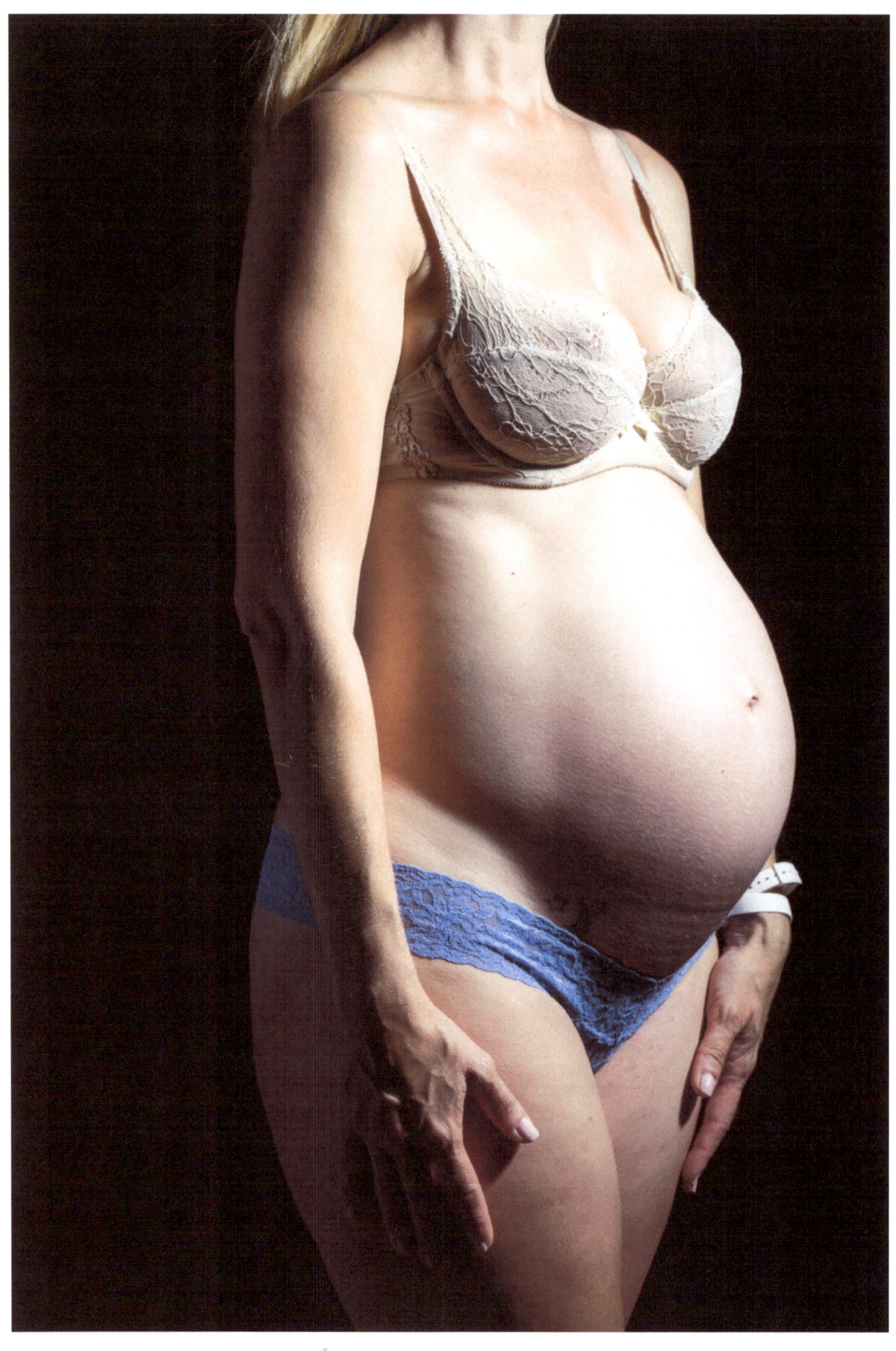

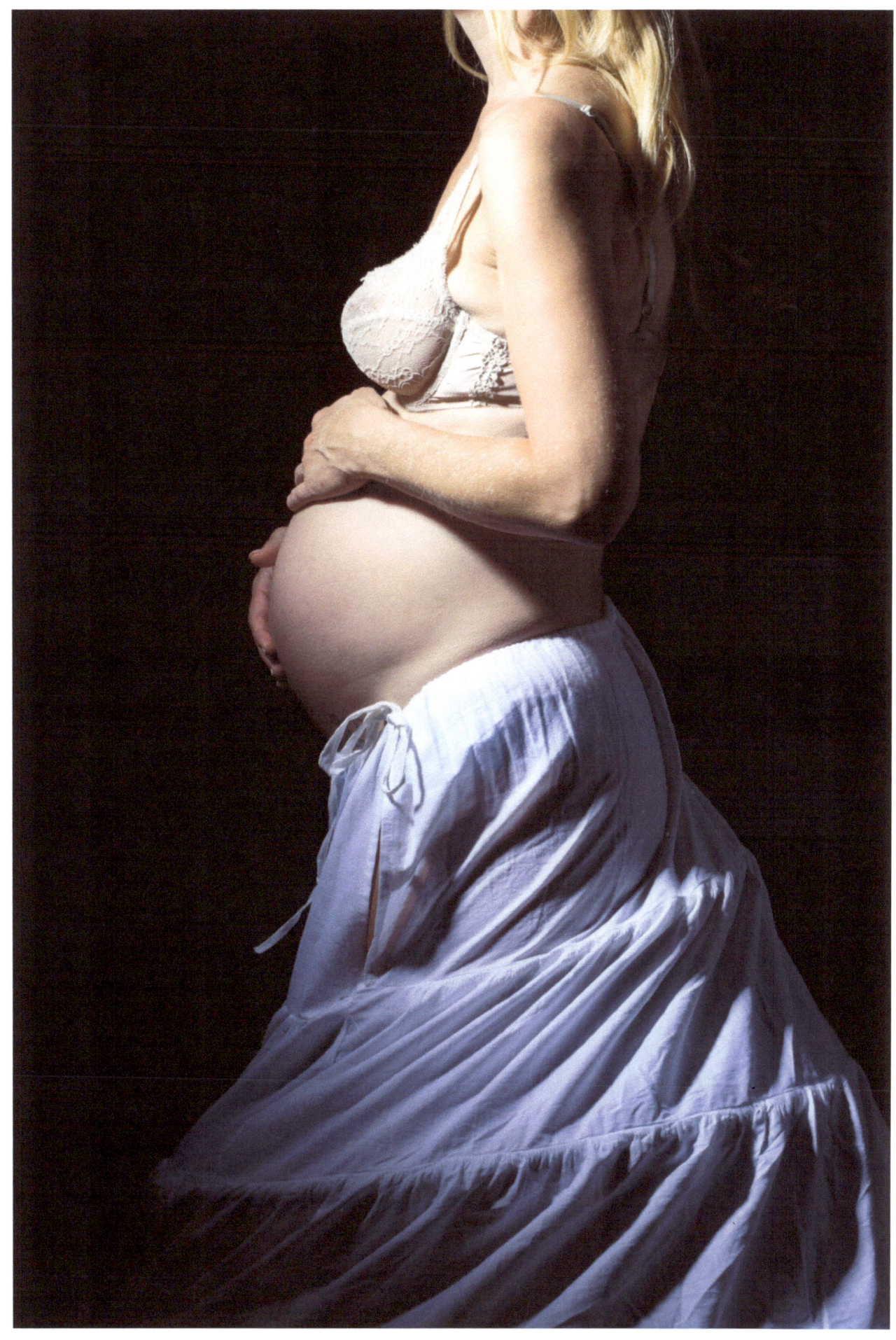

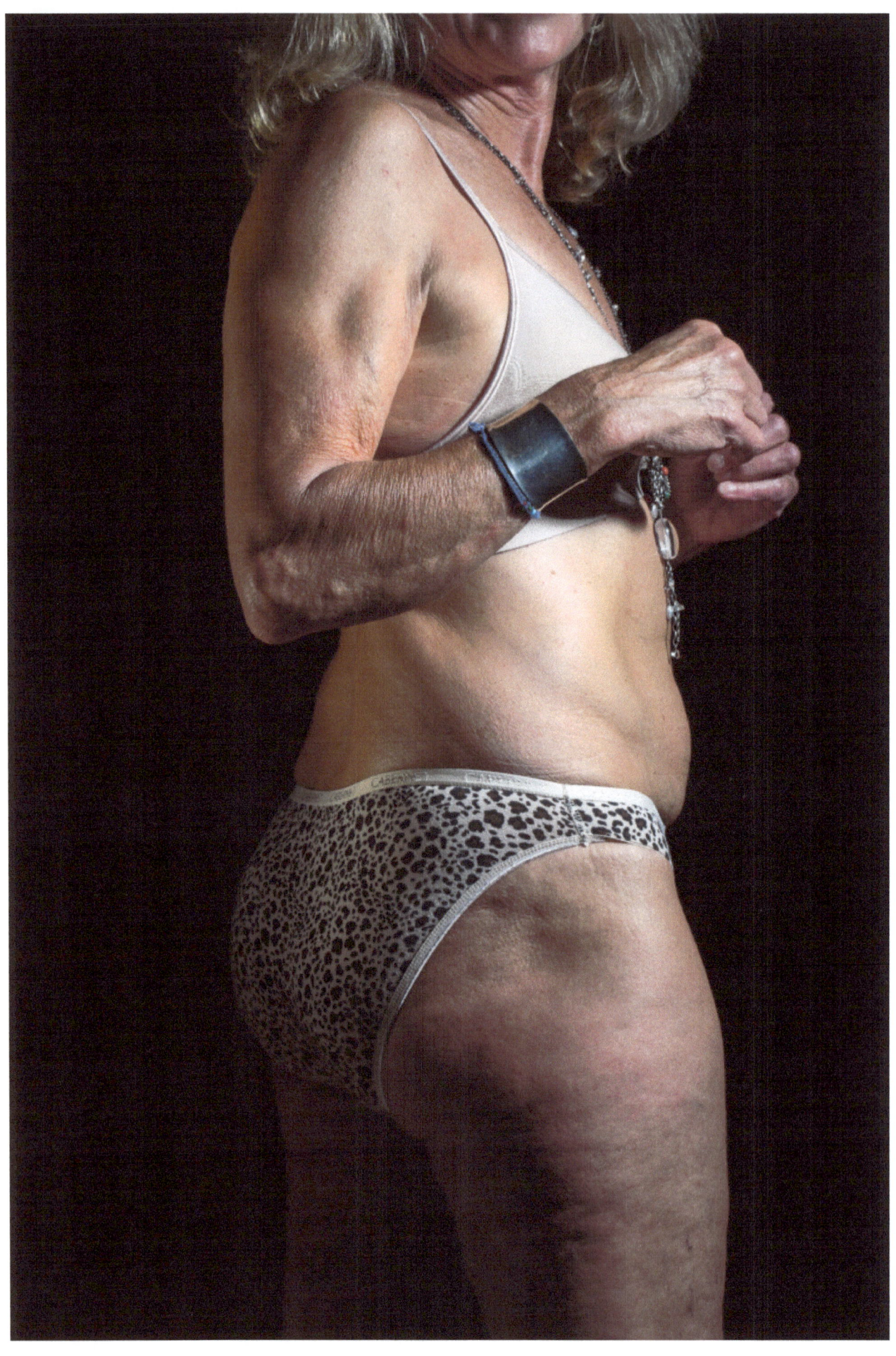

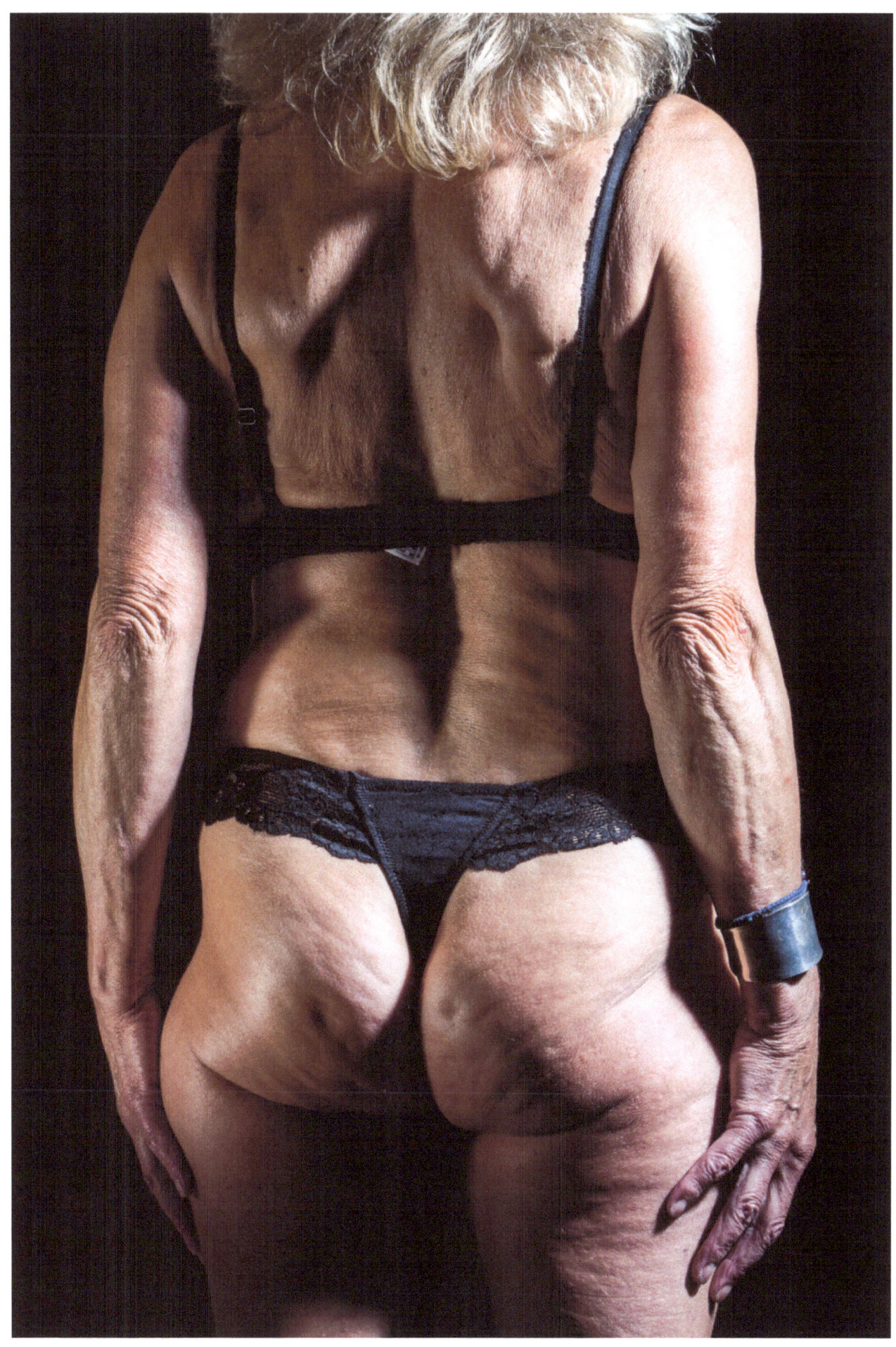

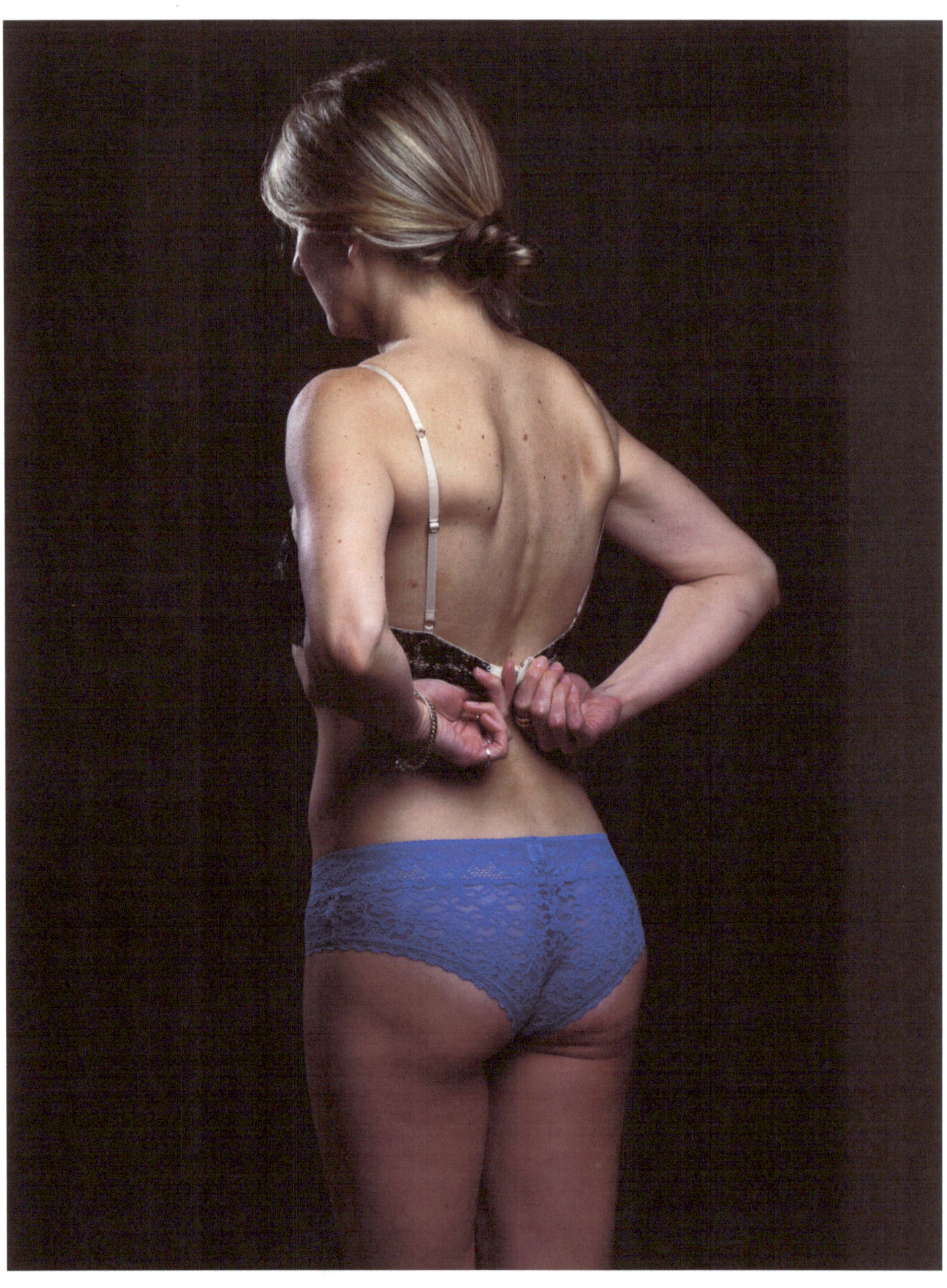

The Out Spouse

"The Out Spouse" is a visual journal of a chapter in my life. In 2013, my husband of 45 years suddenly announced he was divorcing. He said his decision had nothing to do with me but, rather, with him, and he left. Friends, family, and therapists suggested that I journal my thoughts and feeling, no matter how painful. The photographs in this project are the results of this practice.

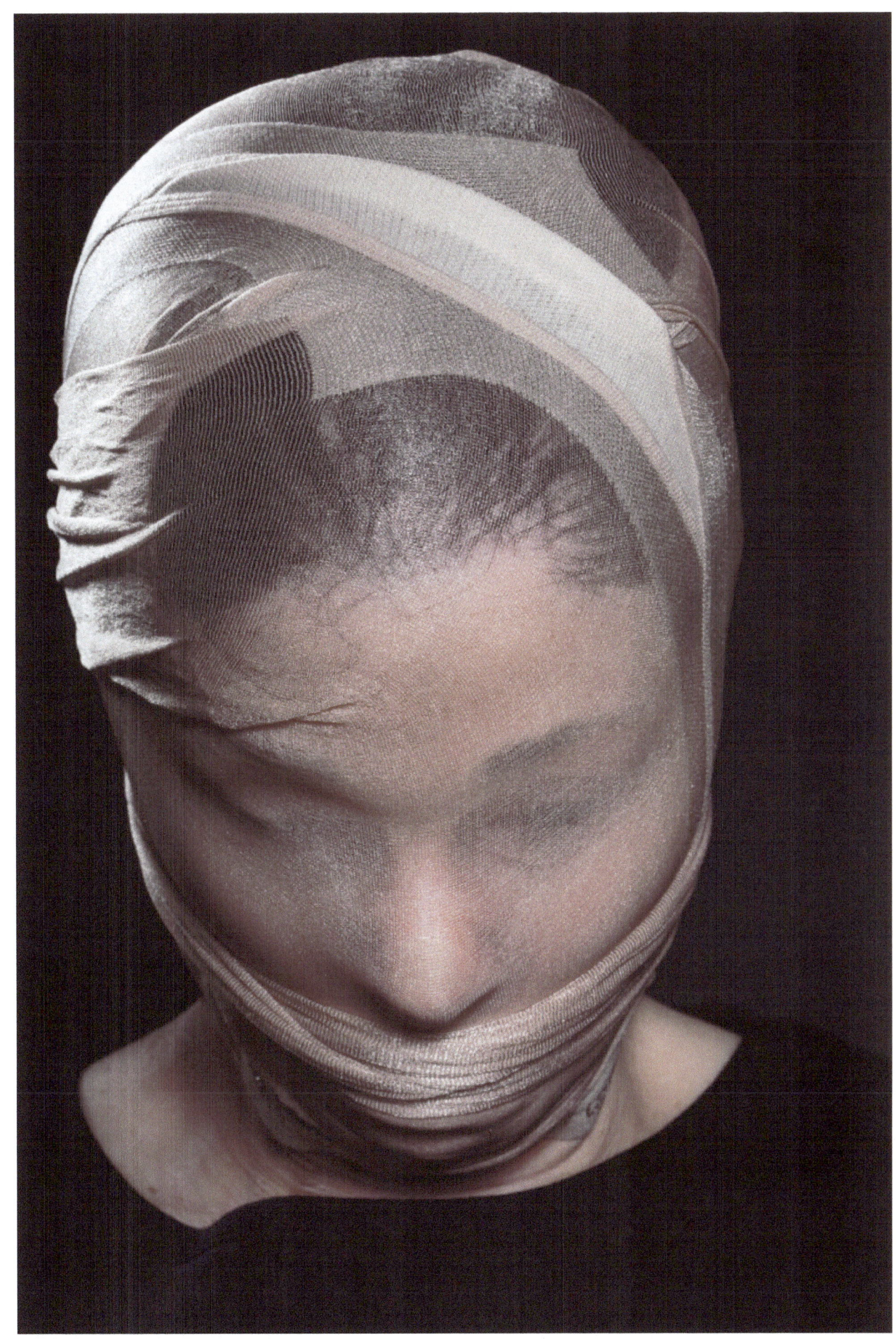

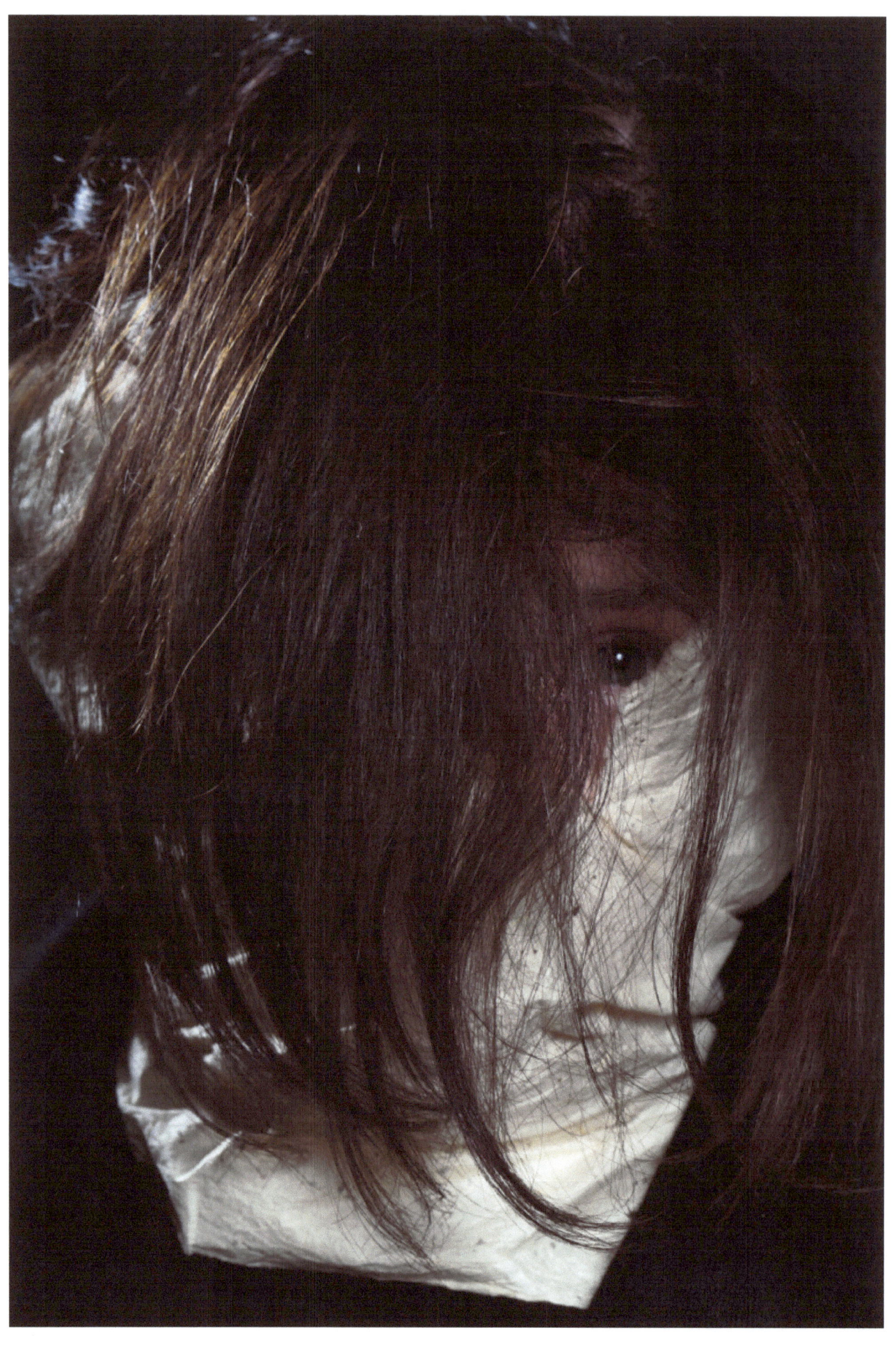

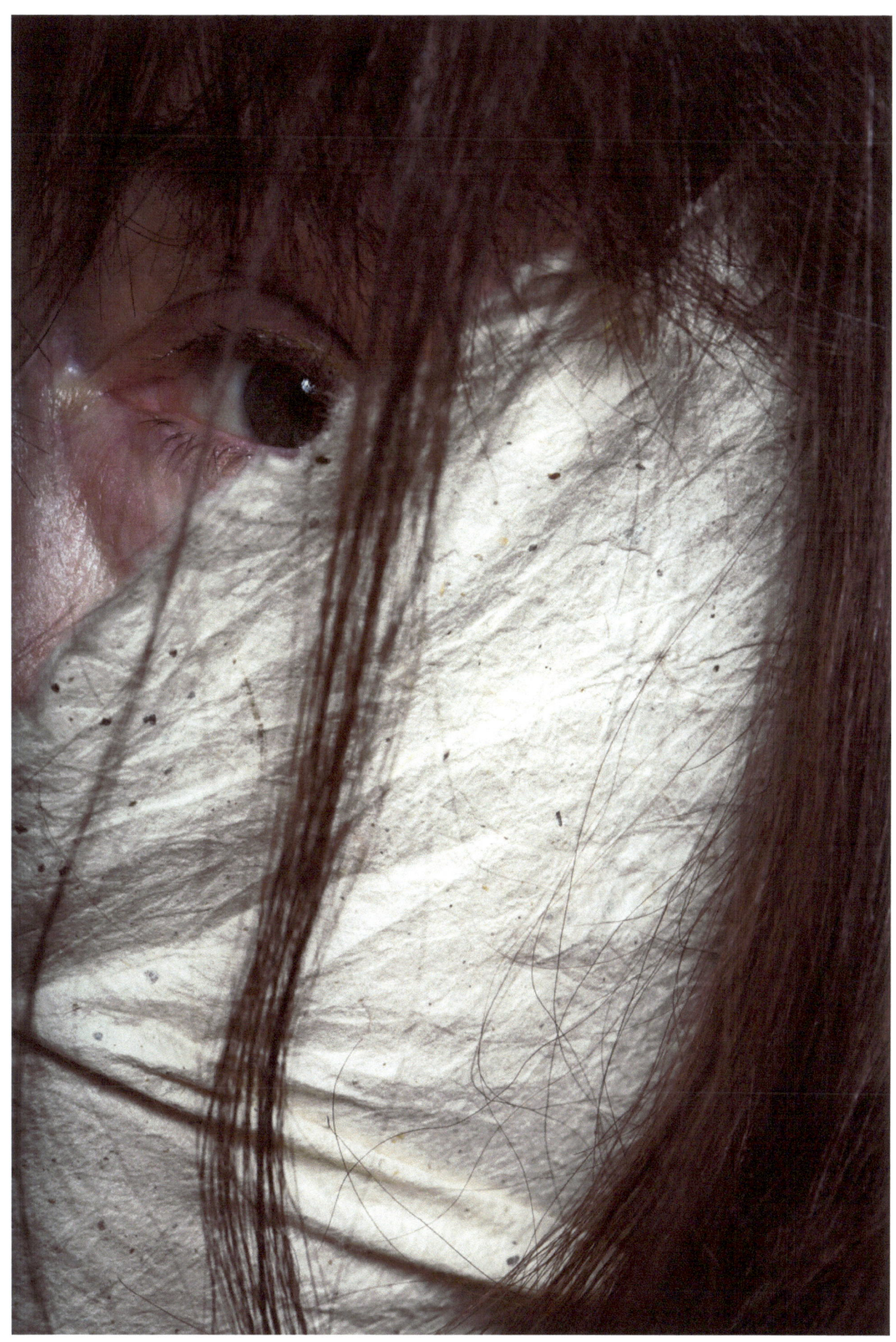

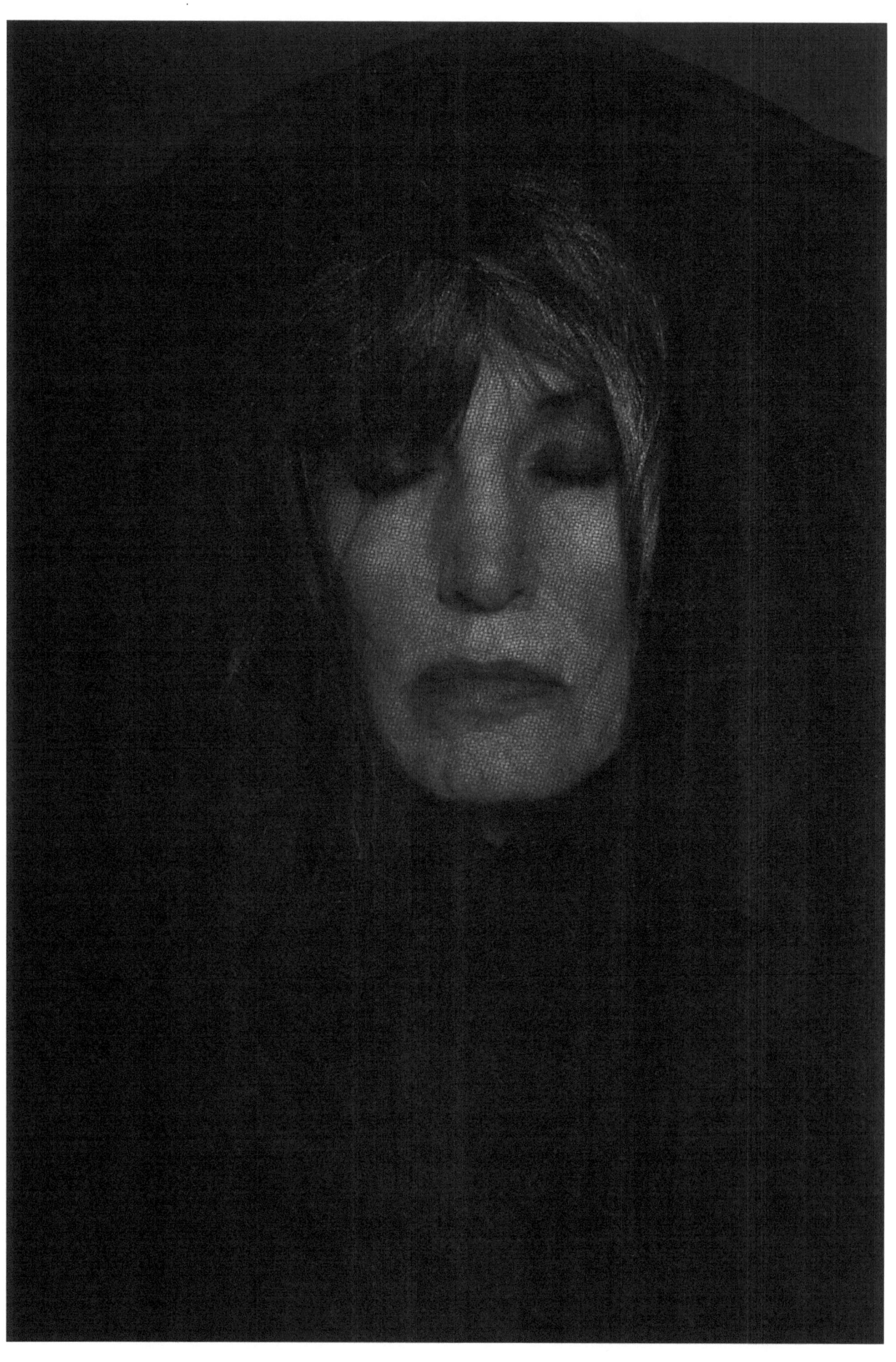

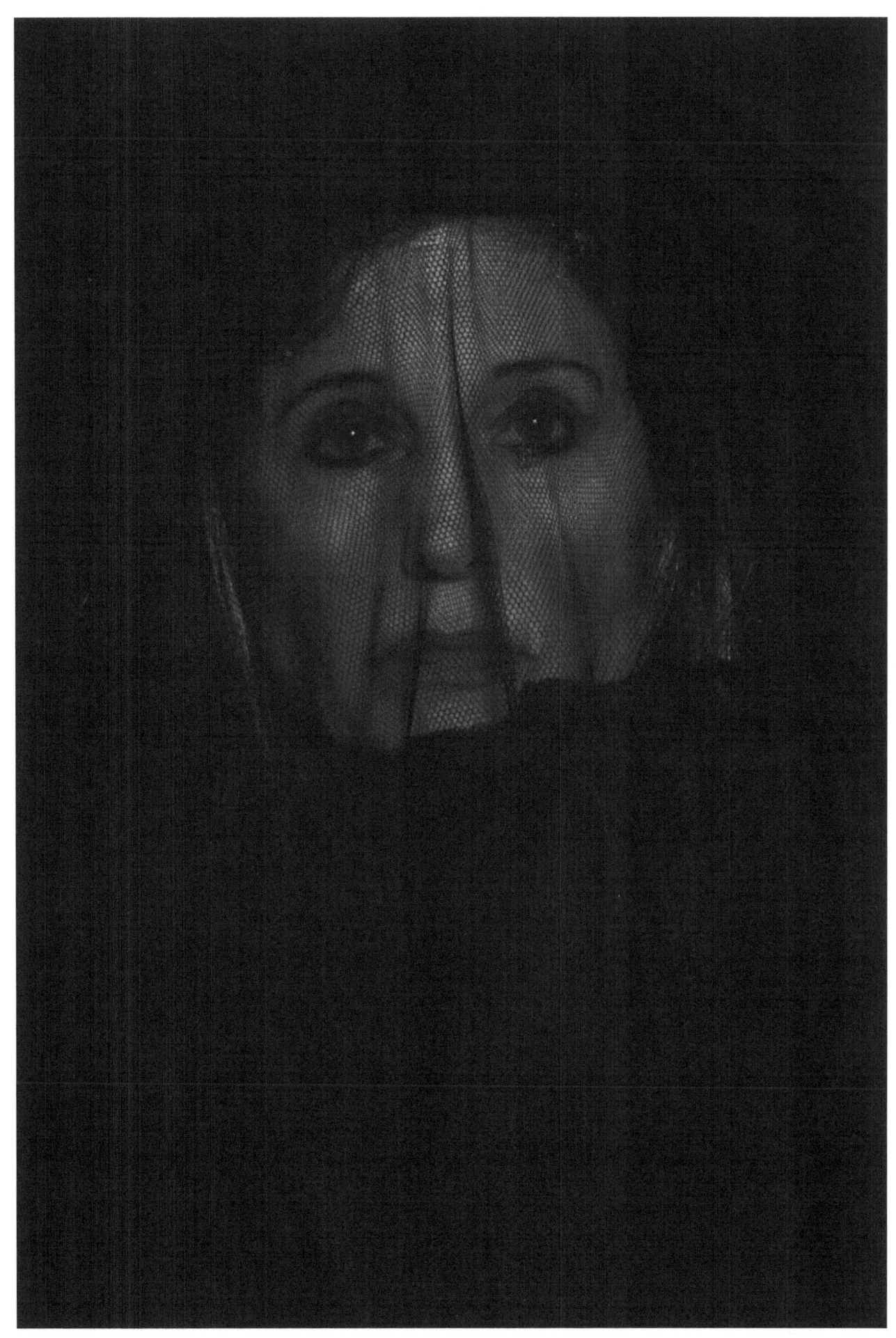

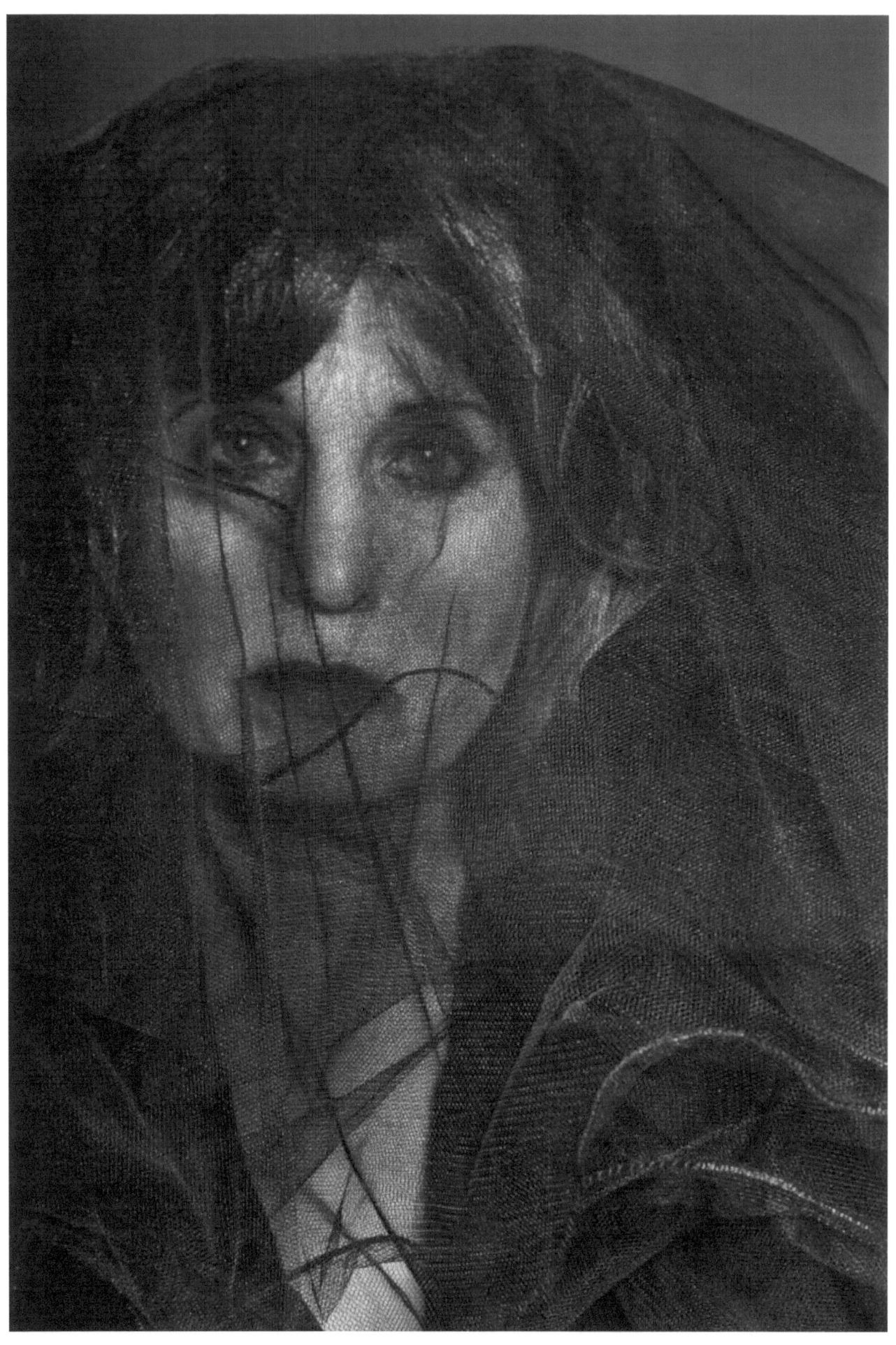

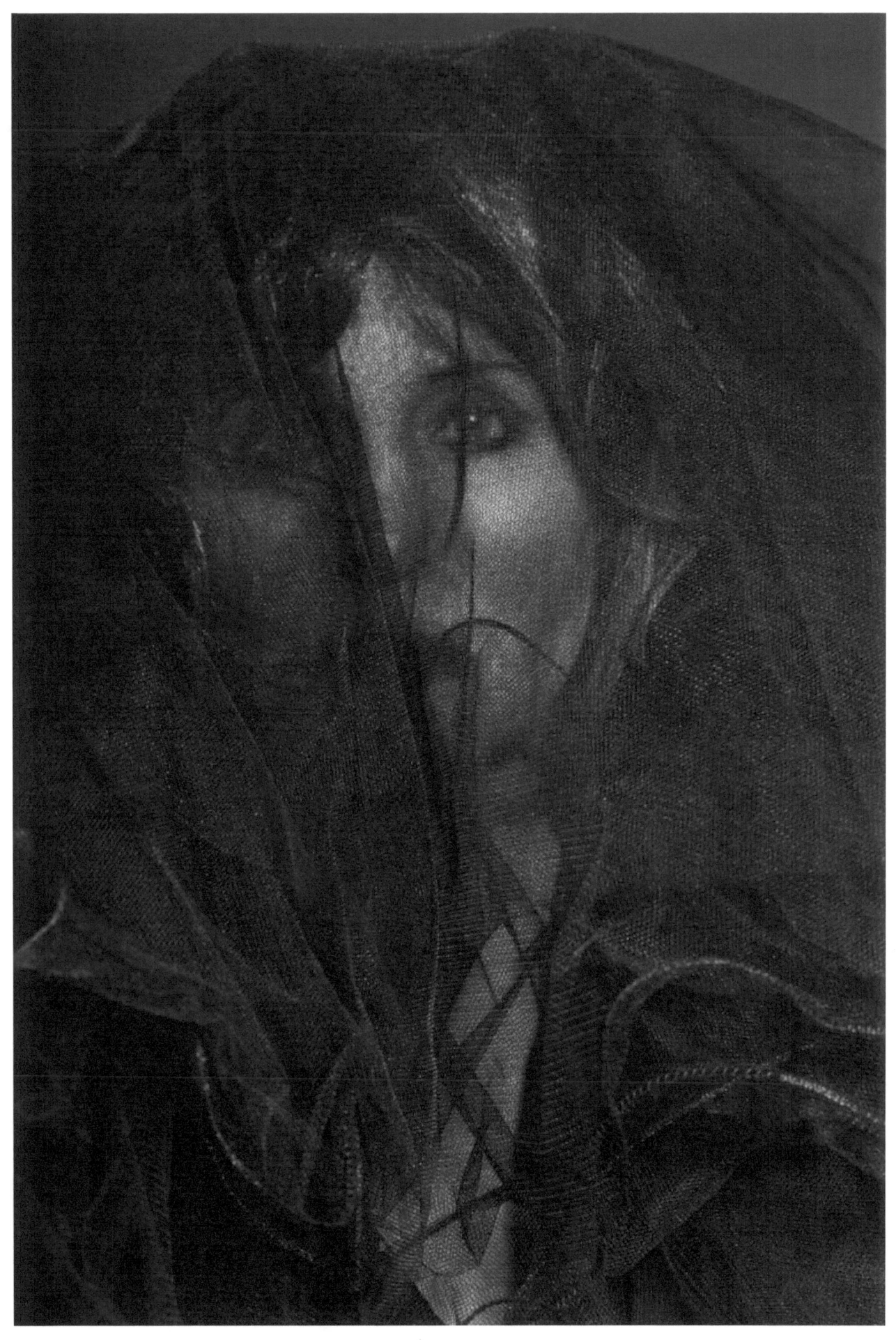

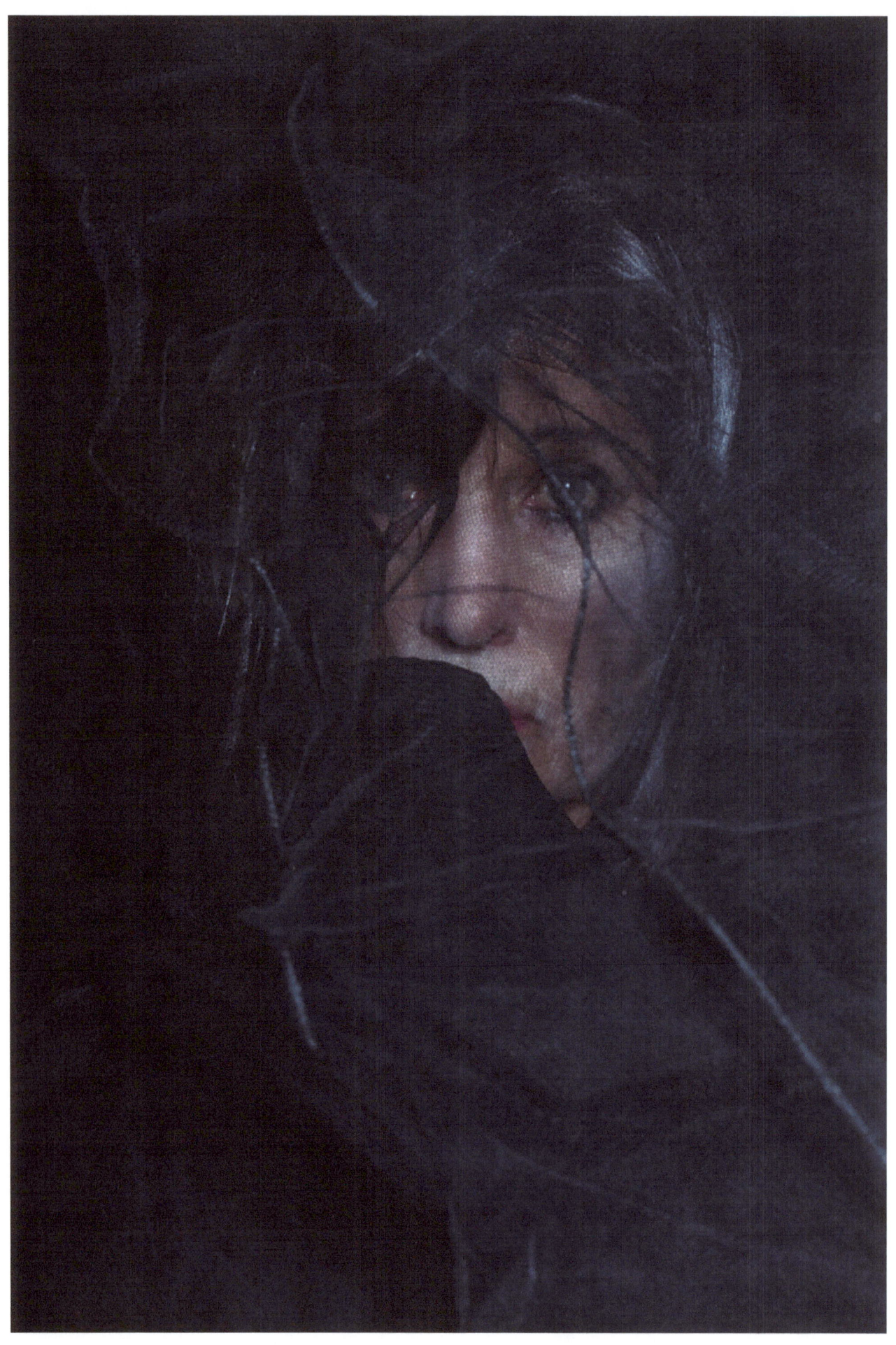

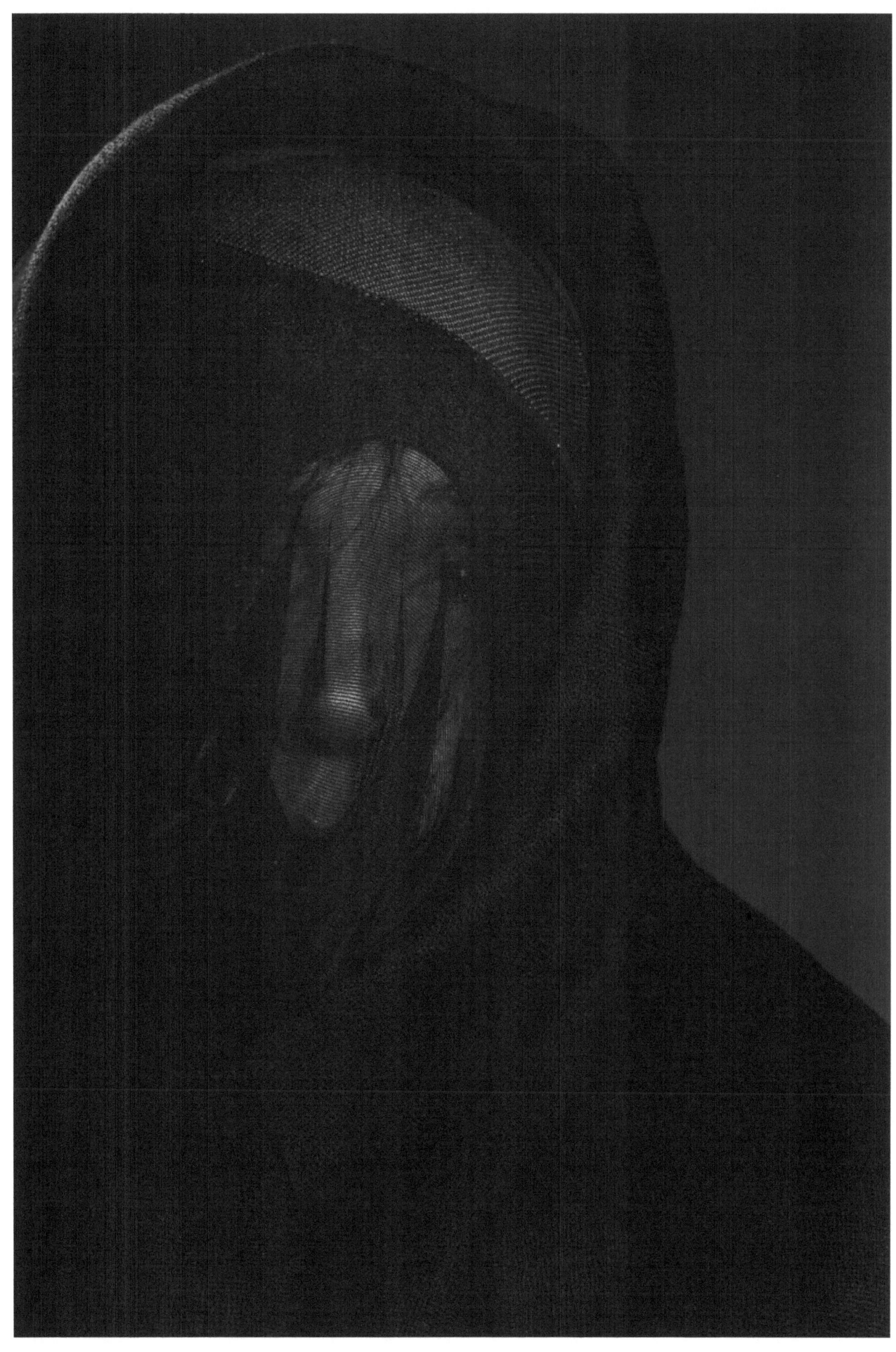

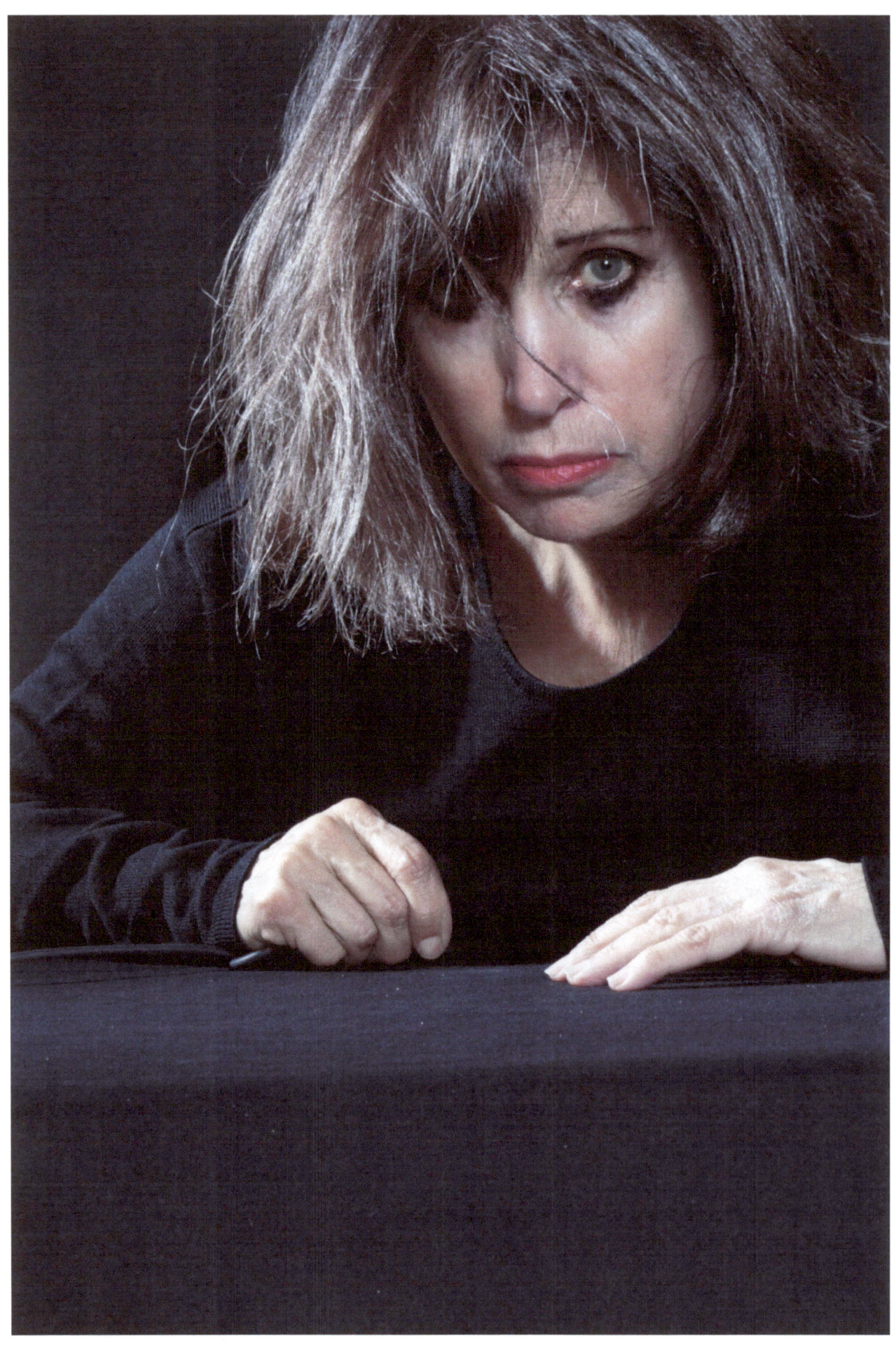

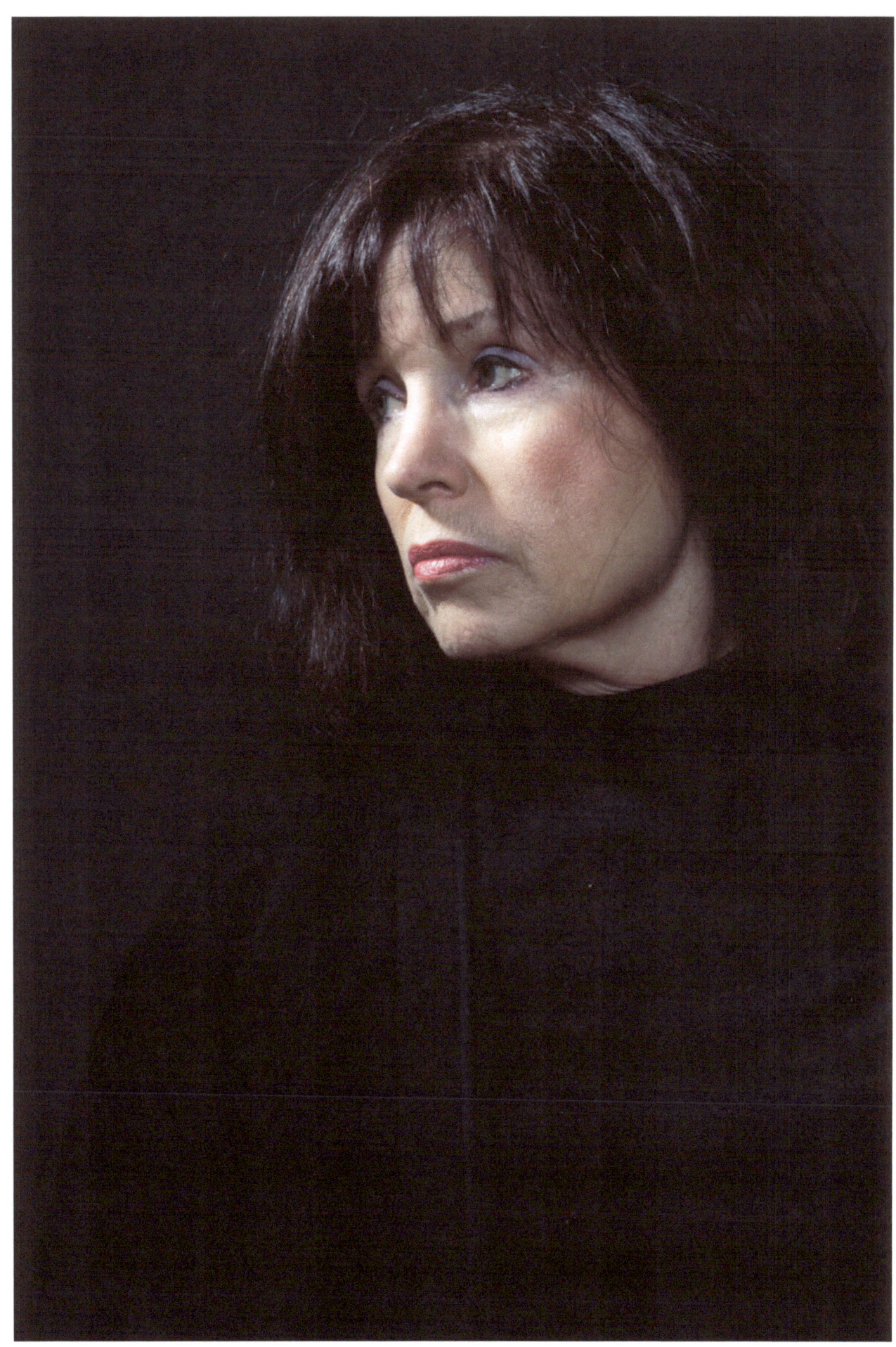

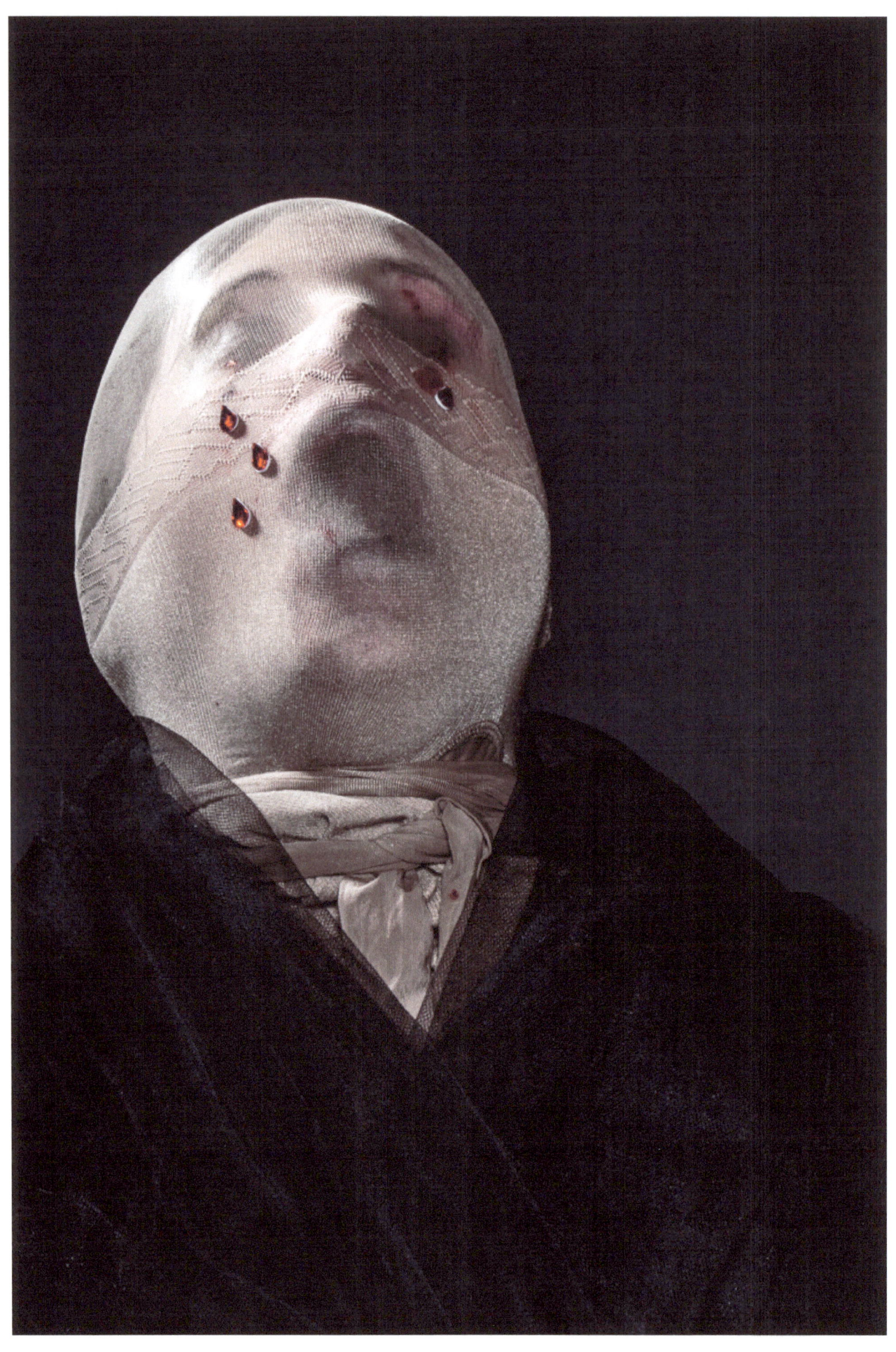

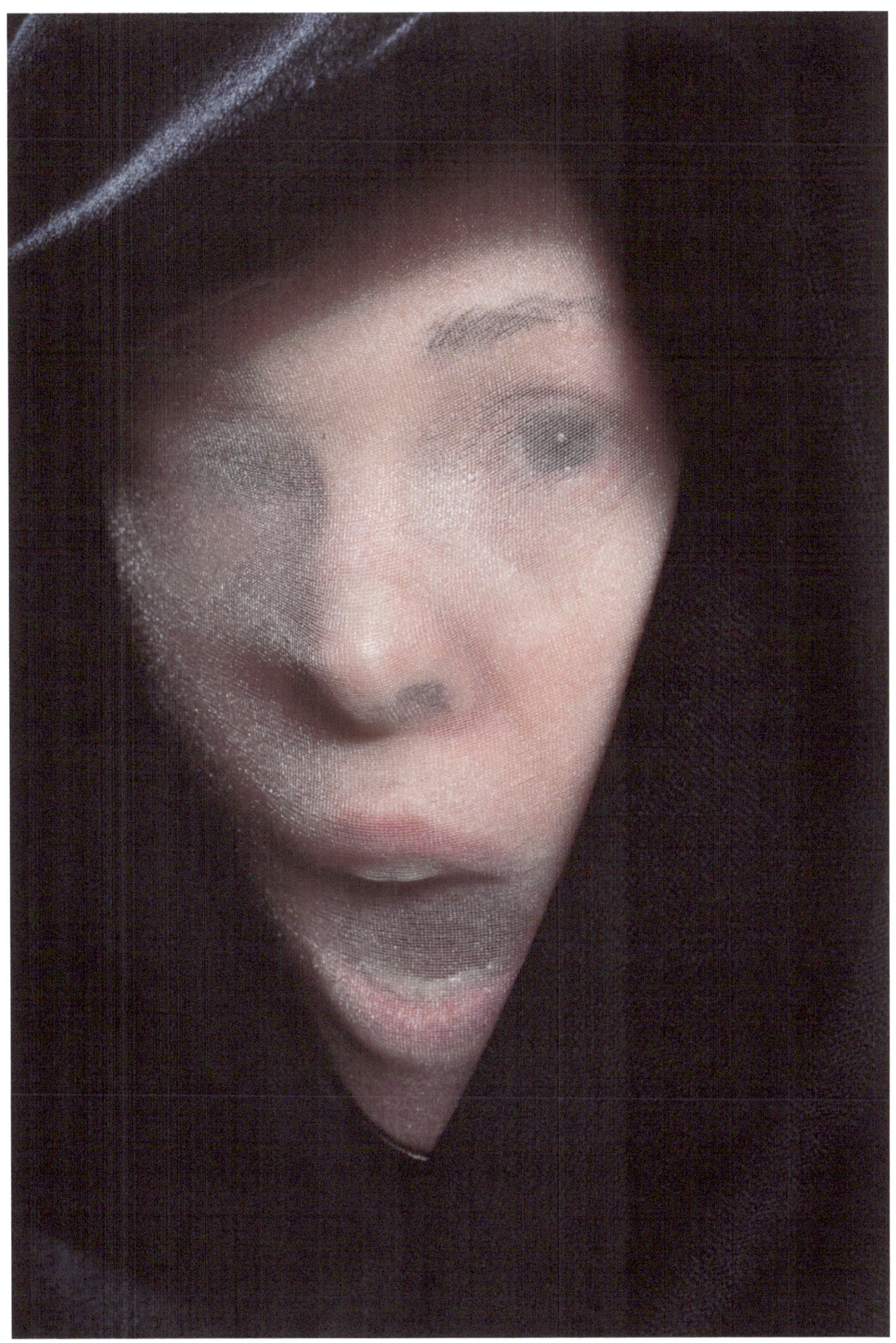

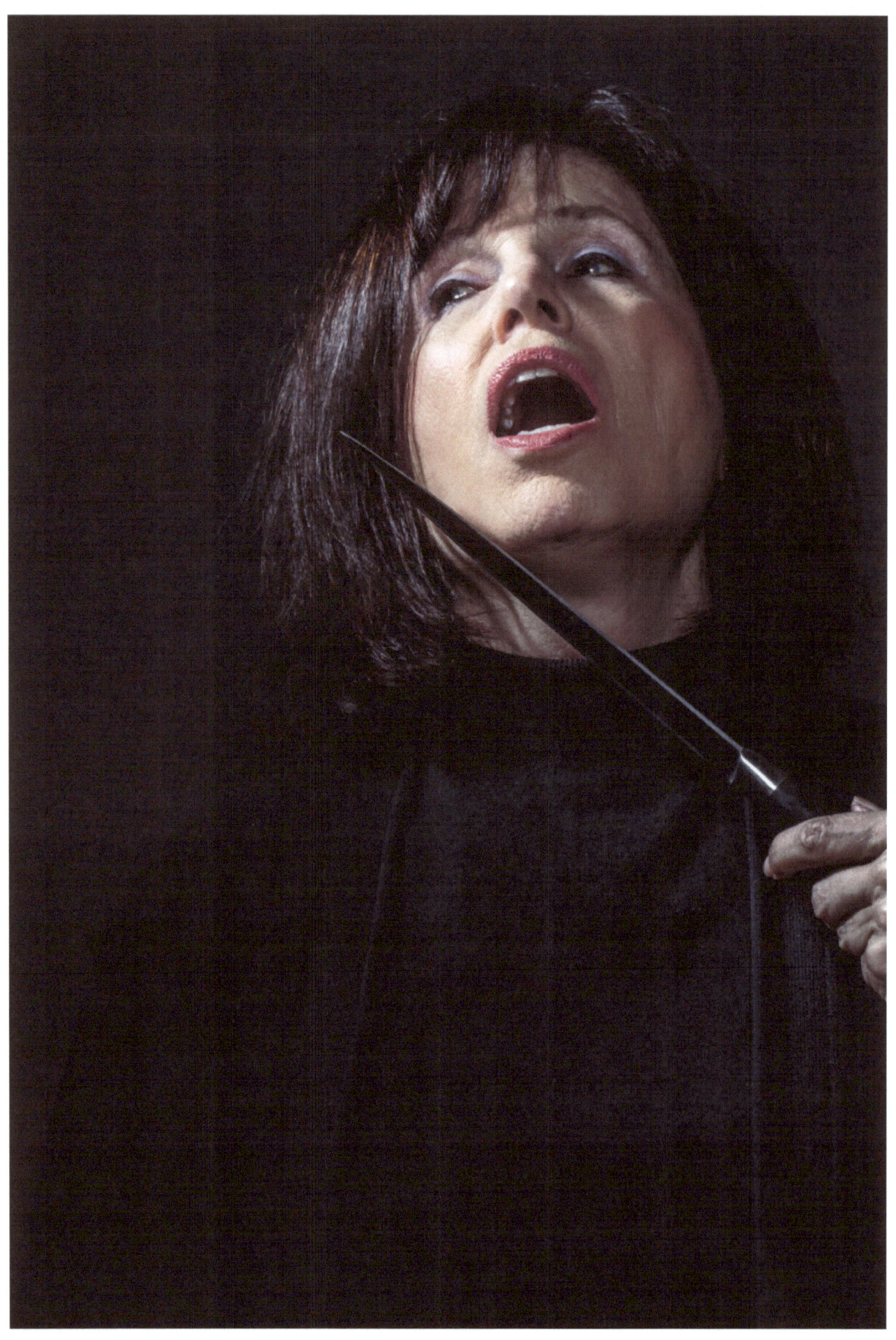

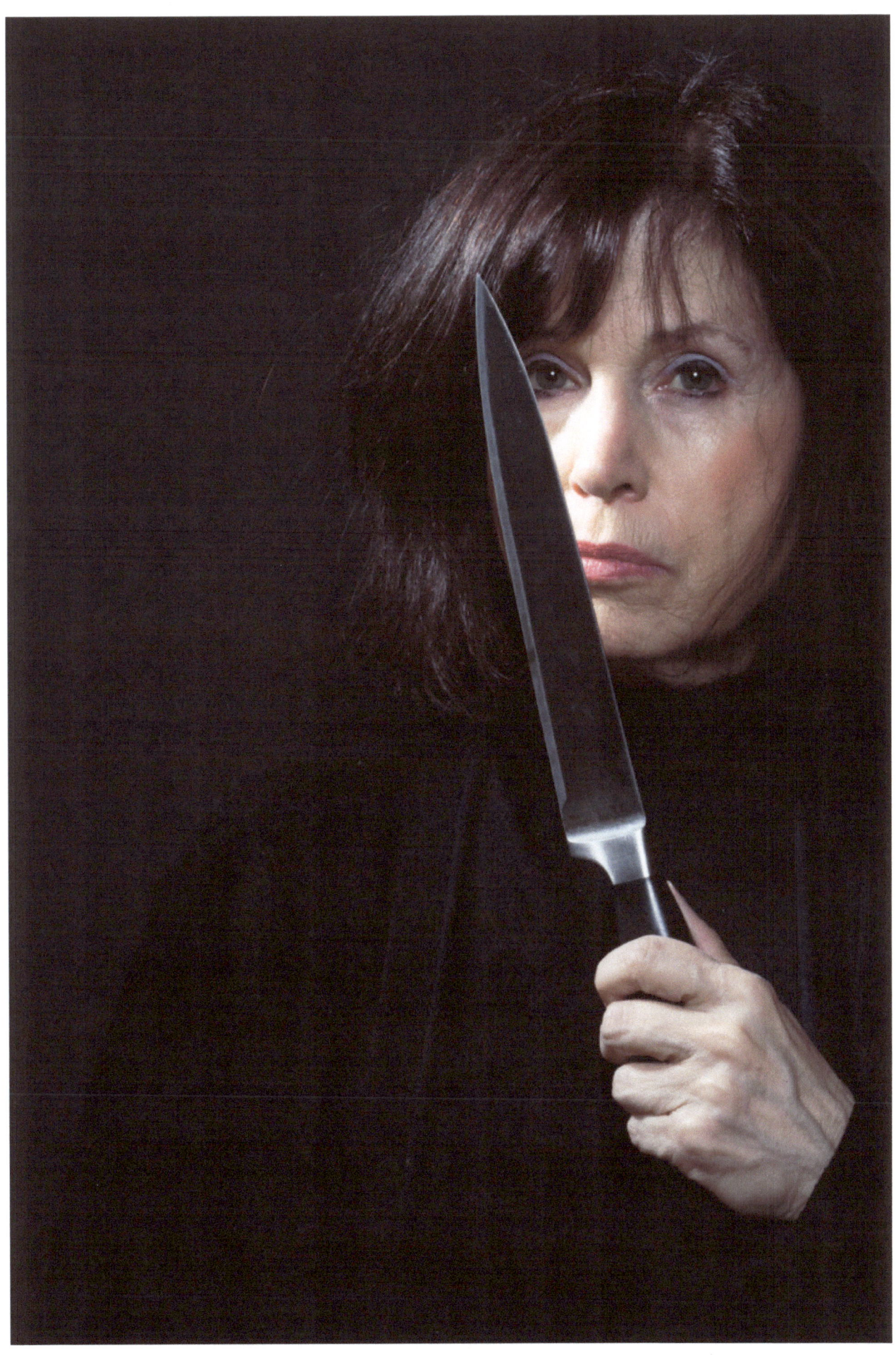

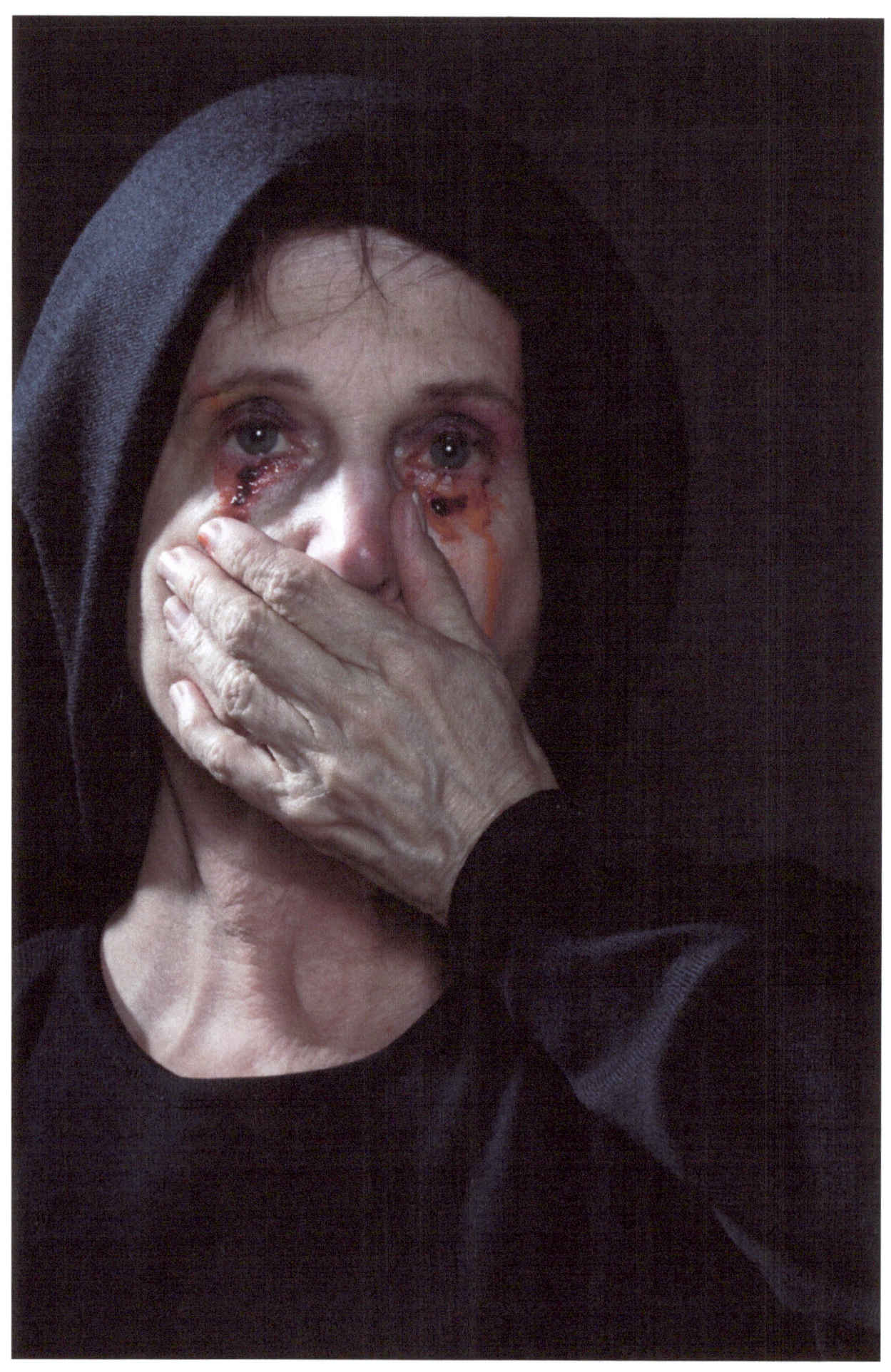

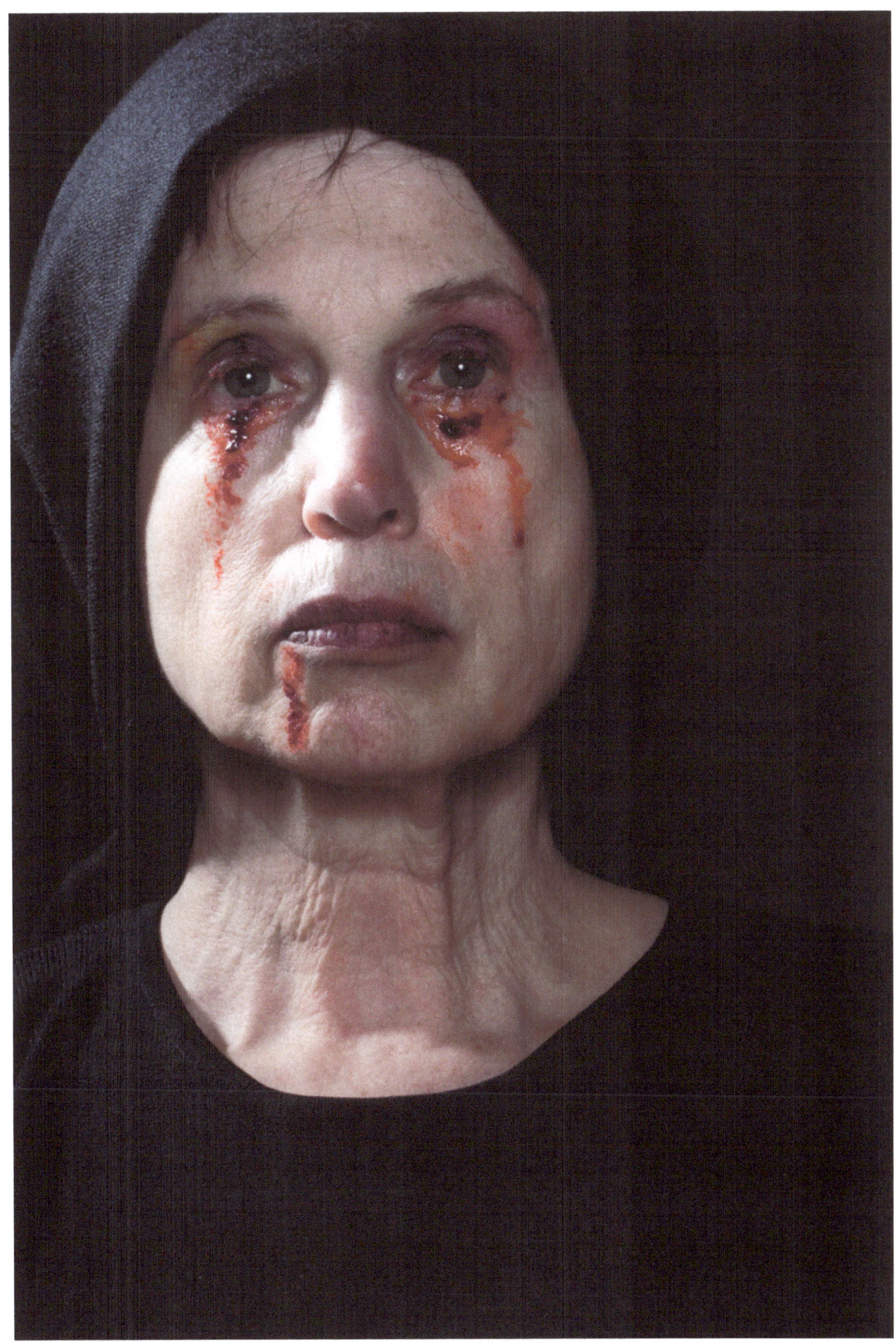

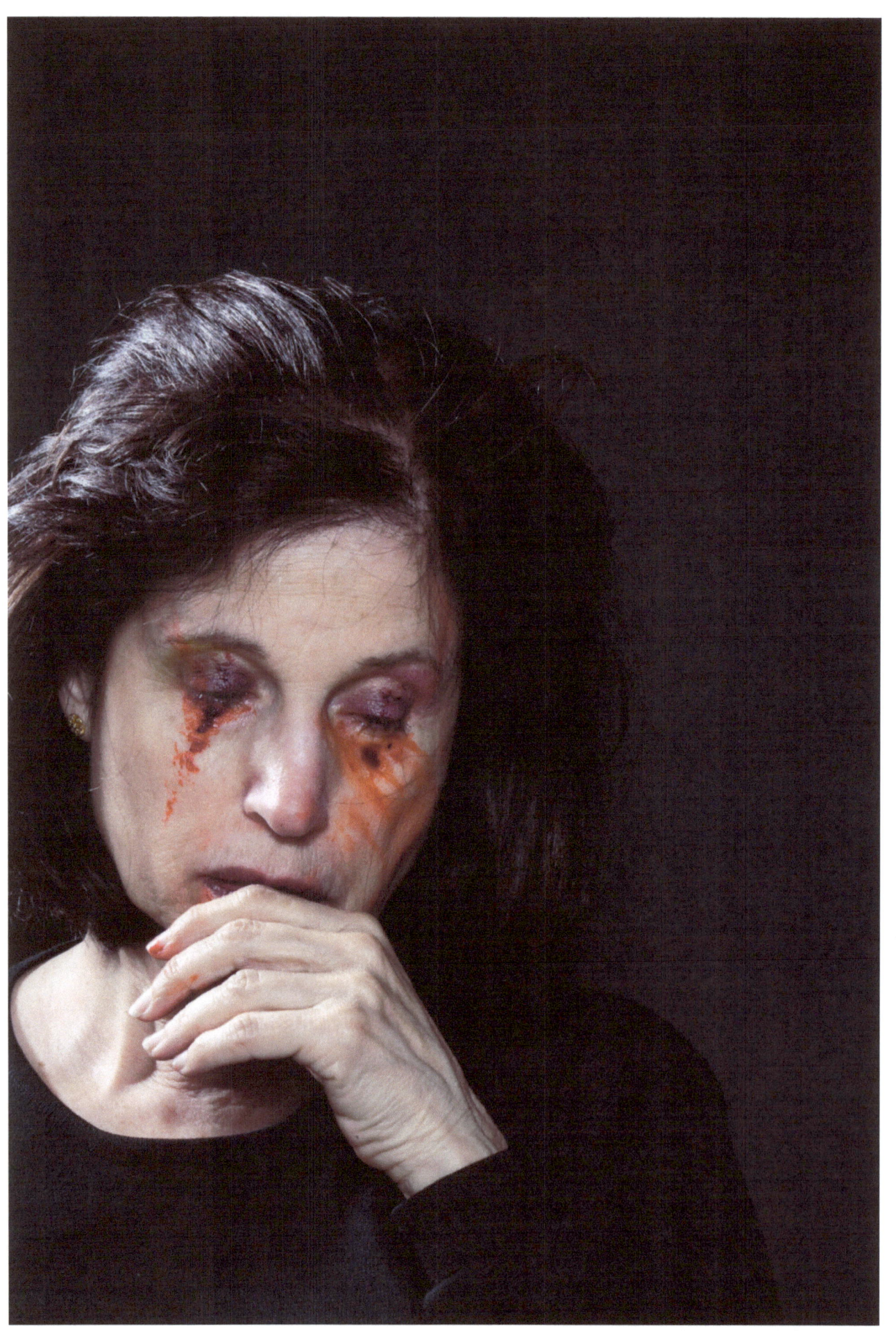

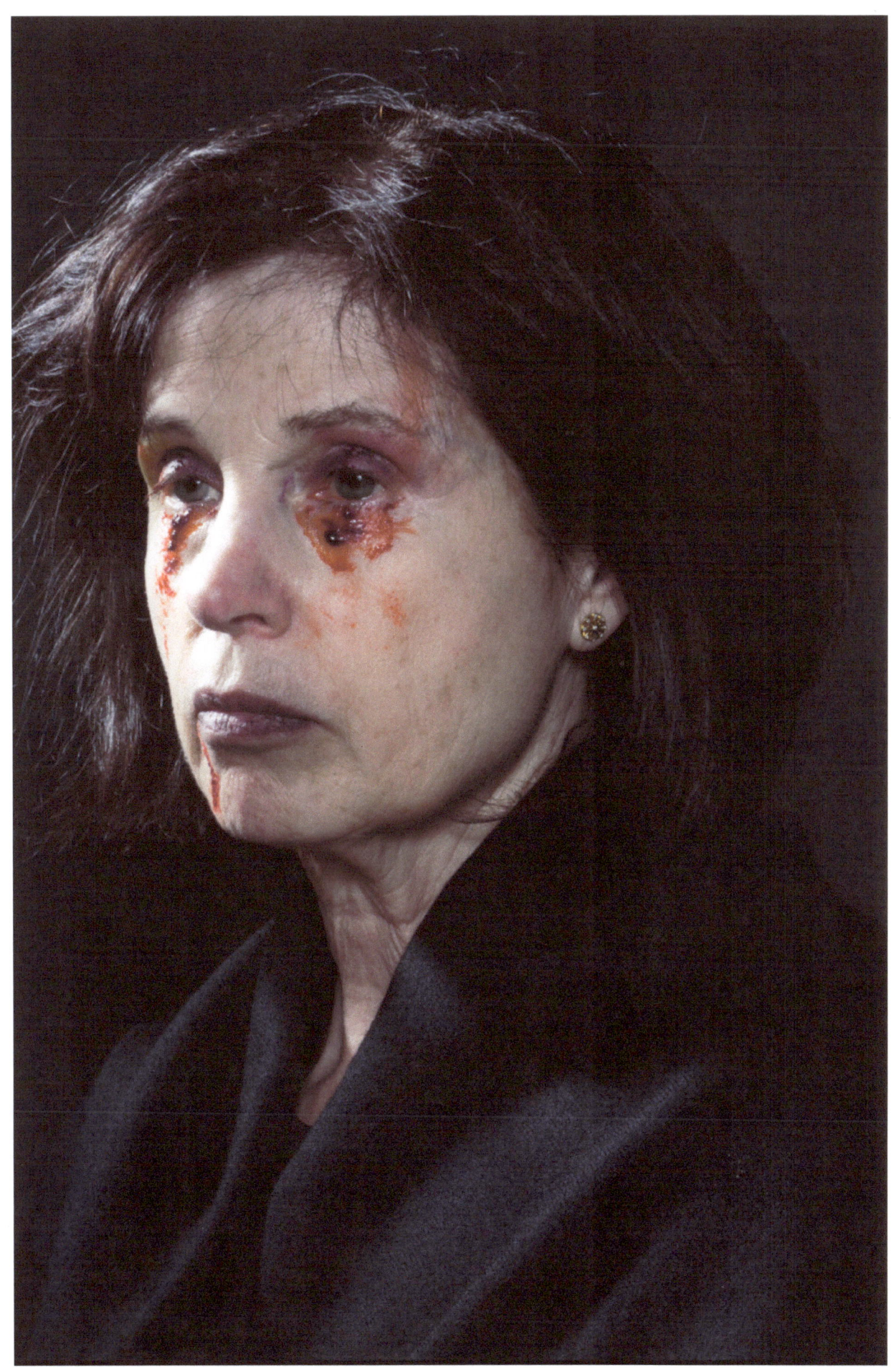

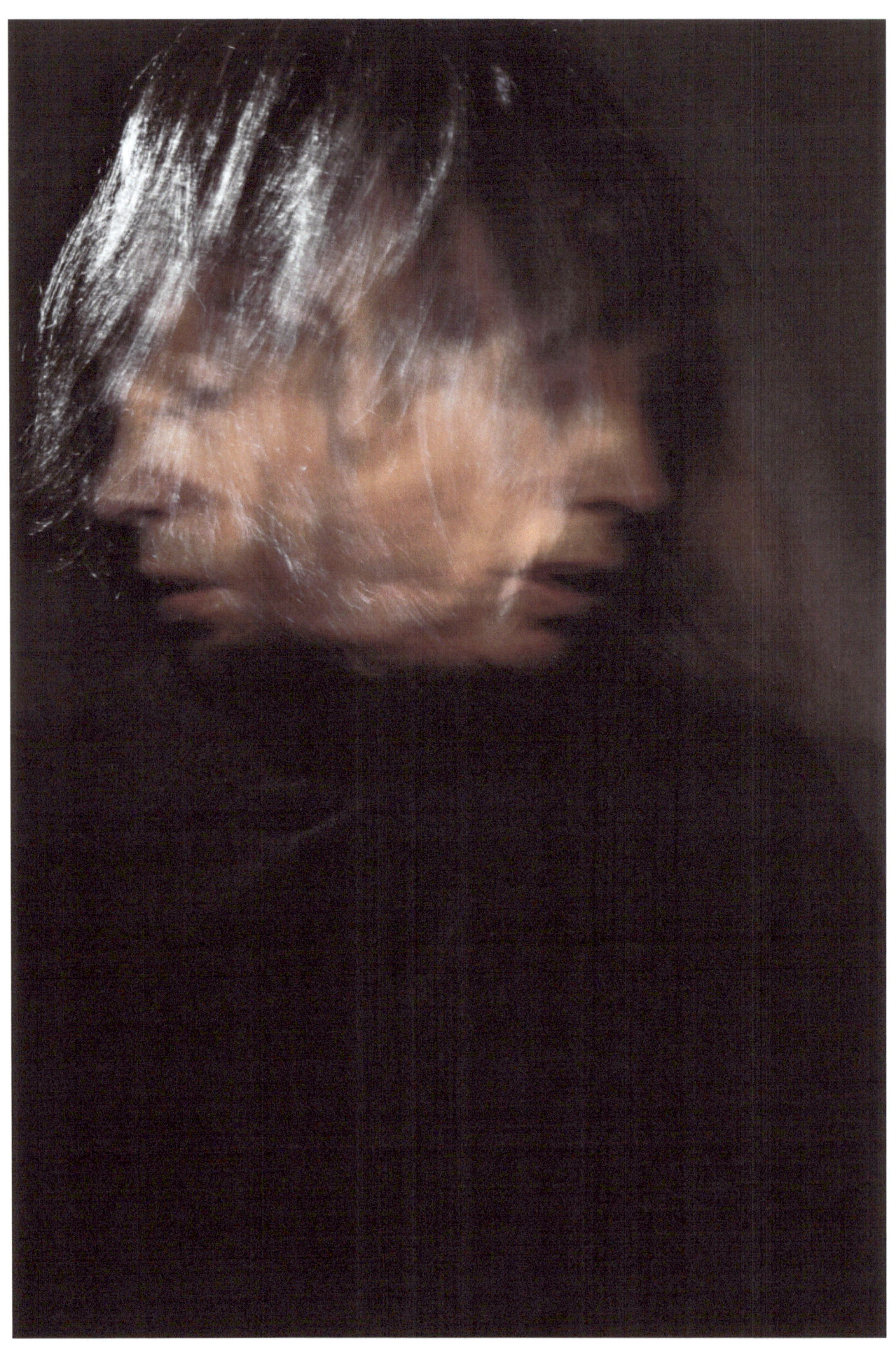

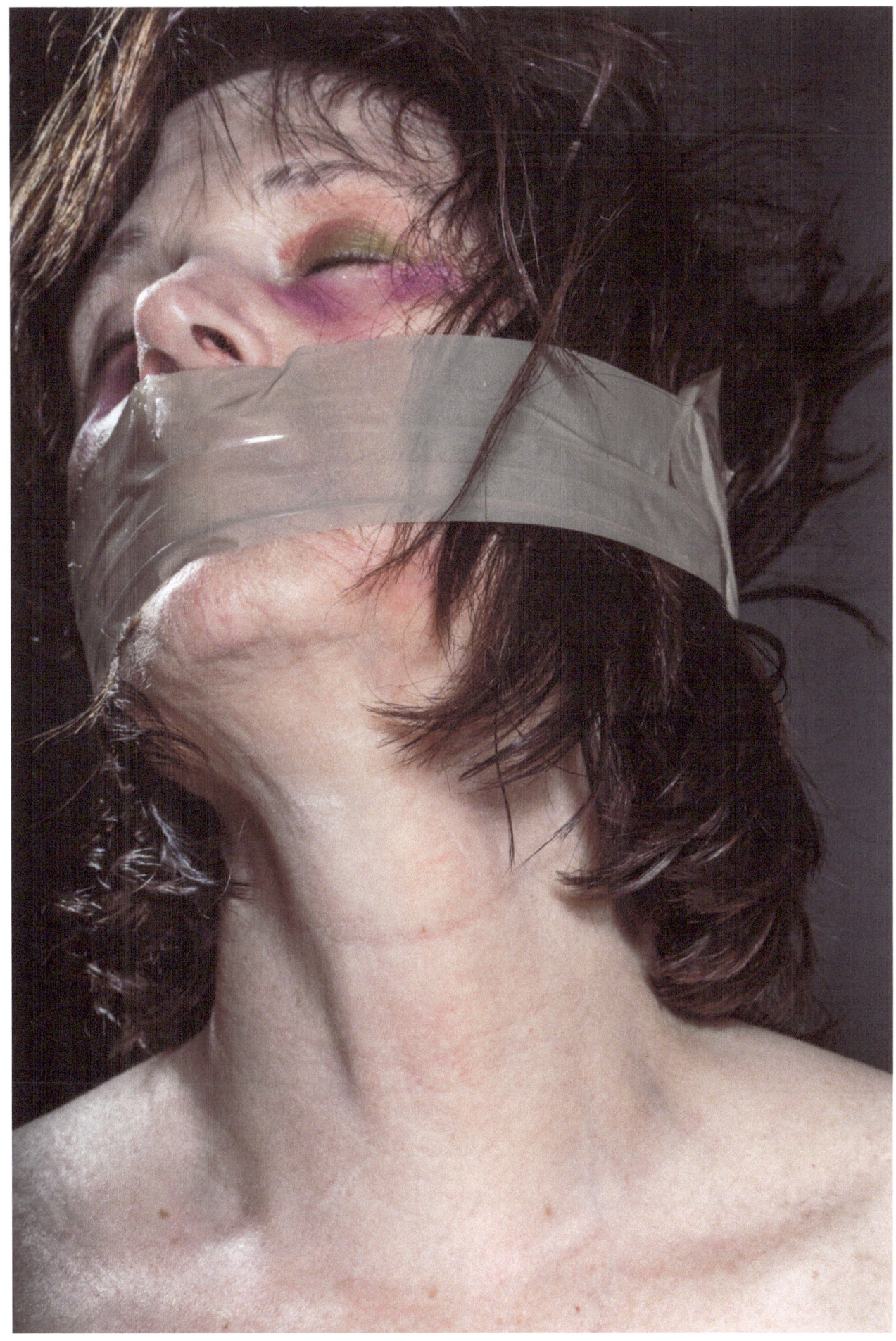

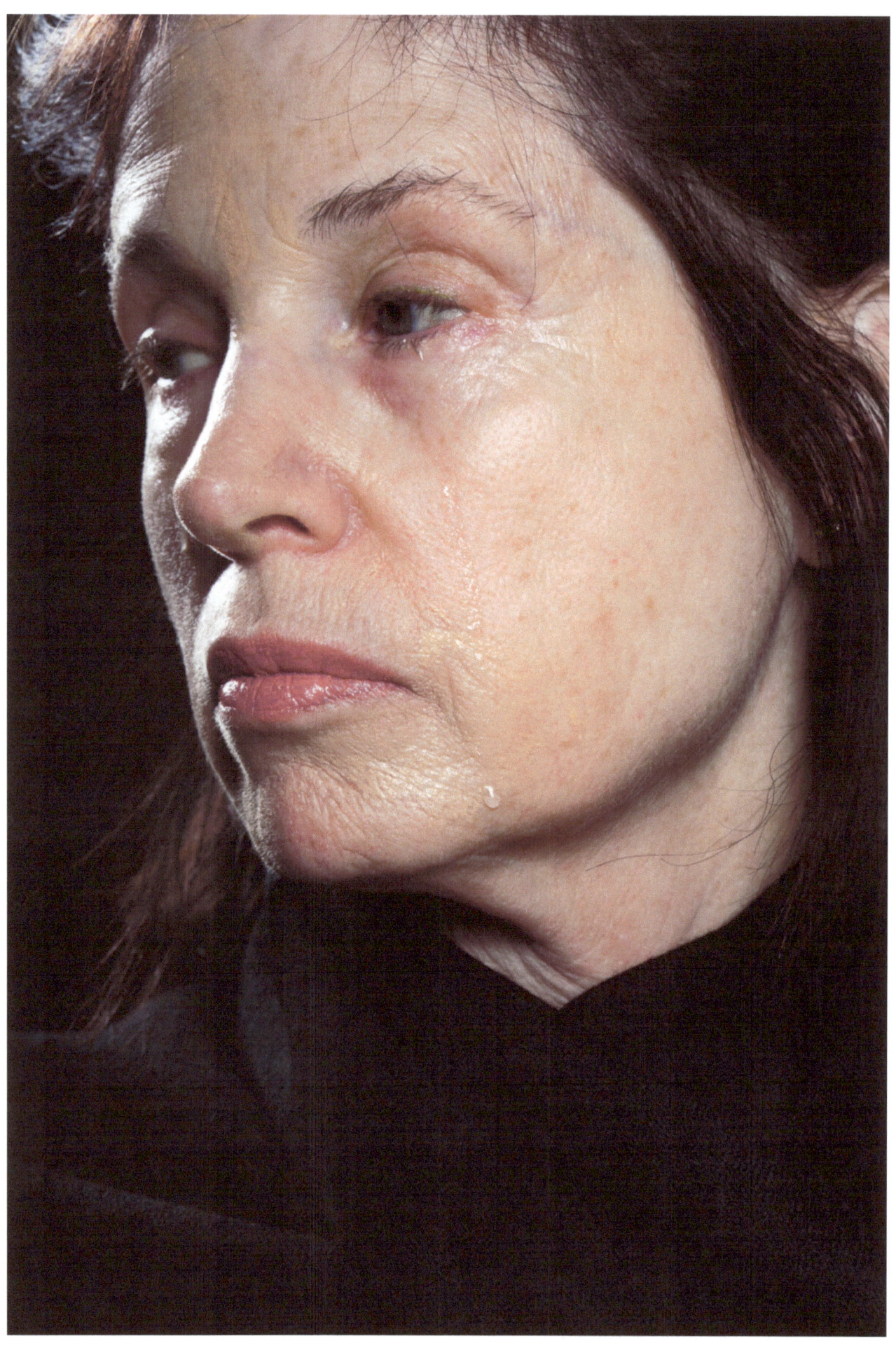

Off the Walls

"Off The Walls" reflects my fascination with the paleolithic iconography found on cliffs in Arizona, where I reside and work for much of the year. The natural beauty of the landscape and the glimpses of historic American Indian cultures has had a profound effect on me and led me to immerse myself in the joy of exploring ancient pictographs and petroglyphs, and interpreting their possible mystical meanings.

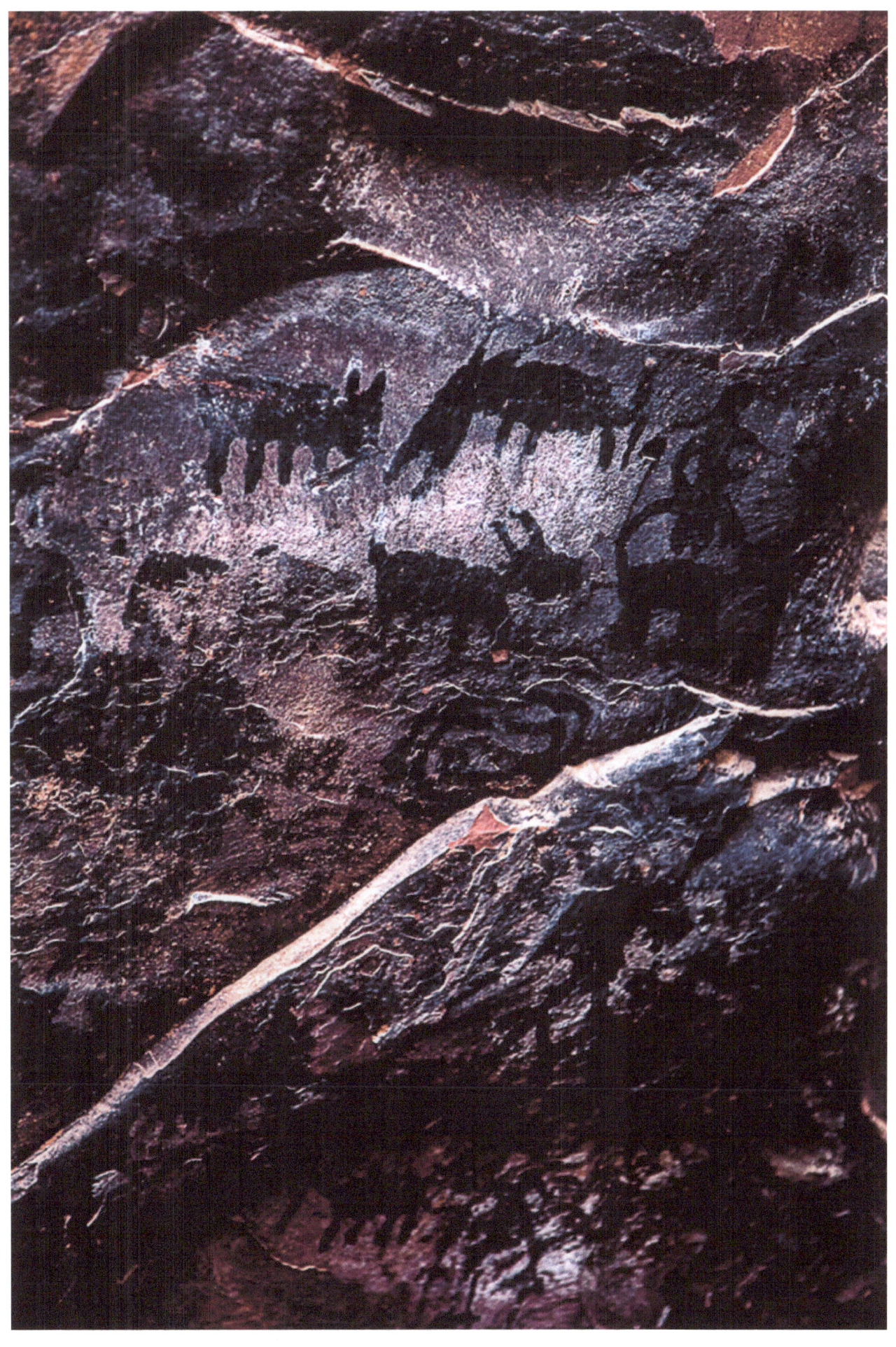

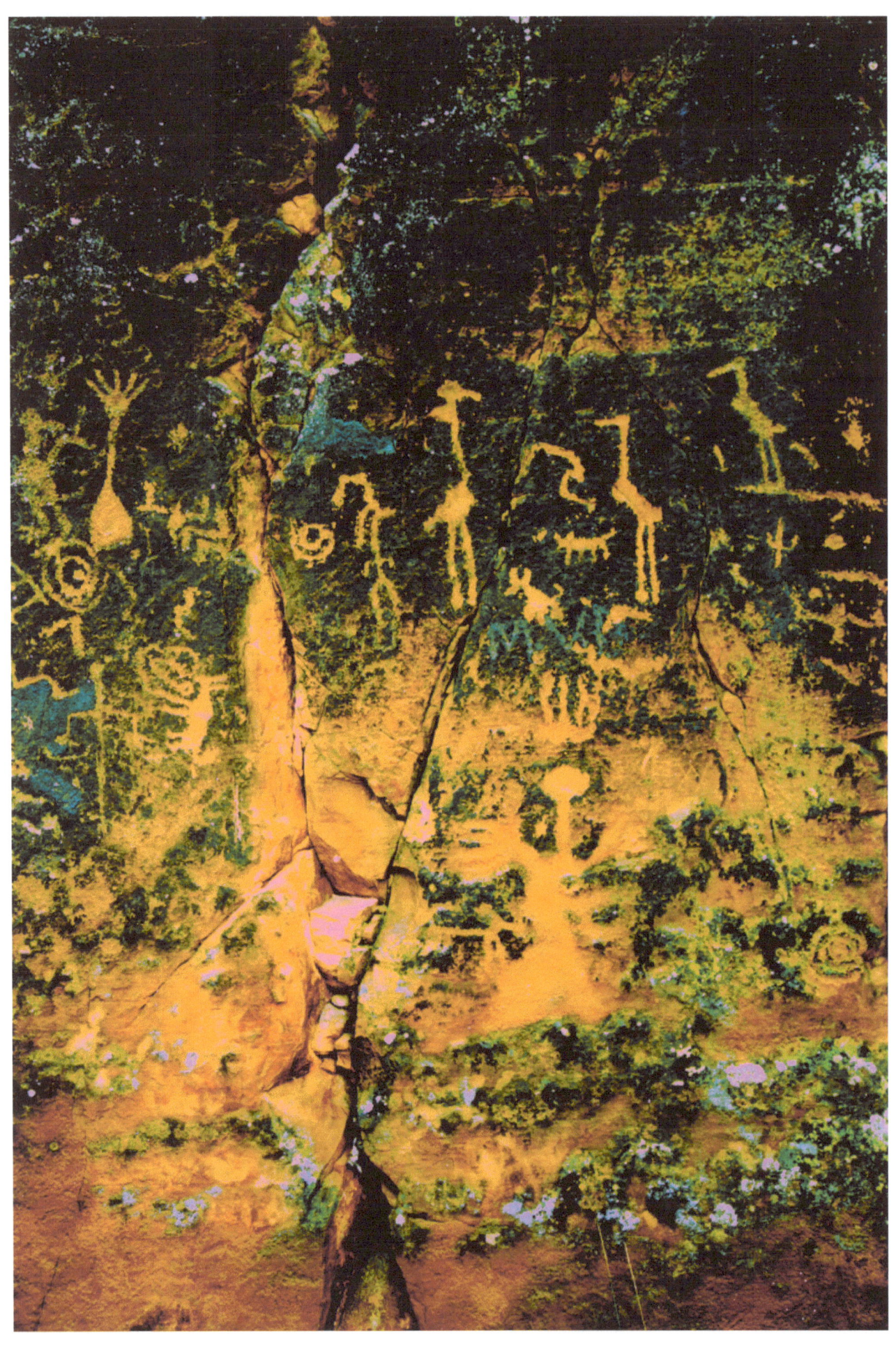

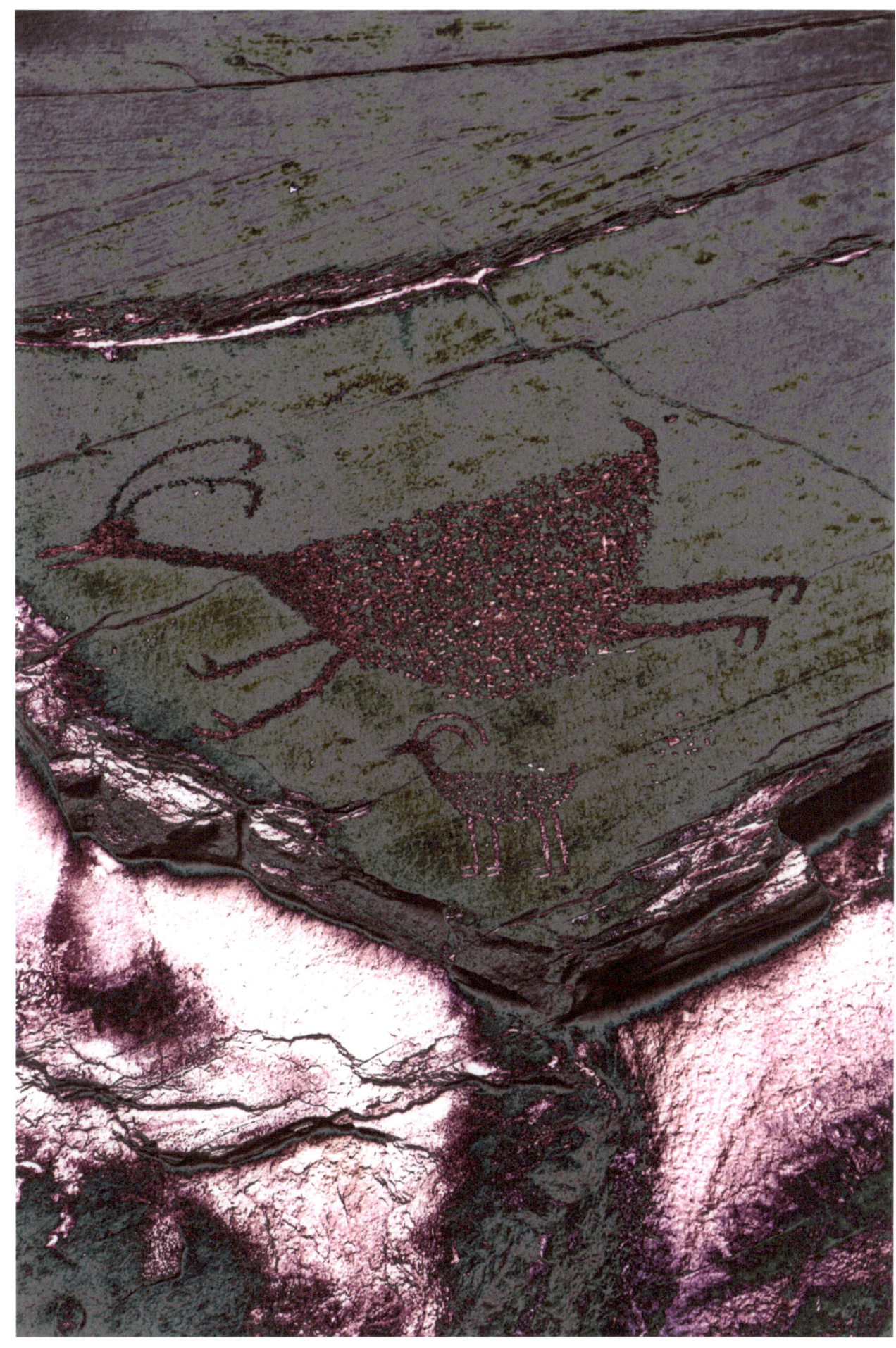

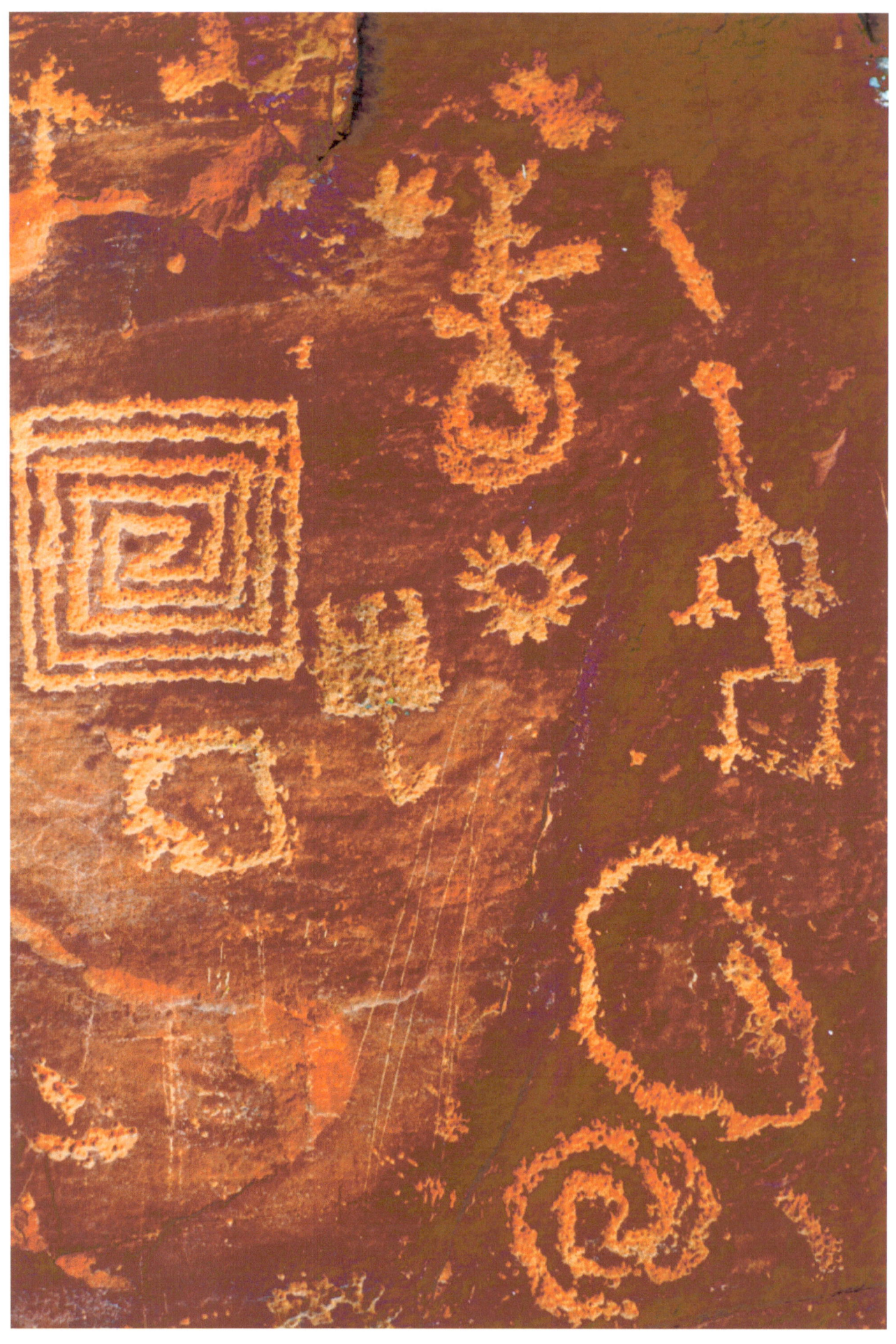

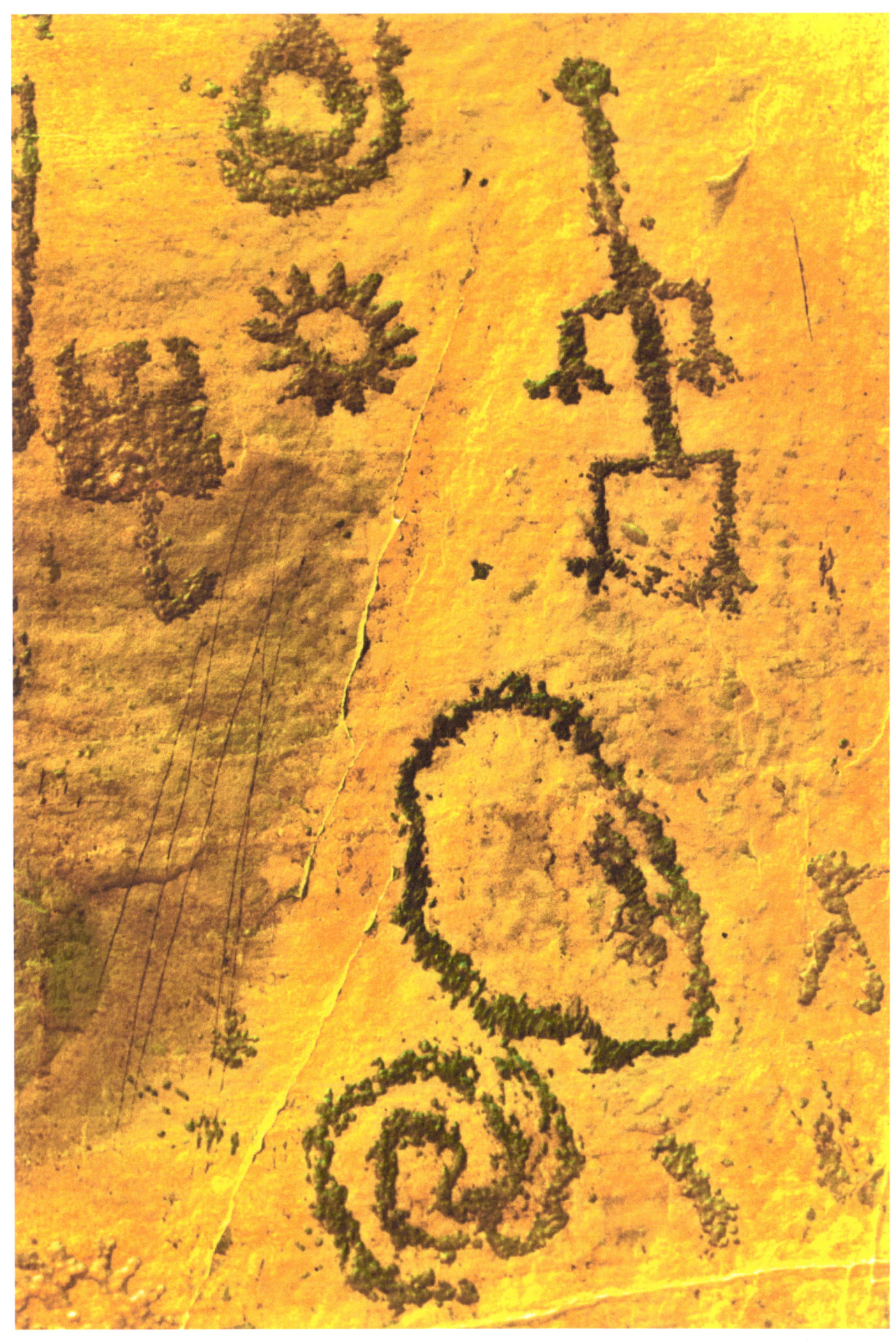

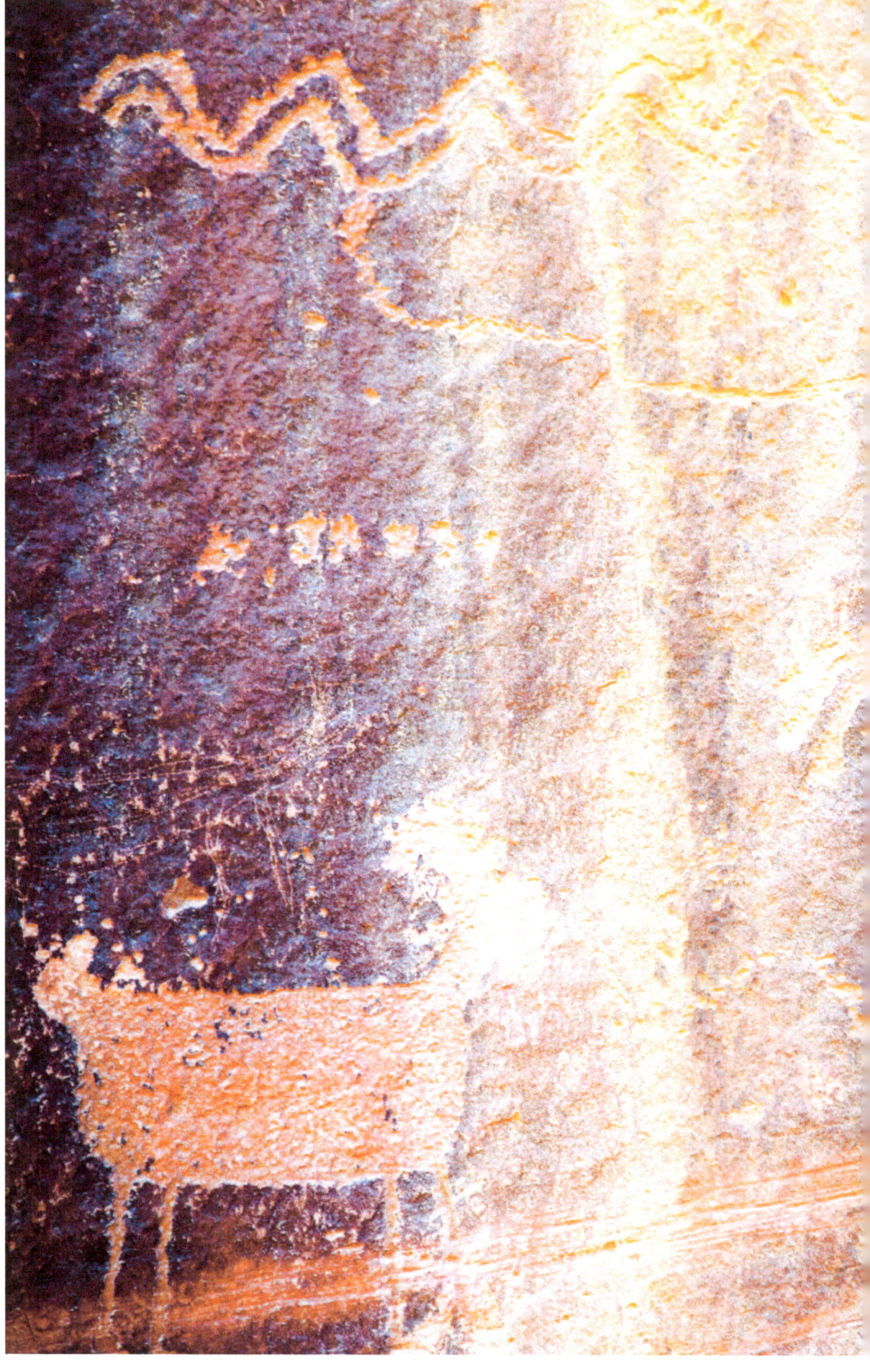

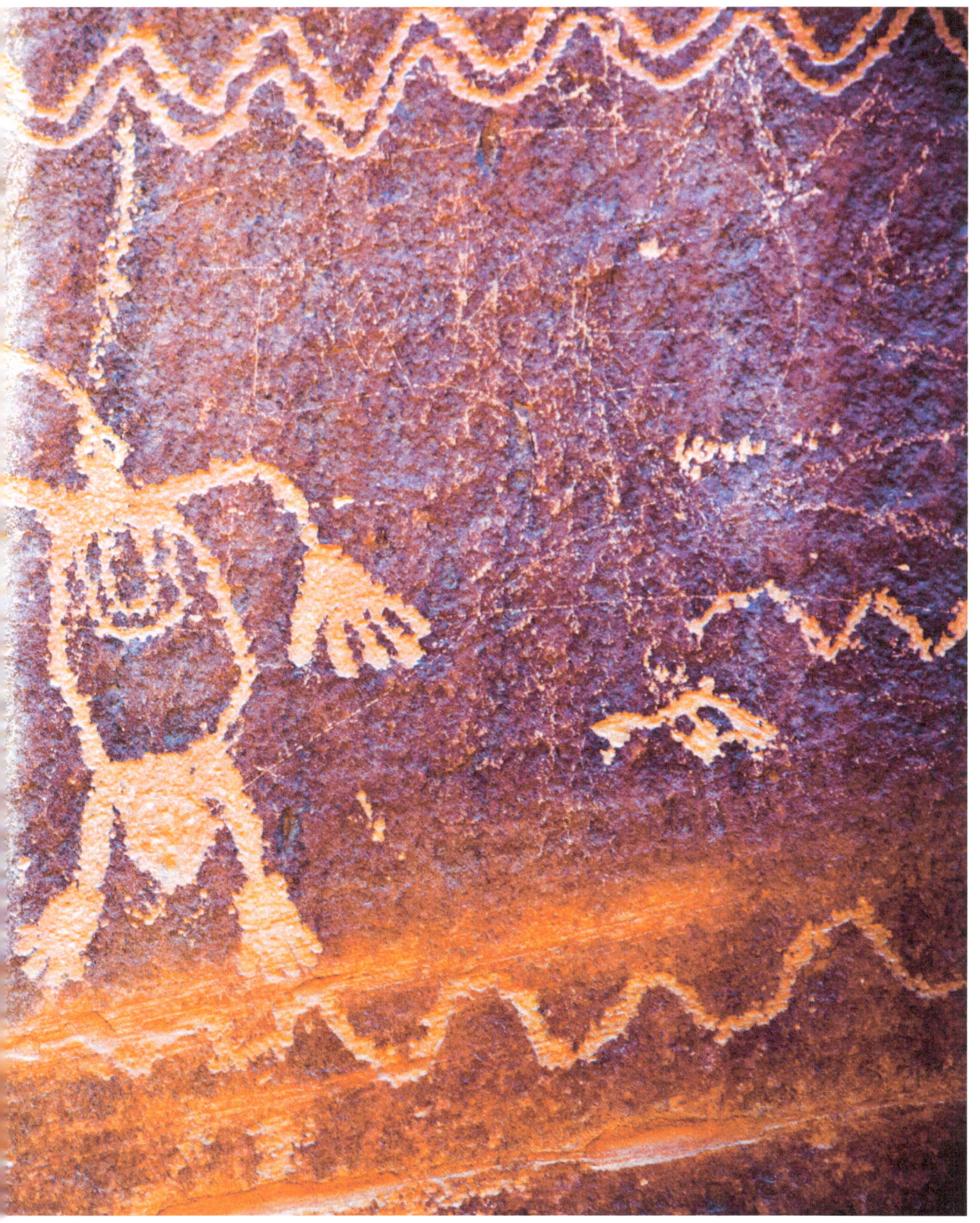

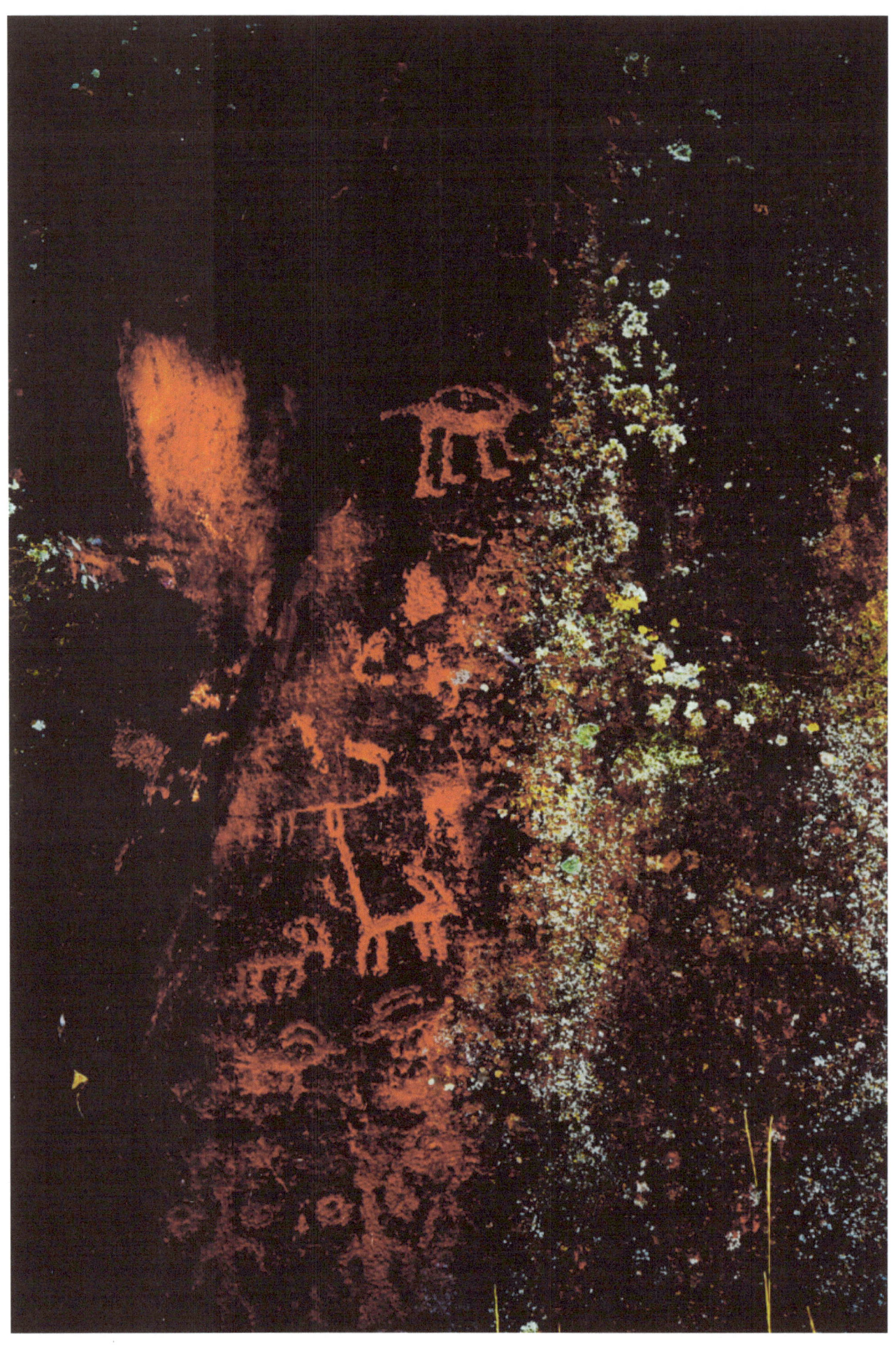

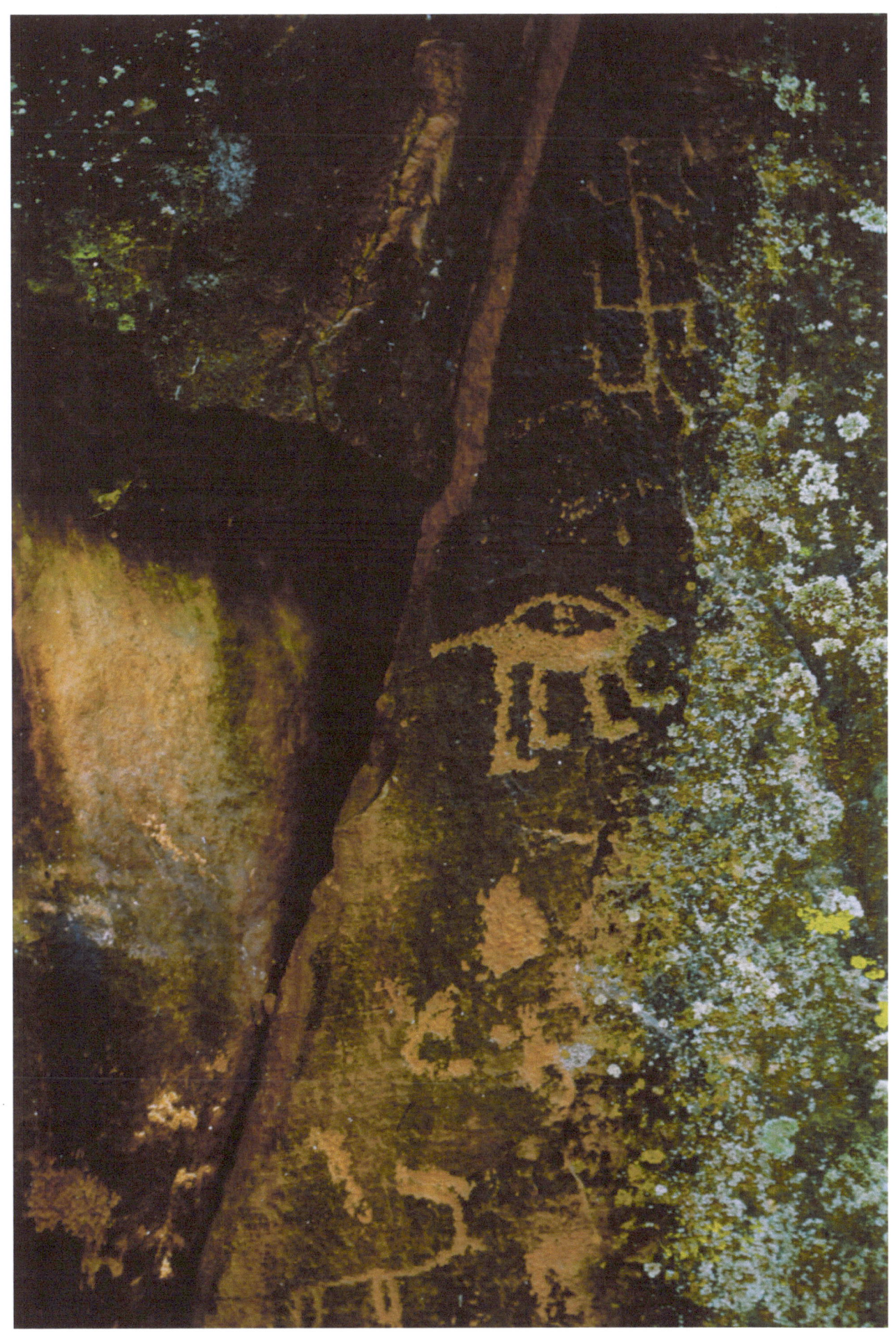

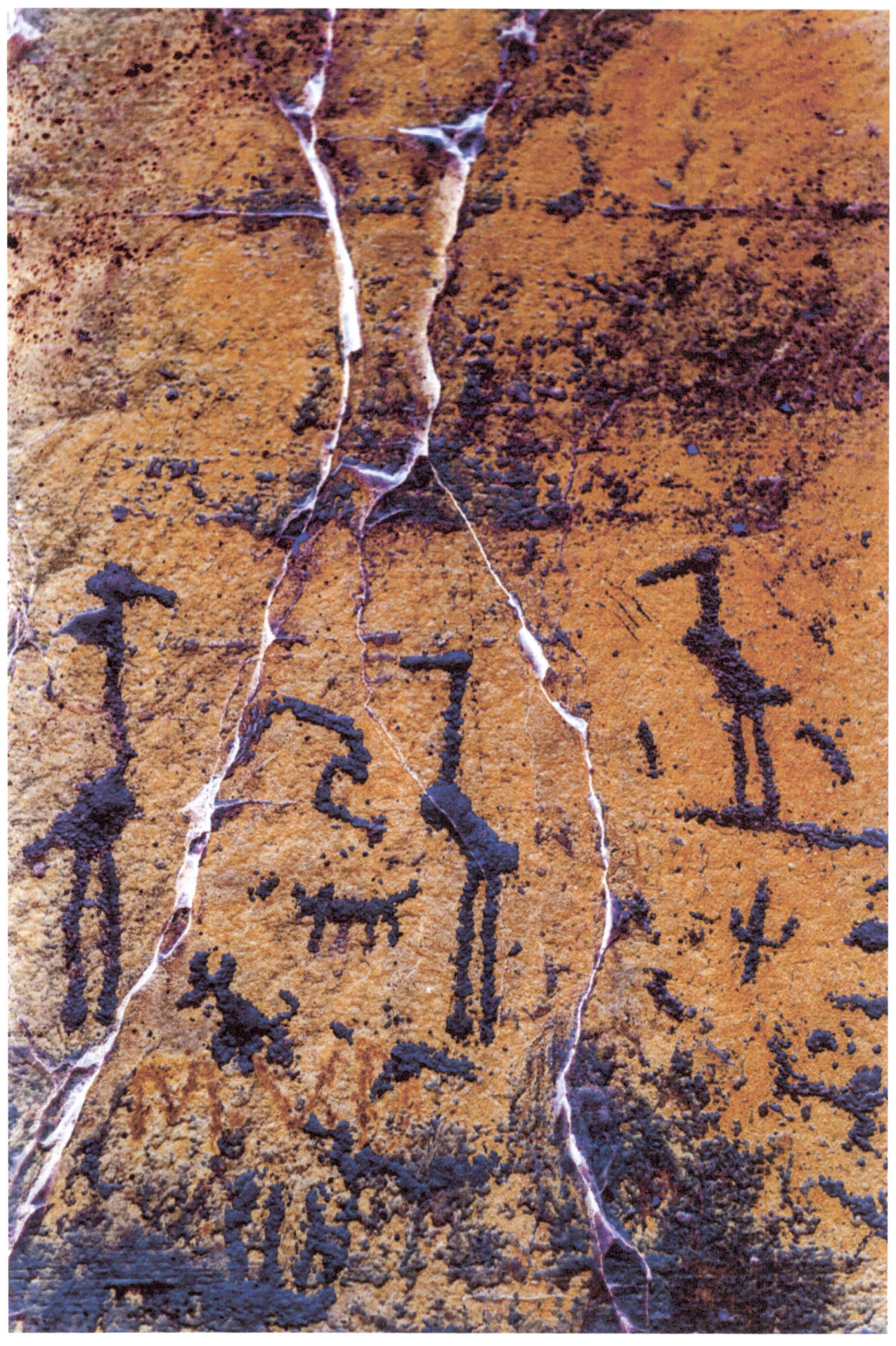

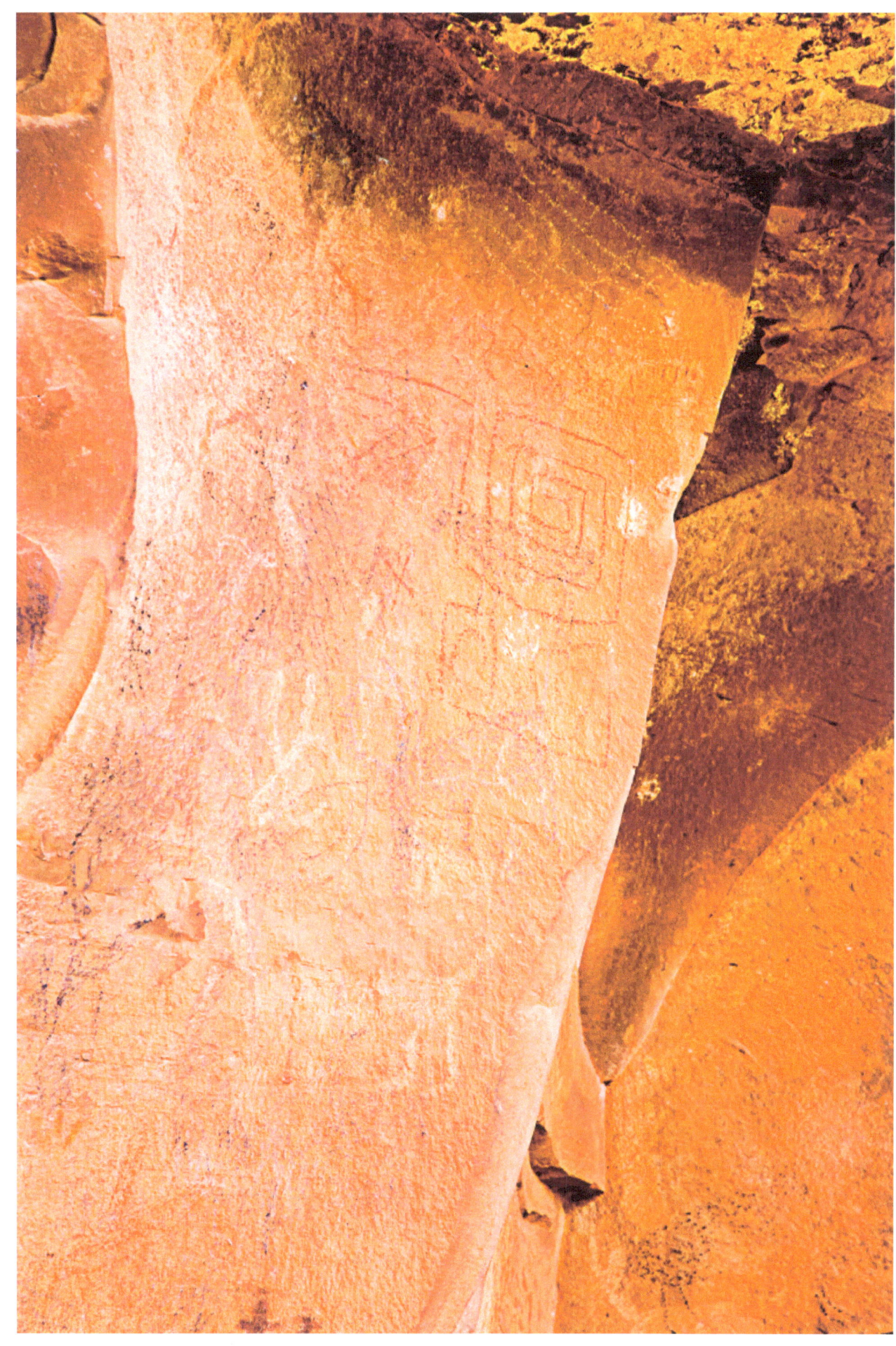

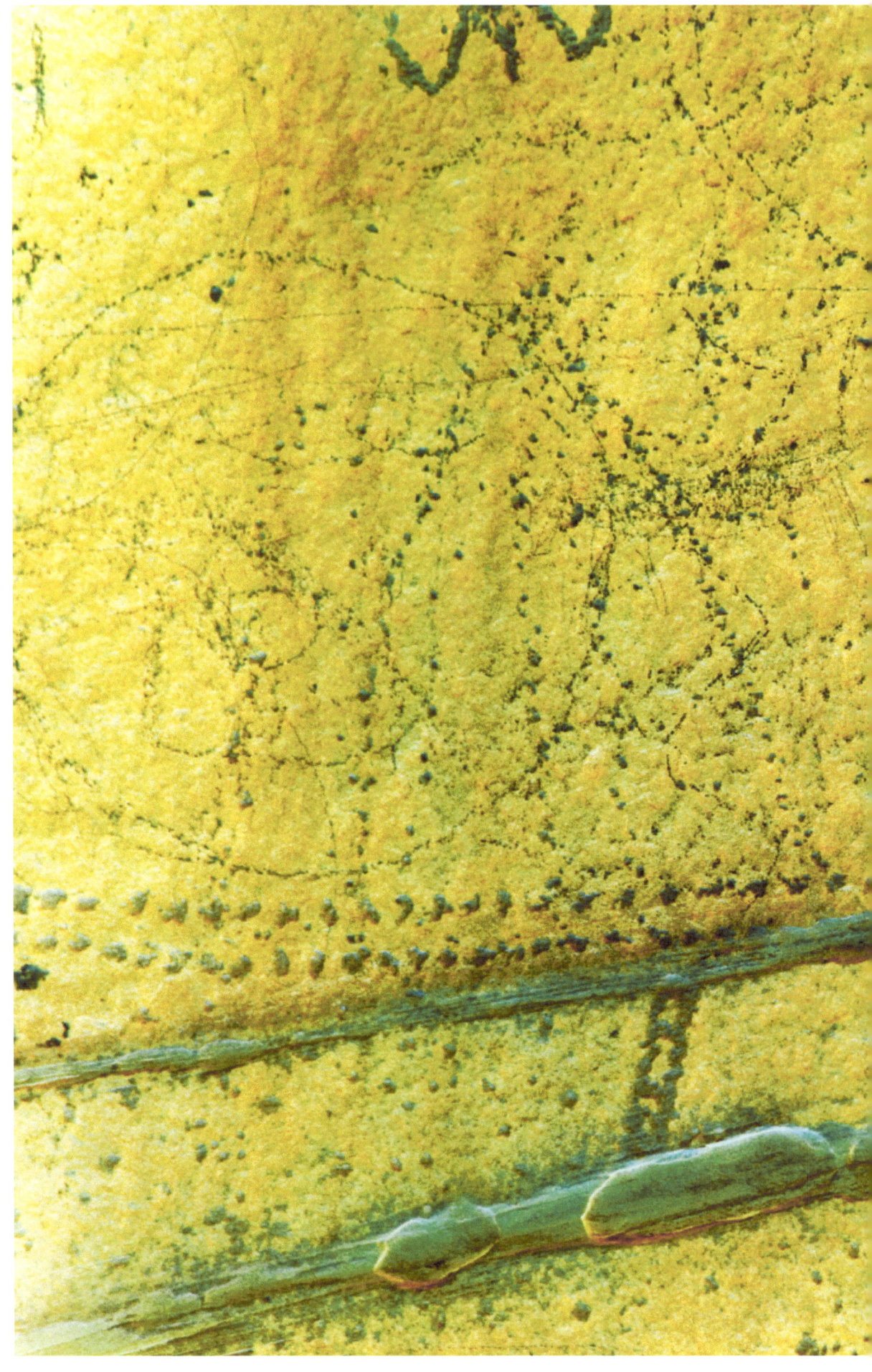

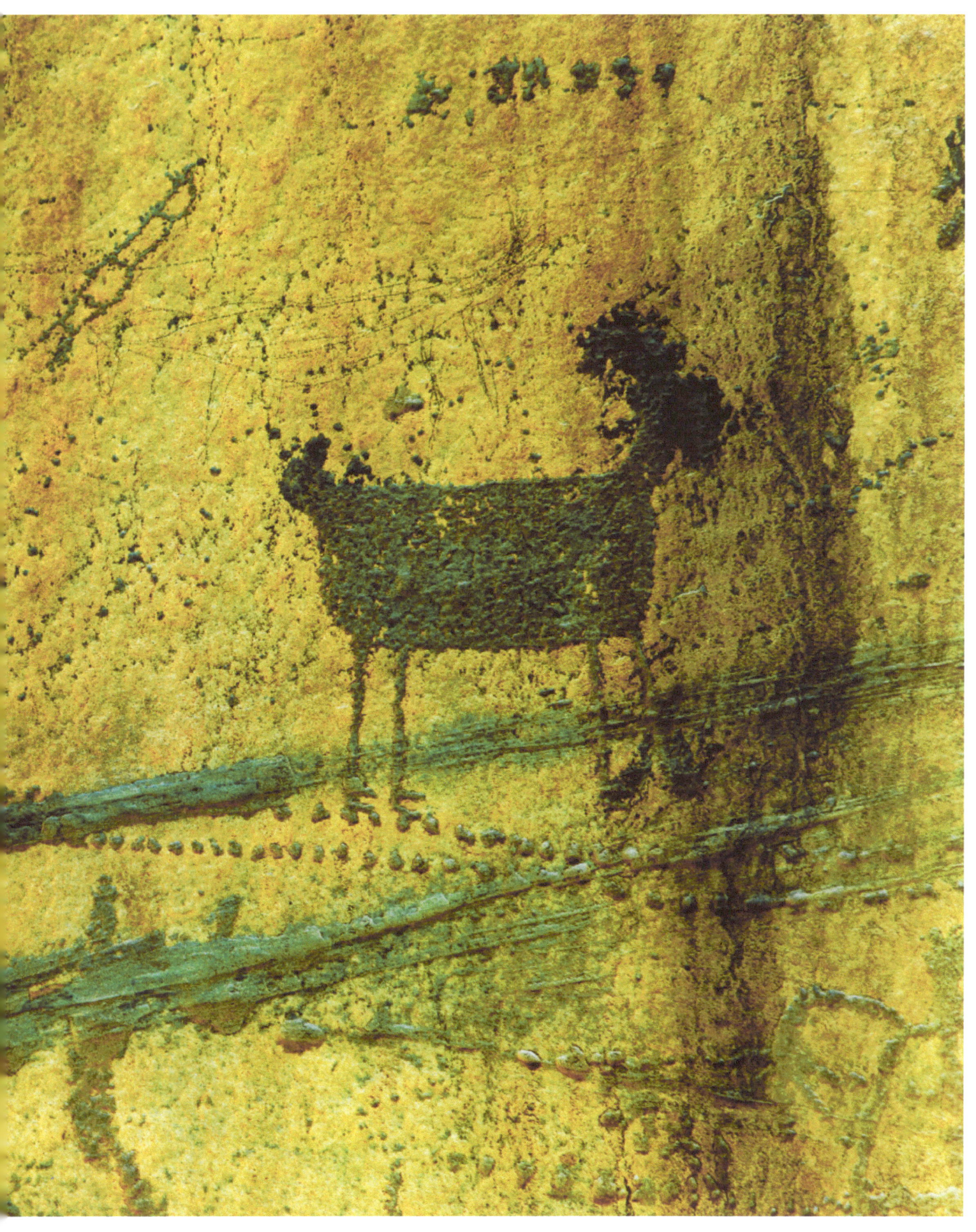

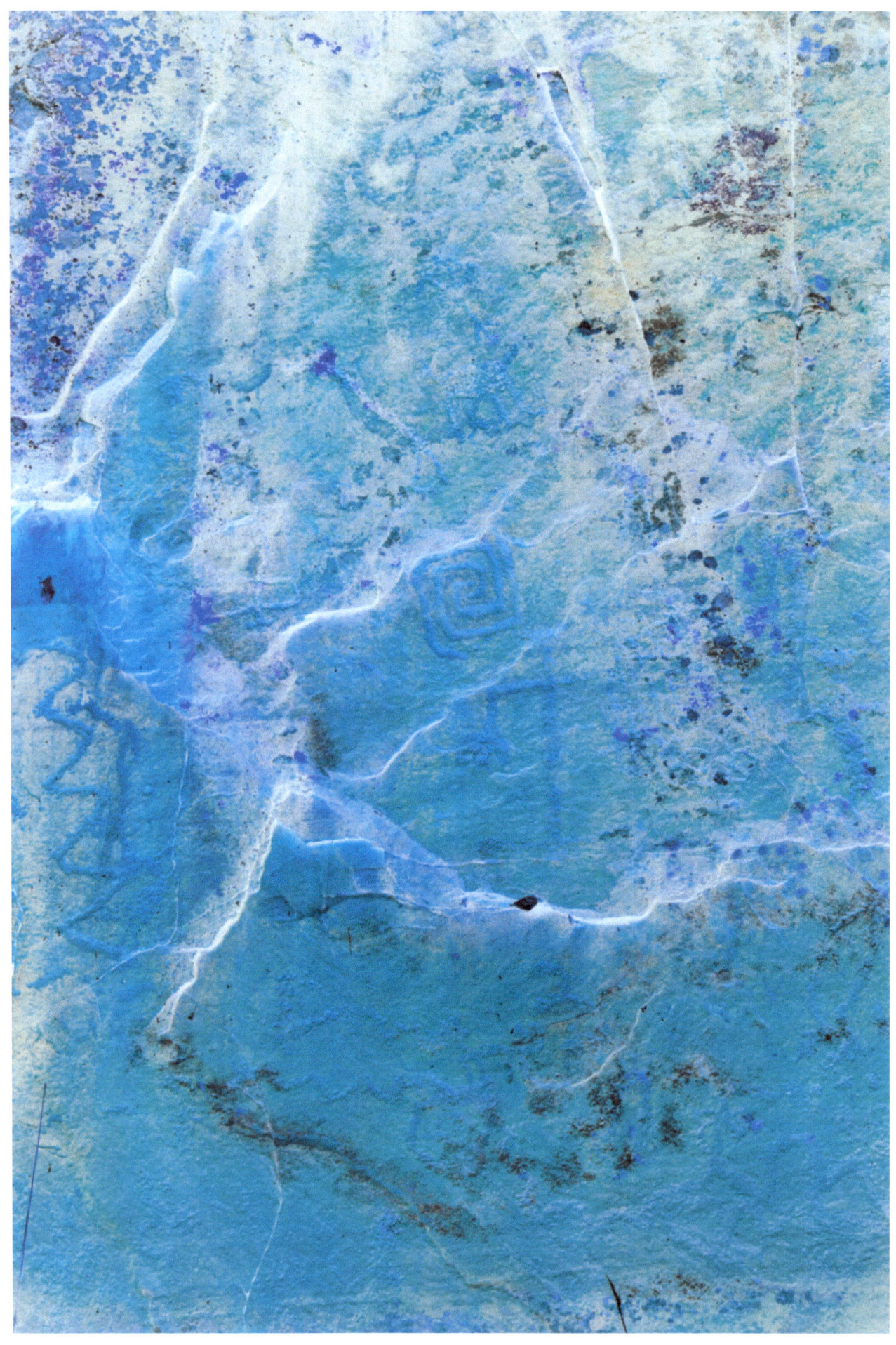

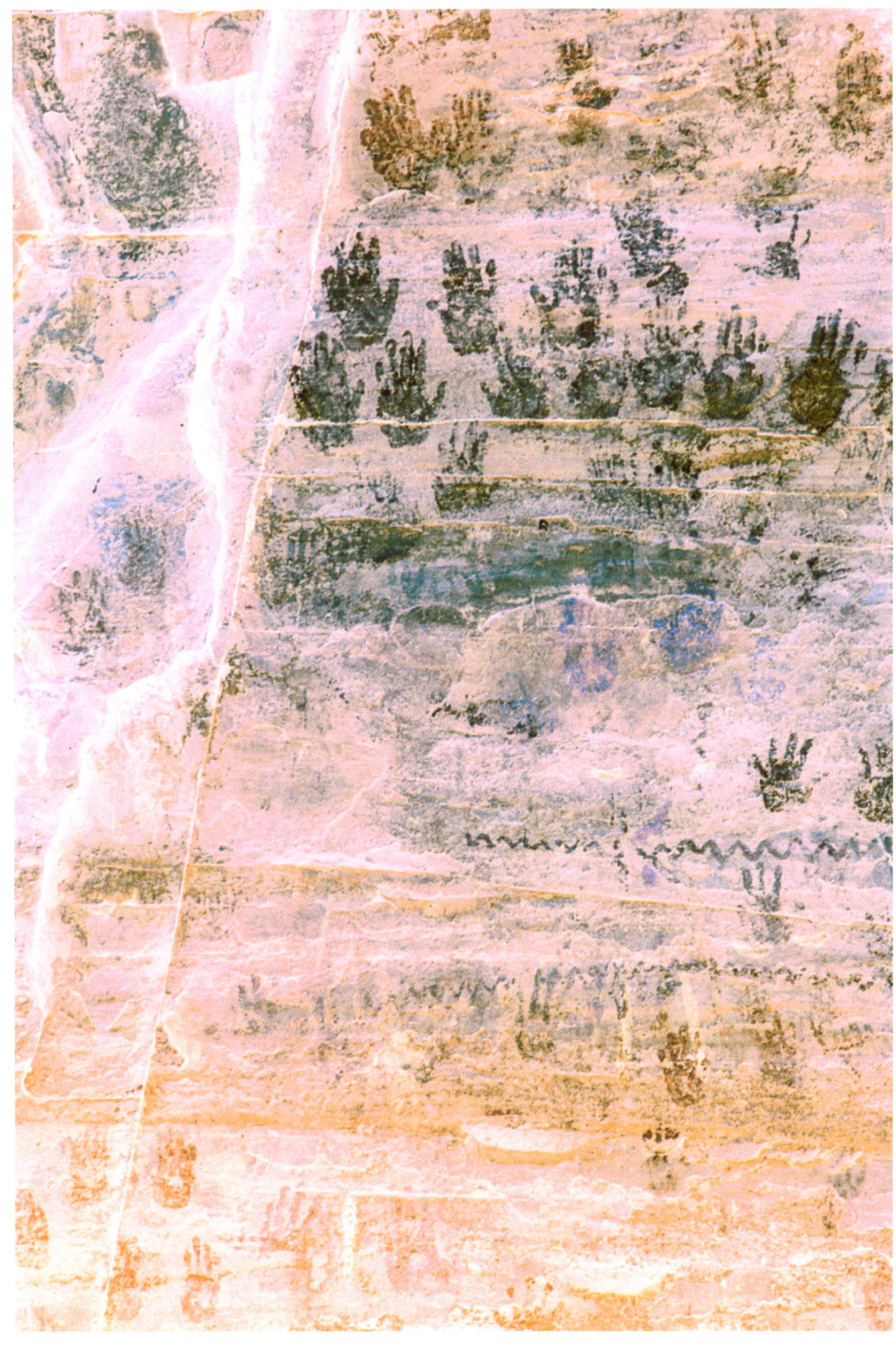

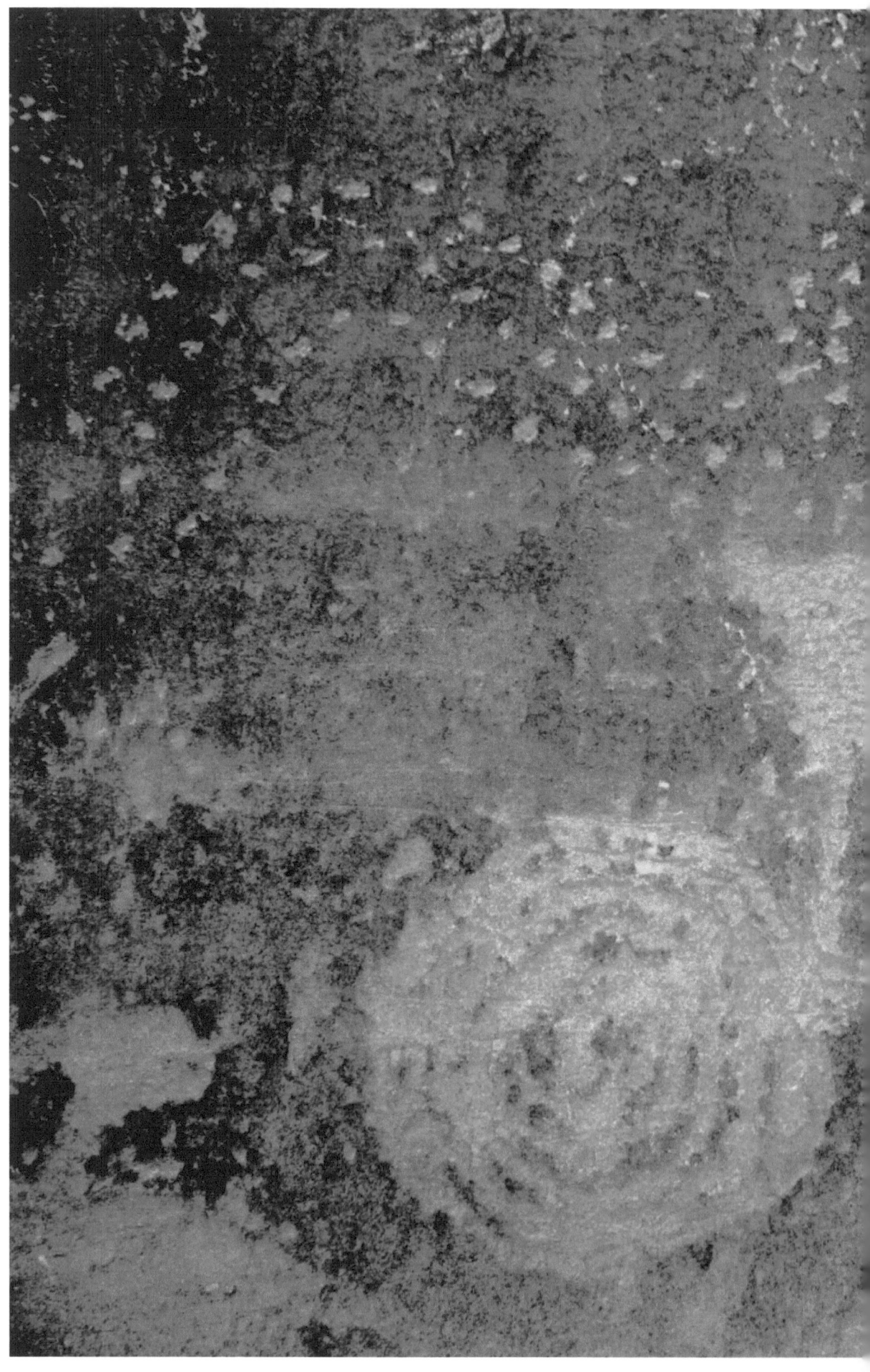

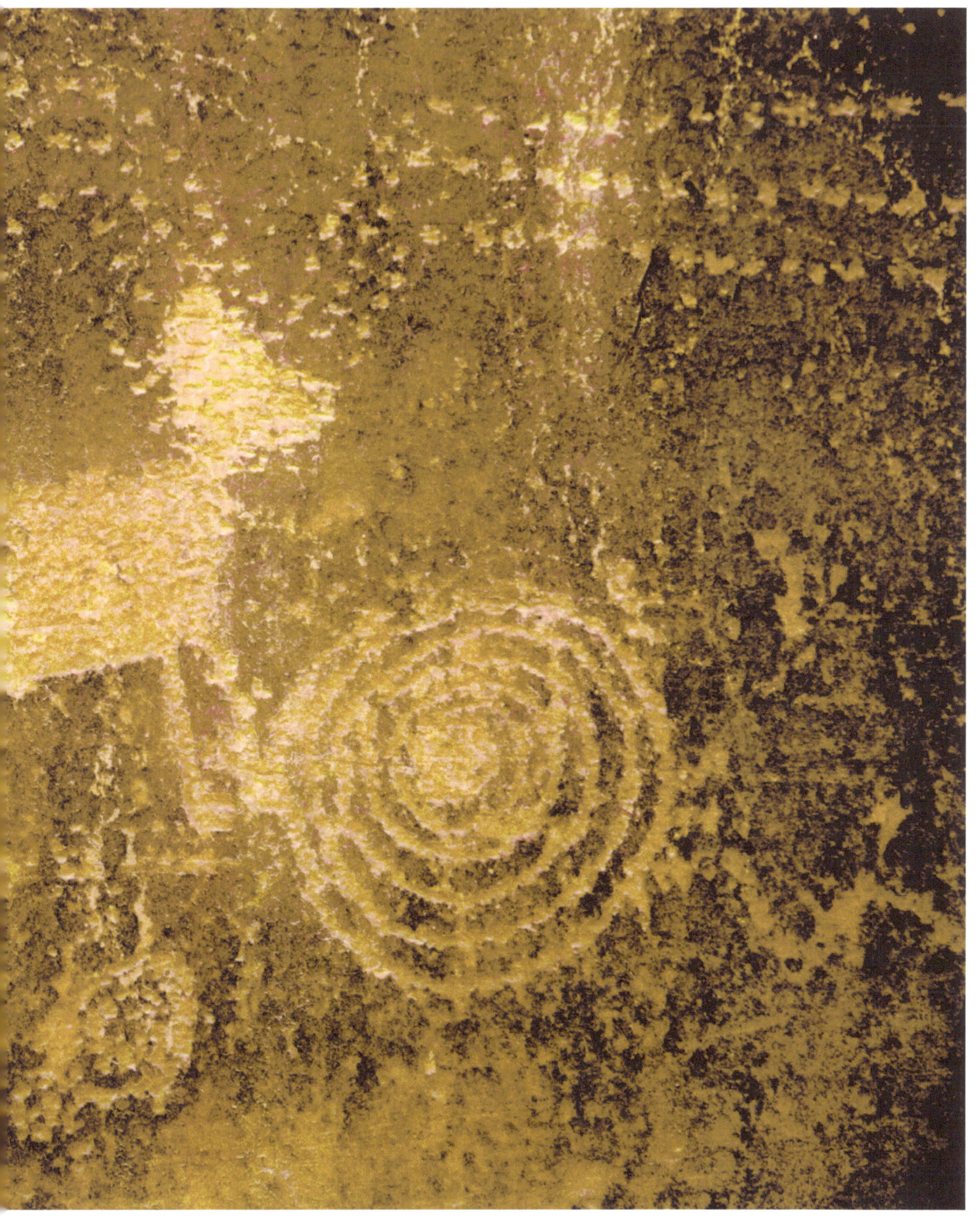

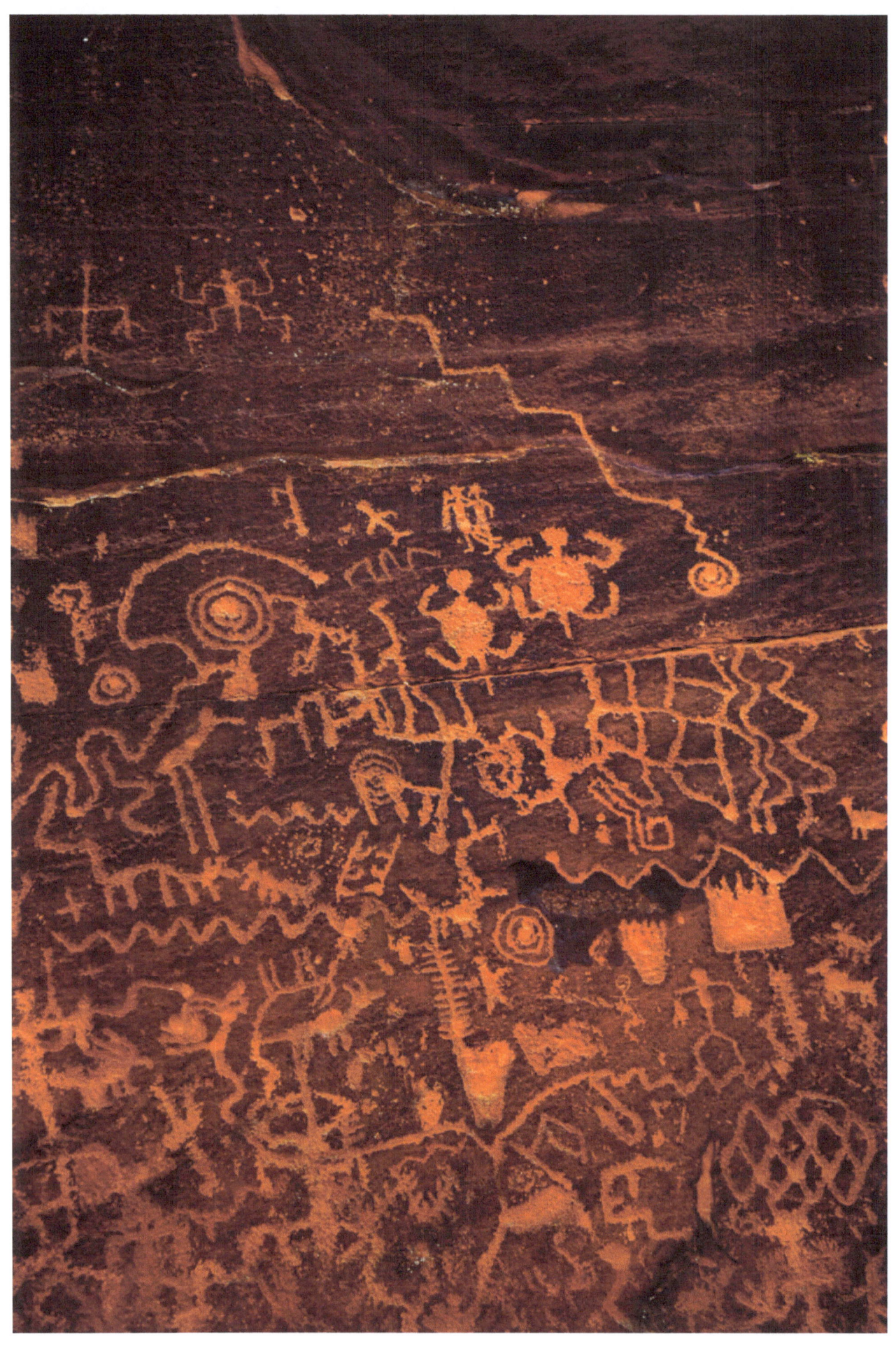

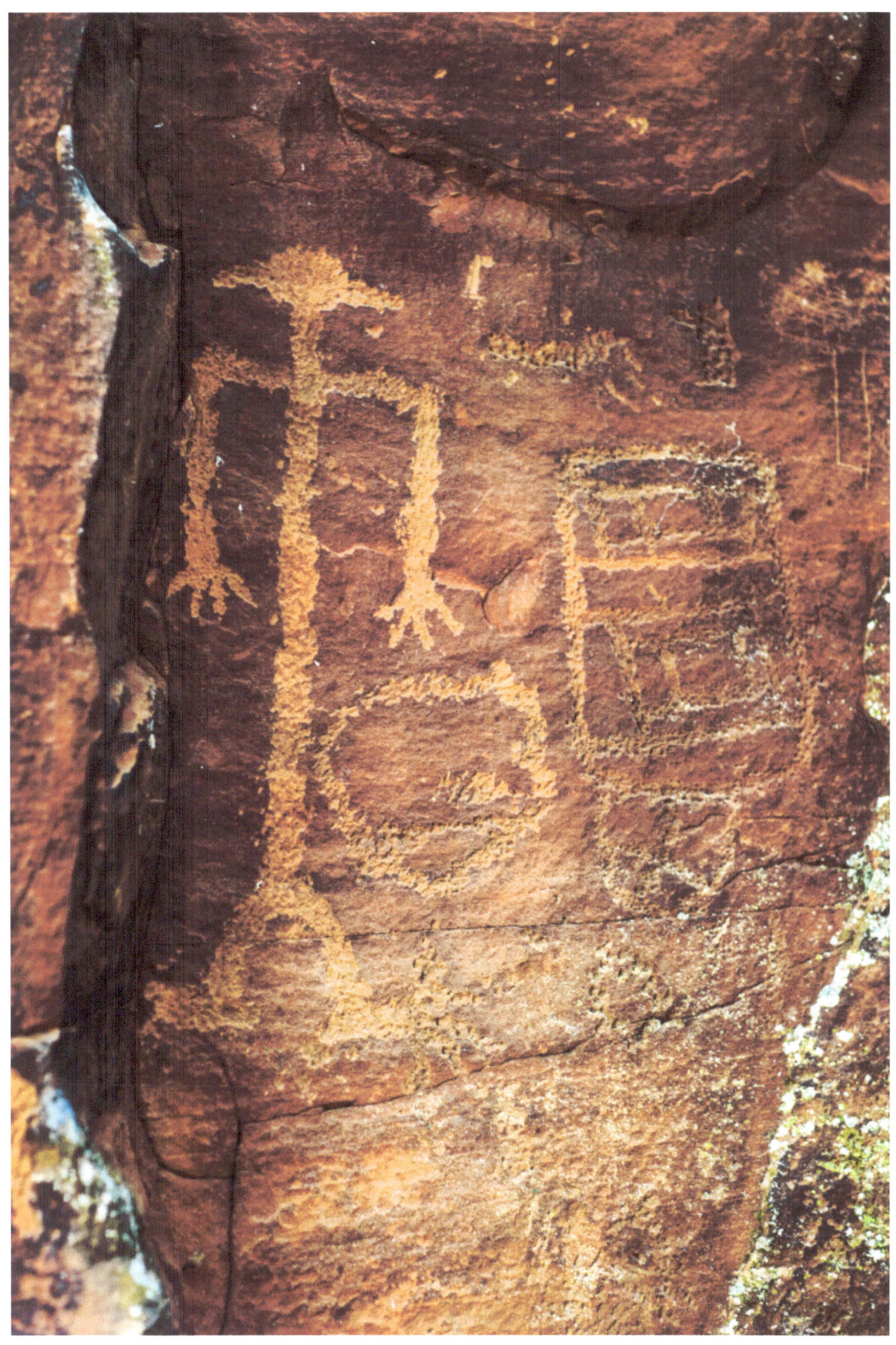

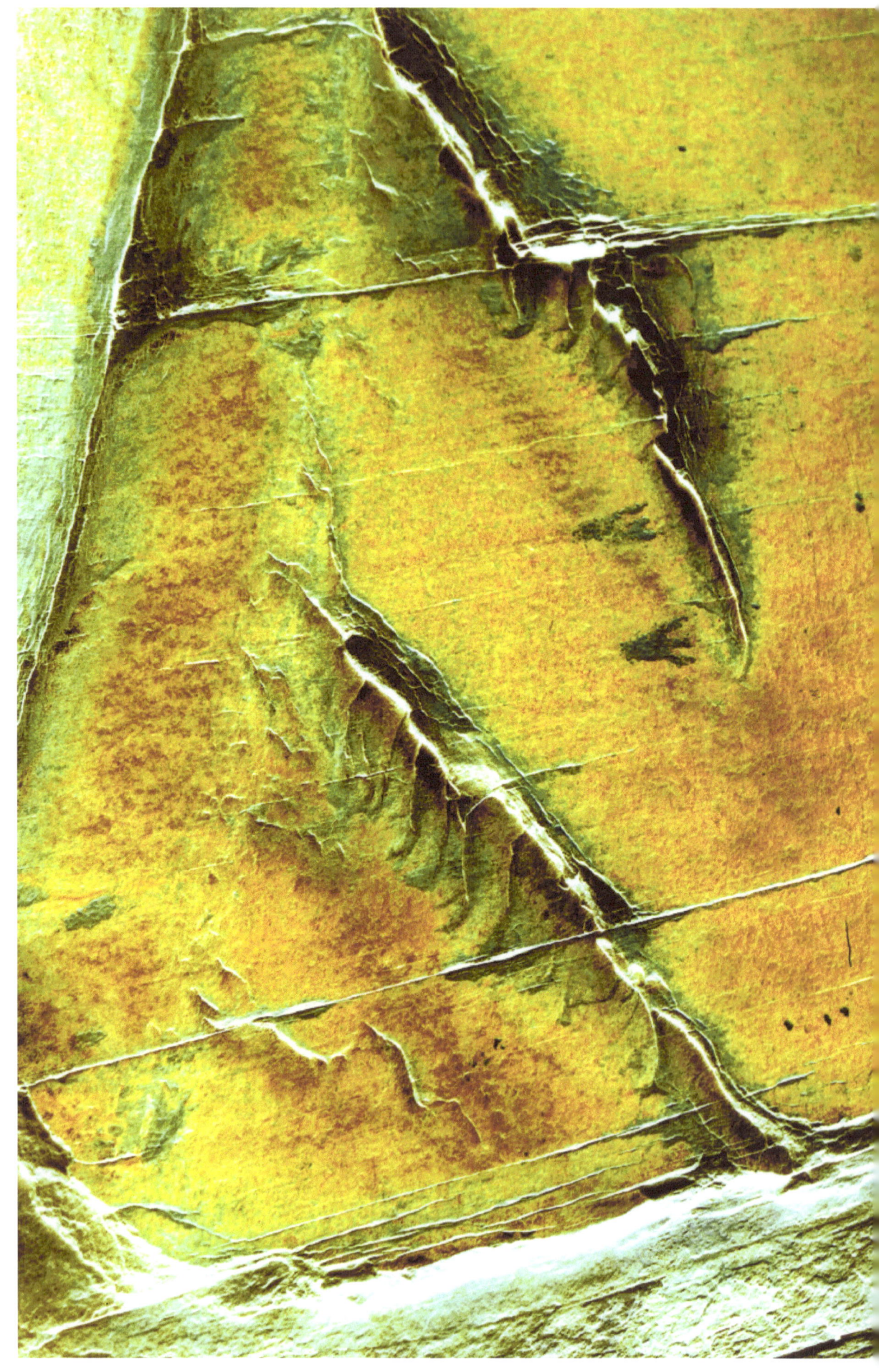

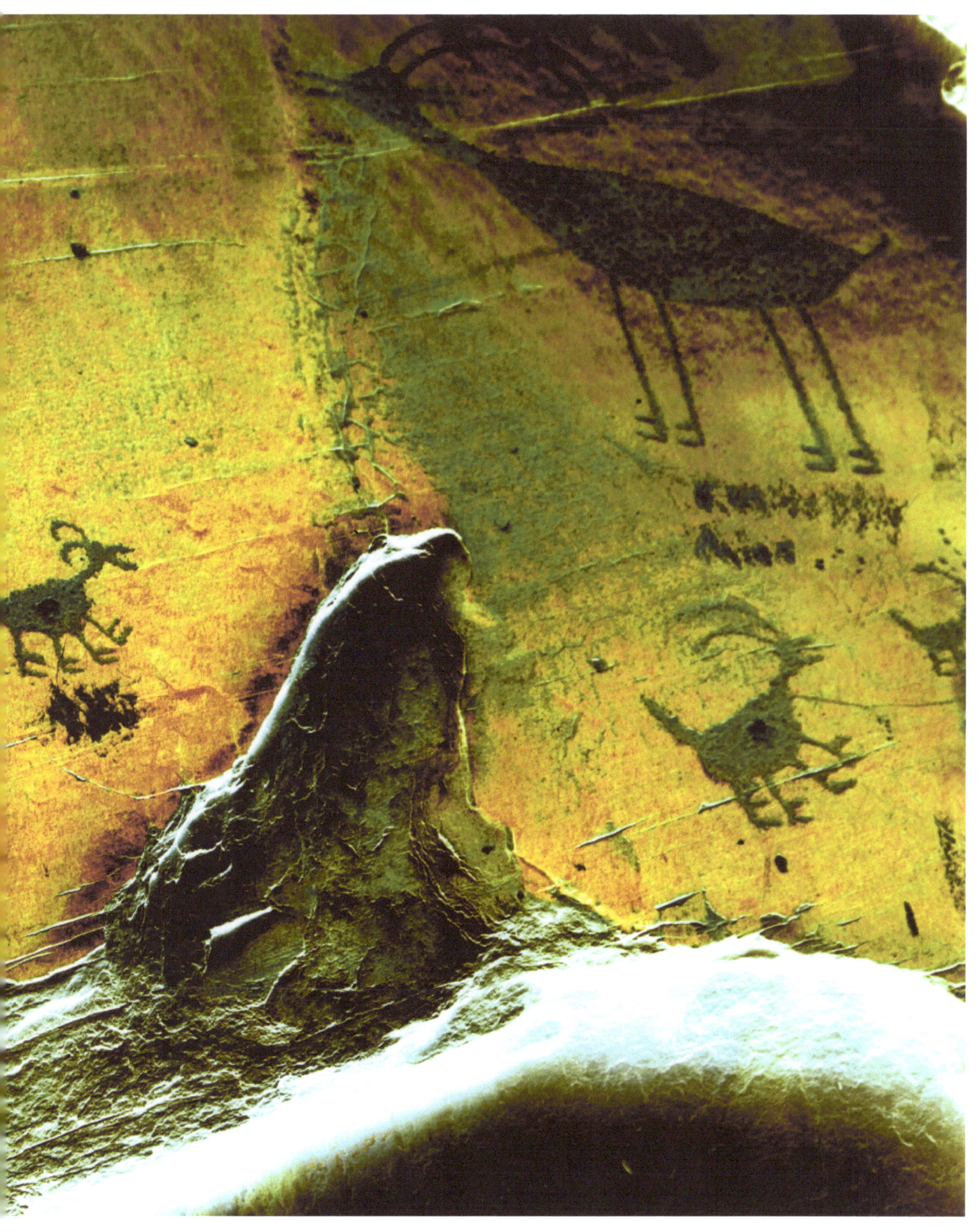

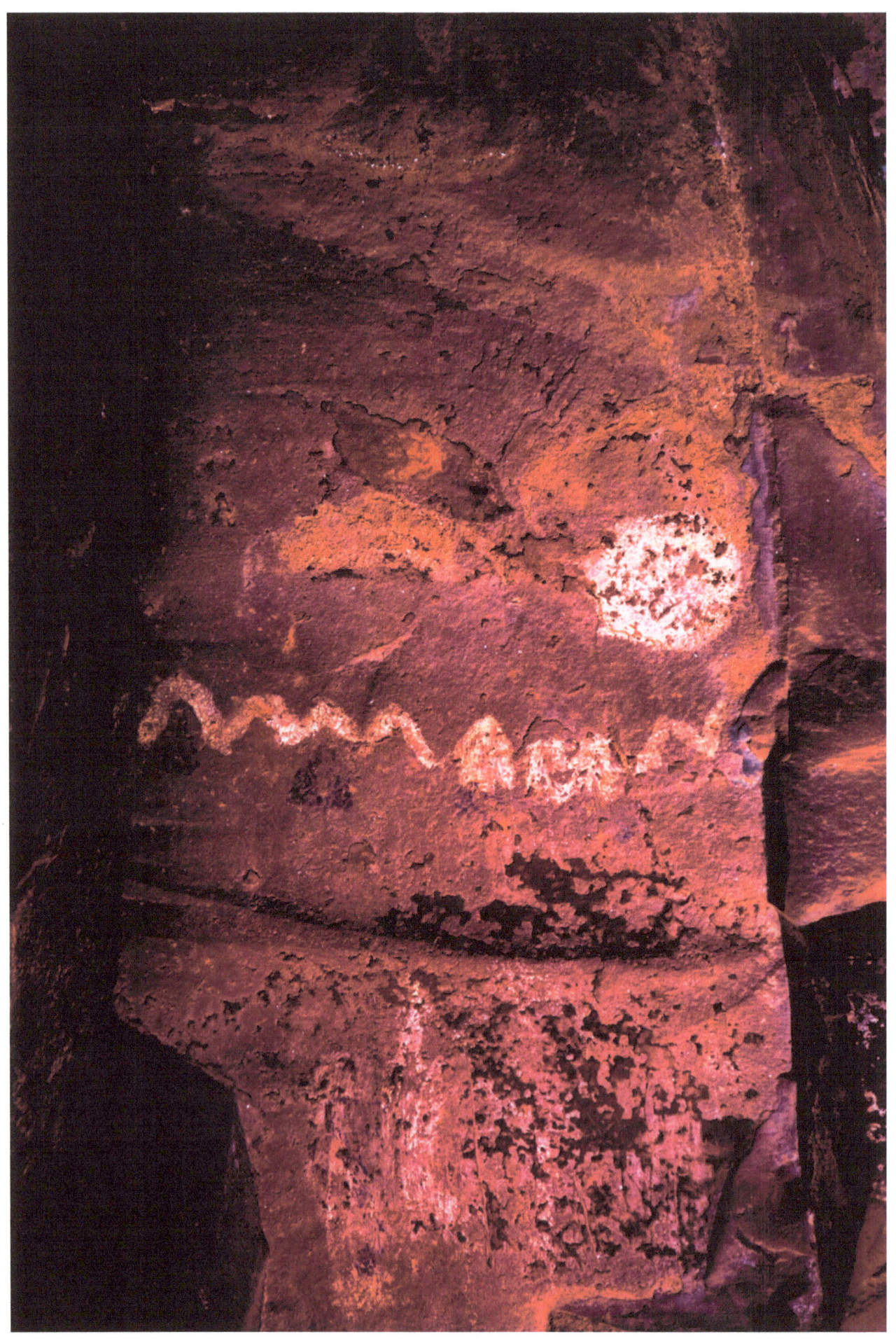

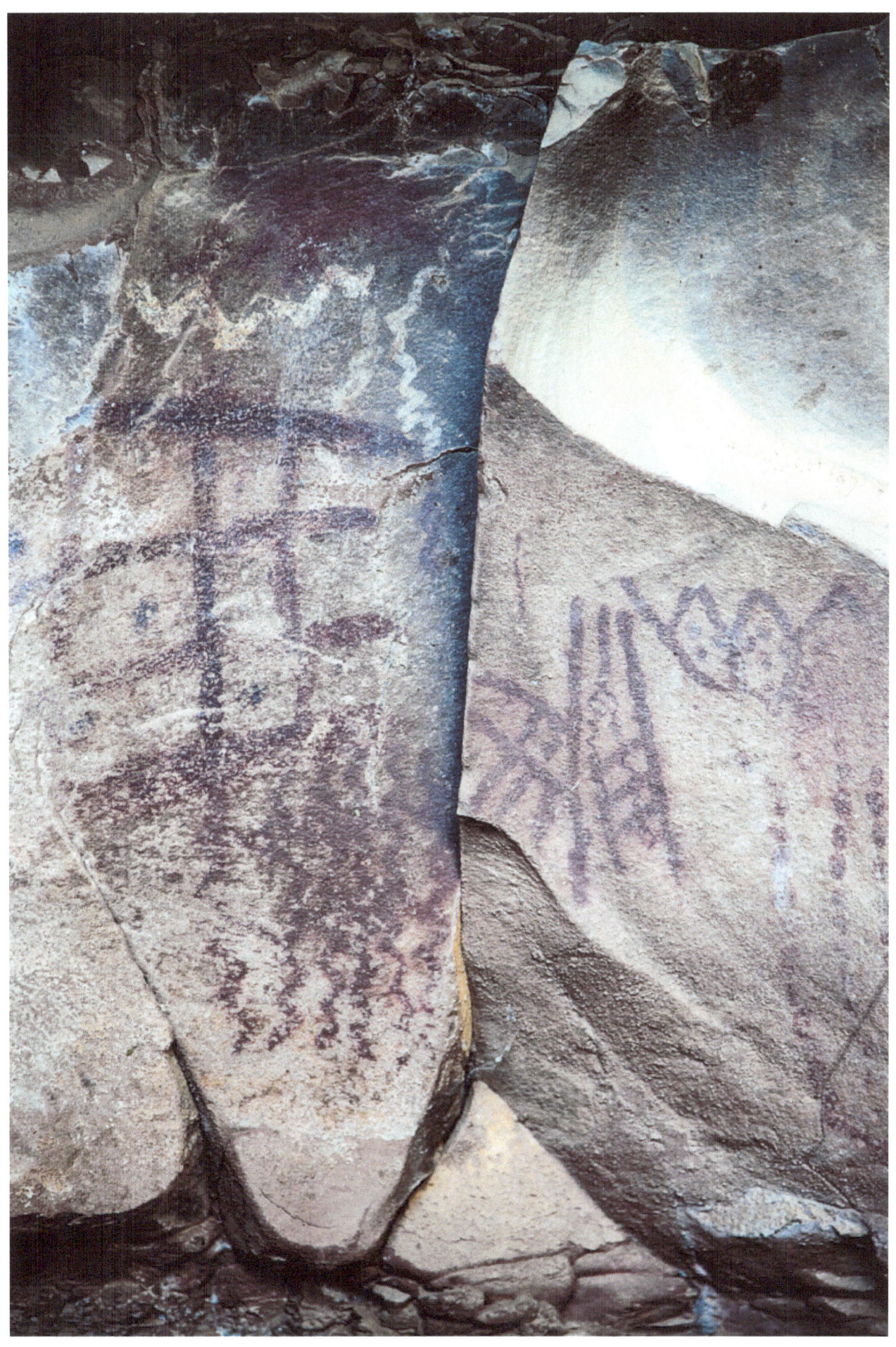

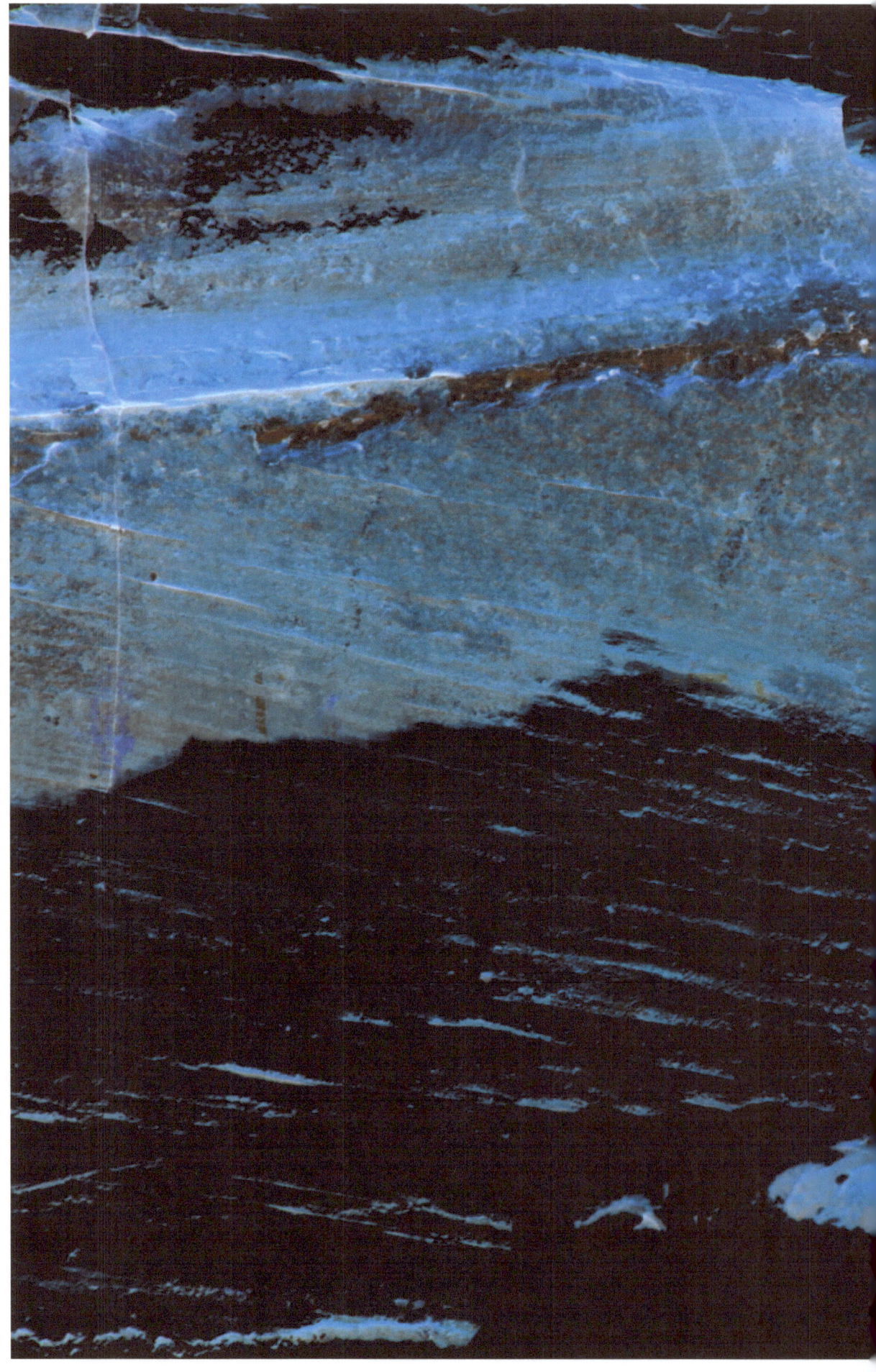

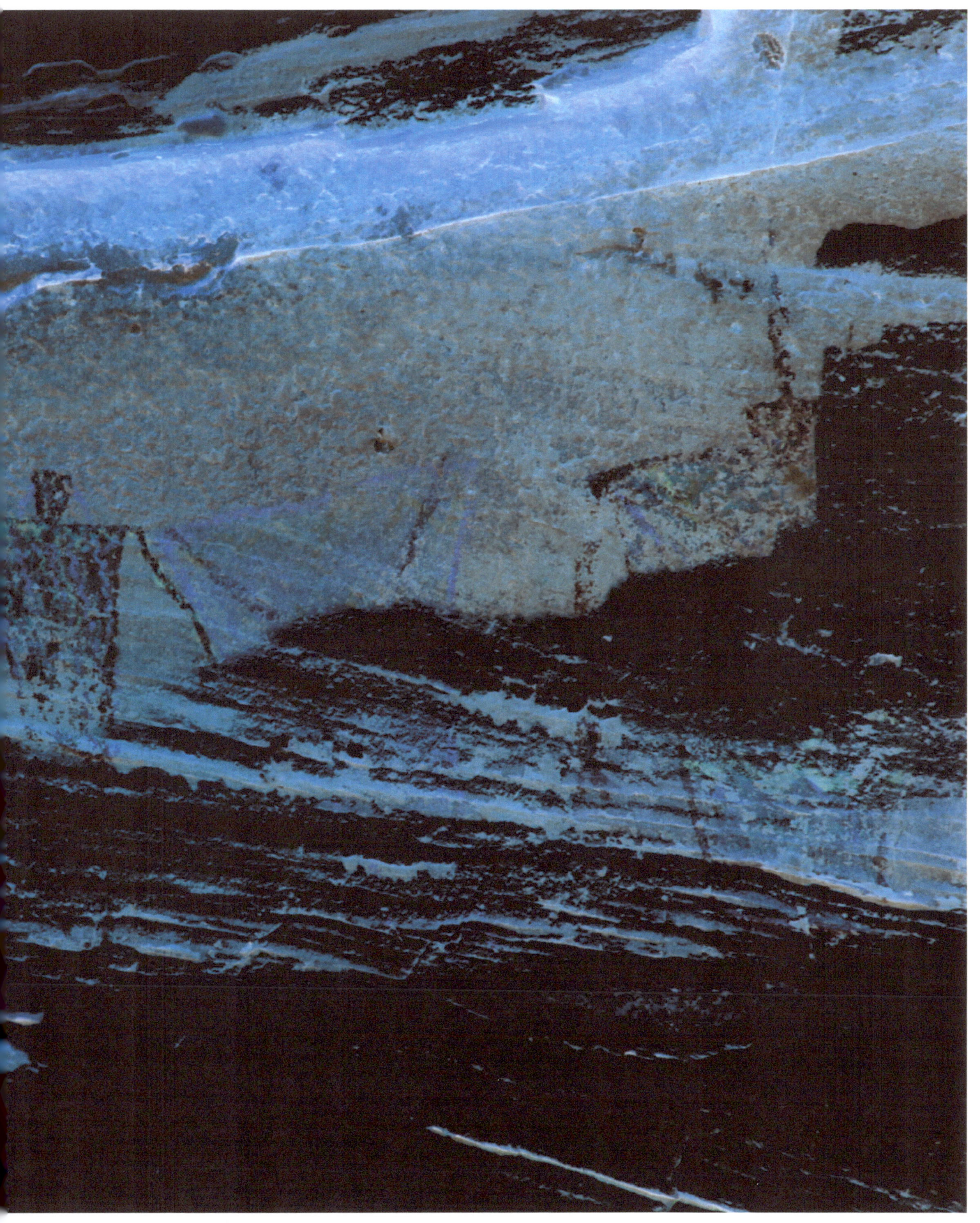

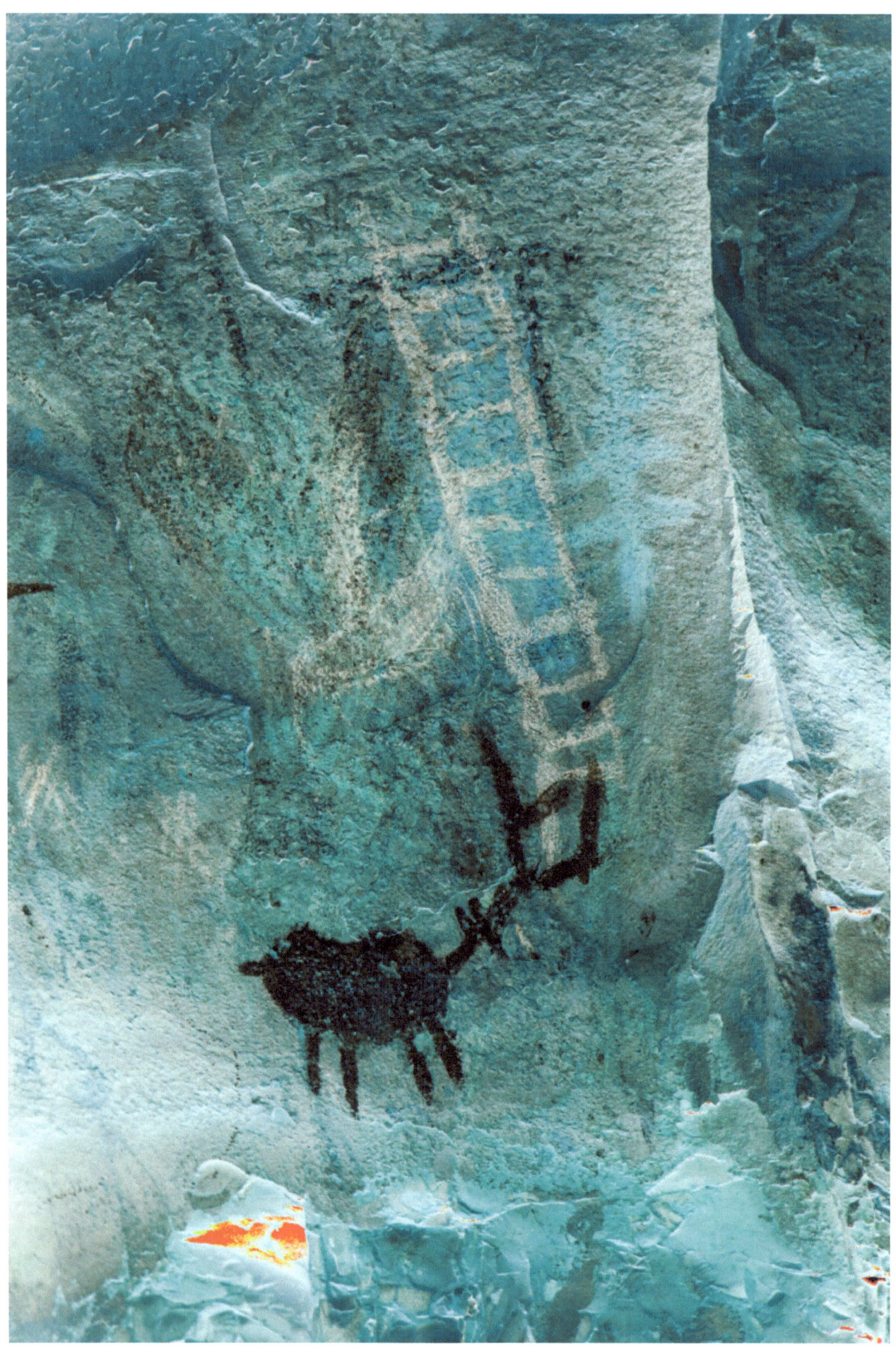

About the Artist

Pamela Fingerhut is a visual artist who explores issues of women's identity, body image, beauty, and aging in contemporary American society. She has a background in both two- and three-dimensional art and is currently working with digital media.

Fingerhut began her studies of fine art disciplines at the age of twelve at the Corcoran Gallery of Art School in Washington, D.C., where she was introduced to abstract expressionist exhibitions that would influence her own work in later life.

Augmenting her early training, she earned a B.A. from the University of Hartford and an M.A., summa cum laude, from Long Island University. She later studied photography, studio lighting, and computer arts at the International Center of Photography.

EXHIBITIONS

2008
International Center of Photography Educational Center New York, NY. "Sensory Prelude," group exhibition. Five pieces from the "Female Taxonomy" series.

Bromefield Gallery, Boston, MA. "Blow Up," group exhibition. #12 from the "Female Taxonomy series.

Galerie BMG, Woodstock, NY. Solo exhibition, "Female Taxonomy" series.

2009
Professional Women Photographers, New York, NY. Group exhibition, "Somnambulism" #2 and #5.

2010
Calumet Photographic, New York, NY. "Objects of Affection," group exhibition. *Selma* from the "Her Case" series, #4 from the "Somnambulism" series, and *Opera Star* from personal photographs.

2011
Brandeis National Committee [PAMELA: CHECK THIS], Phoenix Chapter Art Study Group, Phoenix, AZ. Studio visit.

2012
Phoenix Art Museum, Contemporary Forum, Phoenix, AZ. Studio visit.

2013
Jewish Foundation Children's Services, Phoenix, AZ. Exhibition and talk.

Phoenix Art Museum, Contemporary Forum, Phoenix, AZ. Art auction gala. #XX [PAMELA: CHECK THIS] from the "Female Taxonomy series.

JURIED AND OPEN PORTFOLIO REVIEWS

2007
Photo Nola, New Orleans Photo Alliance, New Orleans, LA. Open review.

2008
Power House Portfolio Review, DUMBO, New York, NY. Open review.

2009
ACP, Atlanta Celebrates Photography, Atlanta, GA. Juried review.

2010
Foto Fest, Houston, TX. Open review.

PROFESSIONAL ART SERVICES

2008, 2009, 2010
F.E.G.S Health and Human Services, Haym Solomon Division of the Arts, New York, NY. Judge, Haym Solomon Awards for Arts.